IMAGES
of America

WILKES COUNTY

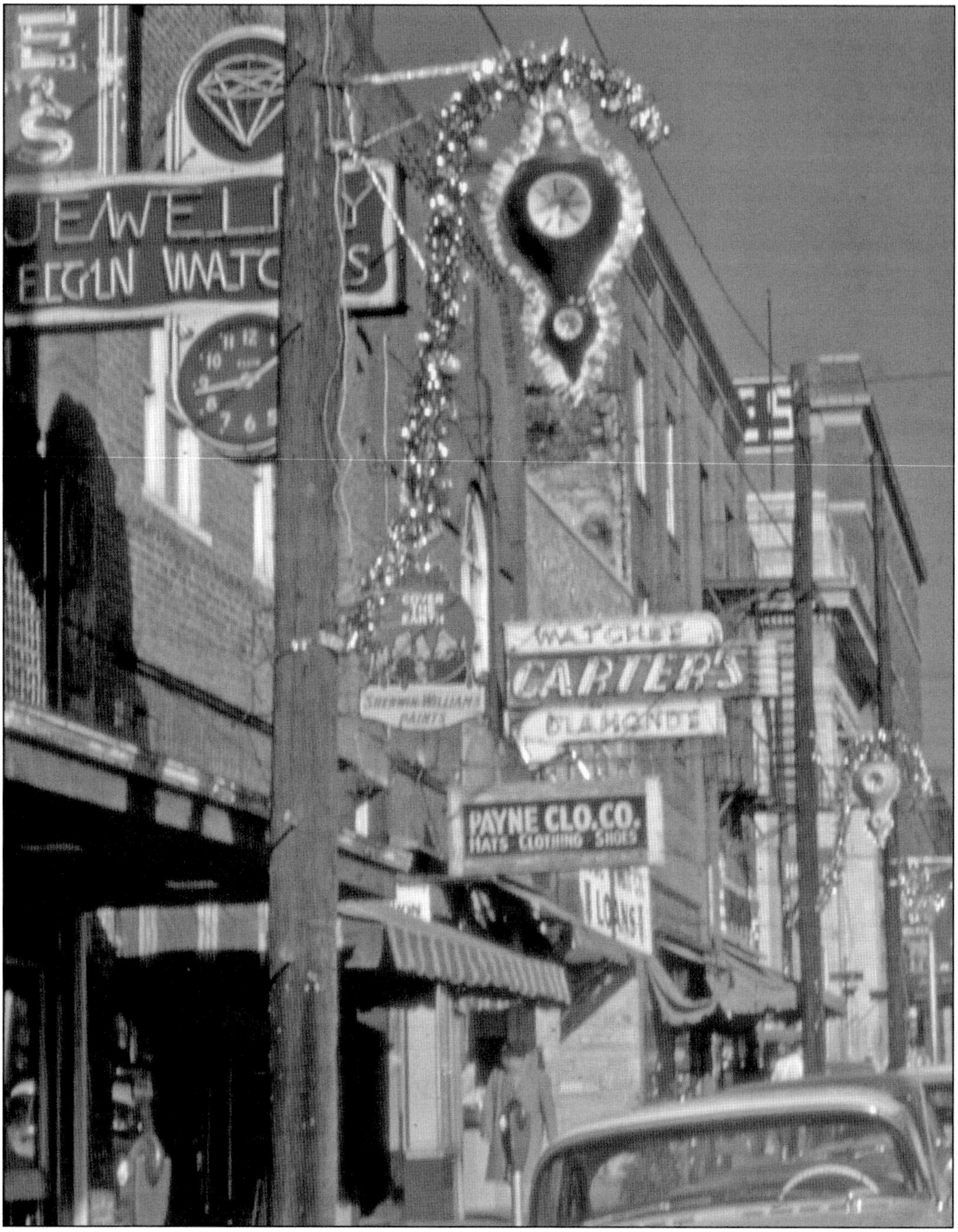

CHRISTMAS IN NORTH WILKESBORO. Pictured is a street in downtown North Wilkesboro decorated for Christmas during the 1960s. The Hotel Wilkes is just visible in the rear of the image. Steele's Jewelry is in the foreground. (Courtesy of Wilkes Community College Library.)

ON THE COVER. Watermelon feasts, like the one depicted on the cover, were common social gatherings in the summertime. Often held by church groups, the feasts were a time to celebrate the season with friends and family, particularly around the Fourth of July. (Courtesy of Wilkes Heritage Museum.)

IMAGES
of America

WILKES COUNTY

Misty Bass, Christy Earp,
and Jennifer L. Peña

ARCADIA
PUBLISHING

ISBN 978-0-7385-5308-5

Published by Arcadia Publishing
Charleston, South Carolina

Printed in the United States of America

Library of Congress Catalog Card Number: 2007934700

For all general information contact Arcadia Publishing at:
Telephone 843-853-2070
Fax 843-853-0044
E-mail sales@arcadiapublishing.com
For customer service and orders:
Toll-Free 1-888-313-2665

Visit us on the Internet at www.arcadiapublishing.com

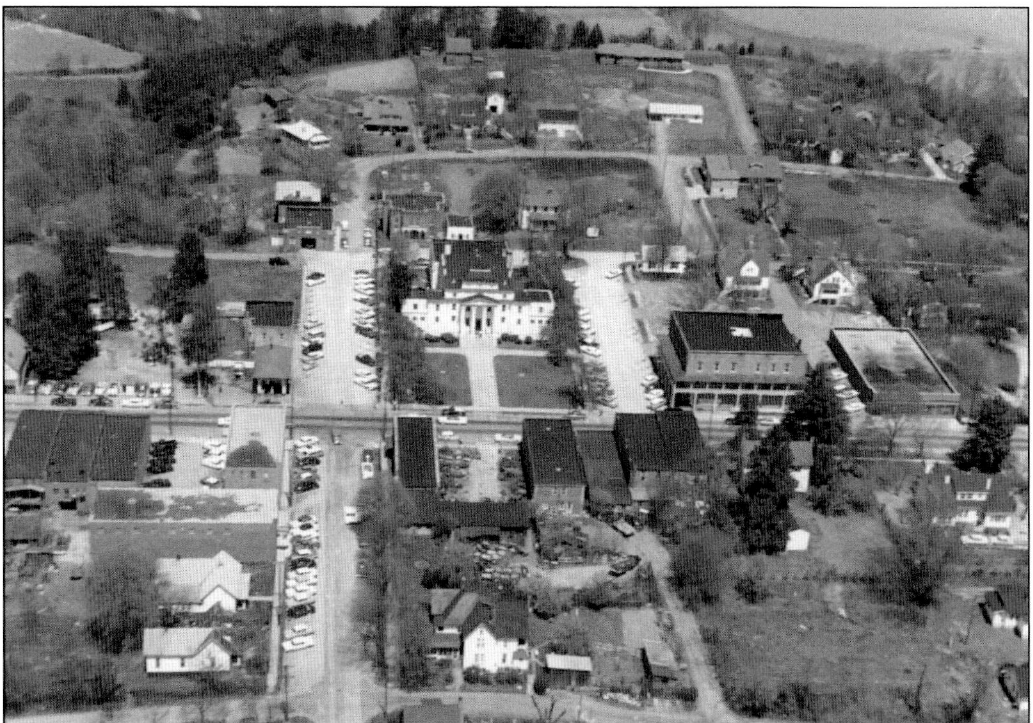

Aerial View of Wilkesboro, c. 1960. The town of Wilkesboro is the county seat of Wilkes County. The town centers on the 1902 courthouse building, now the home of the Wilkes Heritage Museum. (Courtesy of Wilkes Community College Library.)

Contents

Acknowledgments

This is in no way meant to be a comprehensive history. It is a visual celebration of the people and places of Wilkes County. Any mistakes in this work are our own. But the product is not our own; it is a collaboration of individuals who love history. We could not have accomplished this work without the enthusiasm and support provided by Harold Bass, Gary and Gail Haynes, Sheri Hayes, Nicole Brown de Bruijn, and Vickie Cothren. Harold and Gary helped seek out unique images tirelessly, while Gail, Sheri, Nicole, and Vickie not only provided images but also answered endless questions as we sought specific dates, times, names, places, and details.

Other people that provided images, assistance, and support include: Shandra Haynes, Hazel Bass, Barbara and James Adams, Wendy Cubert, Jamie Hamlin, Ton de Bruijn, Eloise Church, Kathleen Calloway, Vergie Foster, Linda Triplett, Tony Hayes, Anne Stallings, James Richardson, Allen Wagoner, Mickey Parsons, Nell Swanson Carlton, Glenn Johnson, Freda Eller, Laura Stroud, Mac and Janet Atwood, Goldie Michael, Jason Duncan, Jeff Weaver, Rita Smith, Jennifer Furr, Marilyn Payne, Laurie Hayes, Trish Collins, Janet Telander, Jan Huggins, Kim Faw, Fay Byrd, Nancy Price, Elizabeth Barber, Audrey Chapel, Nancy Reese, Susan Stinnett, the Wilkes Genealogical Society, and the *Wilkes Journal-Patriot*.

Several collections proved invaluable in the compilation of this book: the James Larkin Pearson Collection at the Wilkes Community College Library (particularly the photographs collected by Jay Anderson), the collection at the Wilkes Heritage Museum, the Jane Carter Ogburn postcard collection at the Wilkes County Public Library, the North Wilkesboro High School Alumni Collection at Benton Hall, the North Carolina State Archives, and the North Carolina Collection at the University of North Carolina at Chapel Hill.

The Save Our Wilkes County History committee brought the three of us together, and for that we are truly enriched. Our editor at Arcadia, Maggie Bullwinkel, was always available to guide us and encourage us through the production process. Most importantly, we could not have accomplished this work without the love and support of our husbands, Bryan Bass, David Earp, and Gus Peña, and the smiling faces of our daughters, Ava Bass and Lora Earp.

INTRODUCTION

In the 17th century, the colony of Carolina was divided into eight sections and conveyed by King Charles II of England to eight proprietors. One of the eight was John Carteret, earl of Granville. The land Granville held encompassed much of the upper half of North Carolina. Native Americans inhabiting this section were pushed back as land agents sold expanses of the Granville tract. The land that comprises the current county of Wilkes was part of this tract.

The first white settler in Wilkes County is believed to have been Christopher Gist. Gist migrated from Maryland, and in 1750, he settled just west of Mulberry Fields in the heart of what is now North Wilkesboro. About two years later, the Mulberry Fields area was sold to Morgan Bryan, who in turn sold the land to his son, Joseph. (Joseph Bryan's daughter, Rebecca, would later wed legendary pioneer Daniel Boone.) Moravian surveyors explored the area at the same time but ultimately settled further east in Winston-Salem. The county was formed in 1777 from a large swath of land in southwestern Surry County. It was officially chartered in 1778.

Many of the early settlers moved to Wilkes County as the frontier moved westward. Most moved because they sought freedom and independence; they stayed because the land was abundant and cheap, the climate was amenable, and the waters of the Yadkin and Reddies Rivers provided an abundant water supply. Other natural resources were plentiful as well.

Wilkesboro became the county seat in 1778. Fifty acres of land were purchased and divided into a grid of streets and lots with a central square designated for the site of a courthouse. In 1890, a railroad was built in North Wilkesboro. Though the county seat remained in Wilkesboro, the coming of the railroad precipitated a boom in development that made the new town on the north side of the river a thriving center of commerce.

Colorful characters such as Daniel Boone, Chang and Eng Bunker (the original Siamese twins), Benjamin "Old Roundabout" Cleveland, Tom Dooley, Benny Parsons, Junior Johnson, James Larkin Pearson, and Zach Galifianakis are some of the county's most famous residents. Industries like Lowe's Companies, Inc., and Holly Farms were born in Wilkes. Equally important to the community are the local and small businesses for which Wilkes County is famous.

Most of all, the folkways and rural lifestyle of Wilkes County make it an irresistible place to live. People in Wilkes have for many years banded together in local organizations like volunteer fire departments, civic organizations, church groups, and other community associations to make this area a safe and inviting place to live. The images contained within this book offer a glimpse into the rich and varied history of this Great State of Wilkes.

One

Readin', Writin', and 'Rithmatic

Formal education evolved gradually in Wilkes County. To early settlers, constructing homes, starting farms, and surviving the frontier proved more pressing than teaching children to read and write. Education often began with apprenticeships: boys learned blacksmithing, carpentry, surveying, and tanning, while girls were taught domestic duties, including sewing and reading. In the early 1800s, churches and religious groups were among the first to establish schools to teach basic skills to students.

Public school districts in Wilkes formed in 1841. Conditions were often rustic; teachers were in short supply, schools were one-room structures, and the system offered little supervision. But students were afforded the opportunity, even under primitive conditions, to attain an education. During the Civil War, enrollment dwindled, and from 1863 to 1864, no students attended school. Private schools began anew during Reconstruction; the Finley School and Mamie Barber's school flourished in the late 1800s. Many women entered the field of education. Academies and institutes like those in Traphill and Mountain View provided advanced education and prepared young people for work and higher education. State funding for public schools was reinstated in 1869.

Champions like C. C. Wright were early advocates of equality in education even though funding for black education was scant. Community members and students eventually raised funds to construct Lincoln Heights in 1924. The school became a tremendous source of pride for the community as students excelled in academics and extracurricular activities.

School consolidation began in the 1920s. It was a slow process but an essential one. Many county schools, especially those in isolated parts of the county, were in terrible condition with few improved roads leading to them. The county had to purchase buses capable of navigating these roads and often could not afford school improvements and construction projects. Consolidation was nearly completed by 1954, when 4 new high schools and several elementary schools were constructed. Today the county boasts 13 elementary schools, 4 new middle schools, 4 high schools currently undergoing renovations, and a vocational center for high school students.

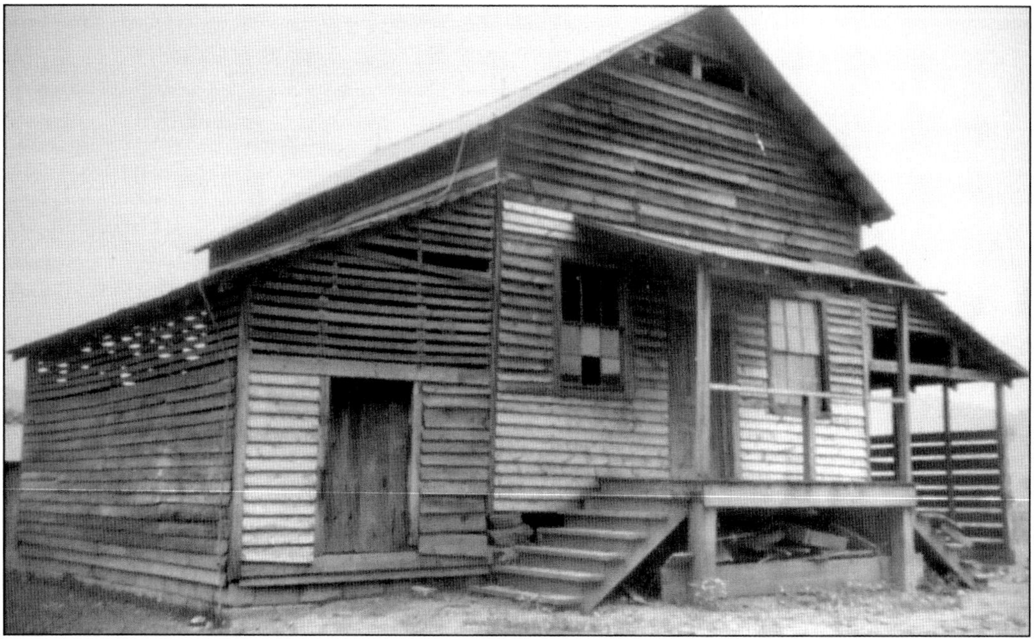

Whippoorwill Academy. Whippoorwill Academy was built in 1880 in Ferguson. The school was open three months out of the year with time off for "fodder pulling and corn gathering," said Tom Ferguson. The building was located on the Peeler farm until 1986, when it was dismantled and reconstructed by Hill and Edith Ferguson Carter for use as a history museum. (Courtesy of Wilkes Community College Library.)

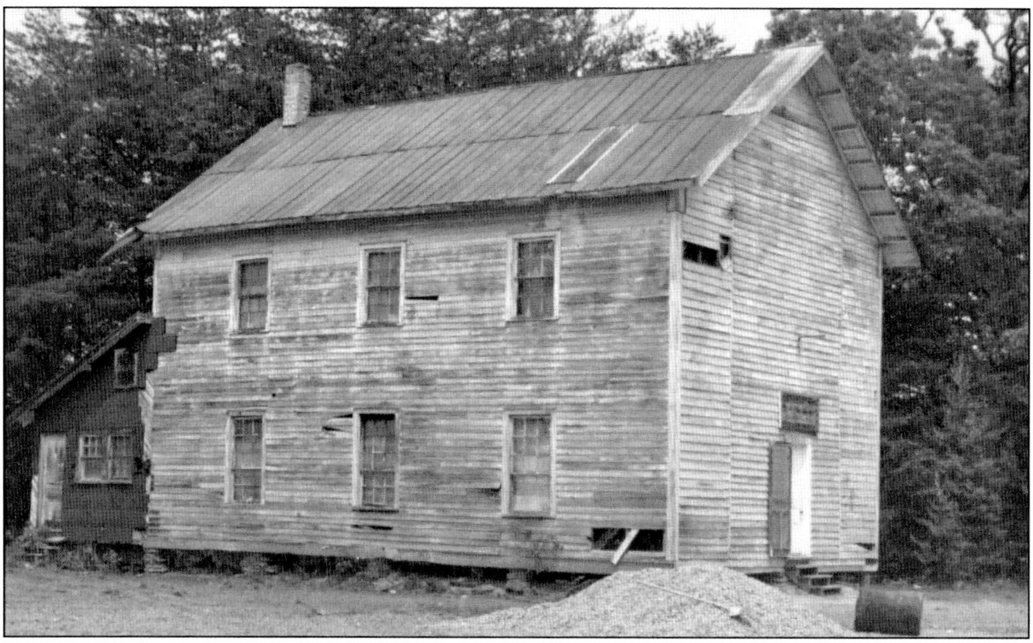

Sulphur Springs Academy. Sulphur Springs Academy was established c. 1875 on donated land in the Mulberry community. Tuition was $10 a month, and lodging cost $7 (including laundry). After 1935, the academy served as a senior citizen's center and as the Odd Fellows Liberty Lodge Hall. (Courtesy of Wilkes Community College Library.)

MAMIE BARBER'S TEACHERS. Miss Mamie Barber's Home School for Young Ladies and Girls was founded by Mary Taylor Barber in 1879. Board at the Barber home was $9.75 per month; girls could also attend as day students. In addition to standard classes, for $3 per month, girls could take Higher English, which included Latin and French. (Courtesy of Wilkes Community College Library.)

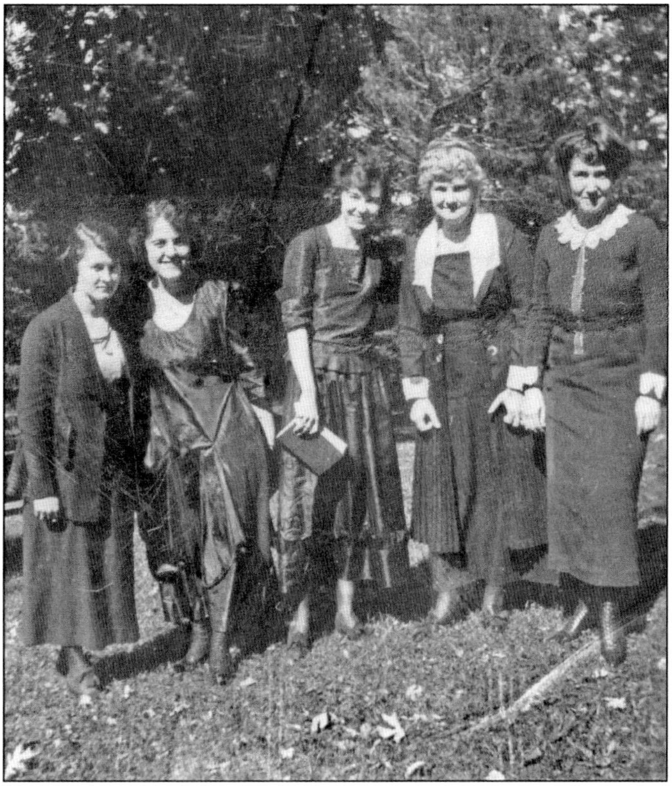

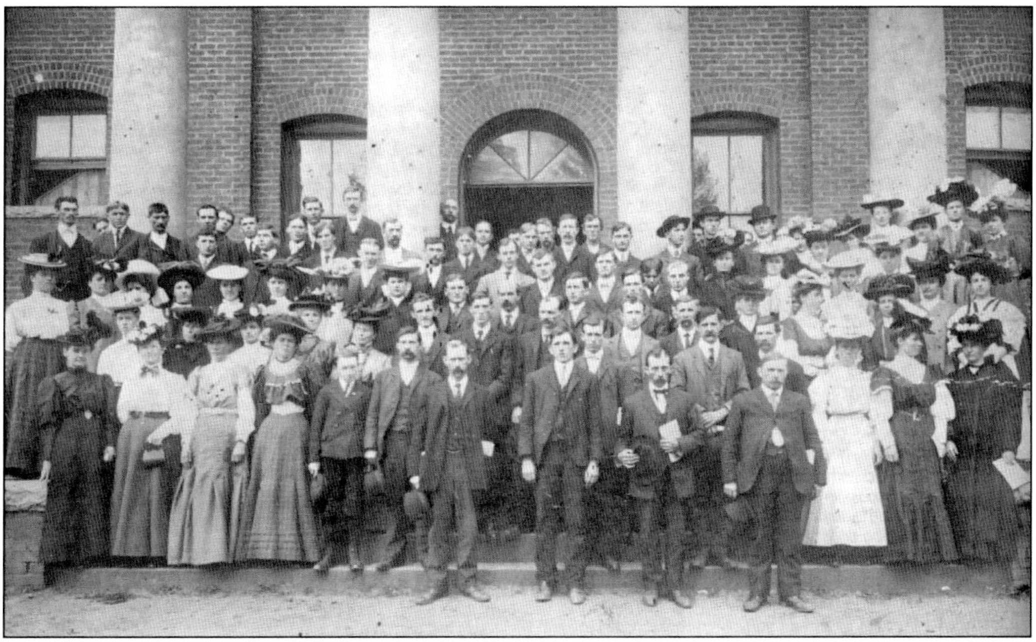

SCHOOL TEACHERS, EARLY 1900S. In 1887, Wilkes County teachers met at the courthouse to organize a teachers' association. Officers elected were James Foote, president; C. C. Wright, vice president; W. R. Hendren, chaplain; and W. S. Surrat, secretary. Topics at the meetings included student retention, discipline, and teaching methods. (Courtesy of Wilkes Genealogical Society.)

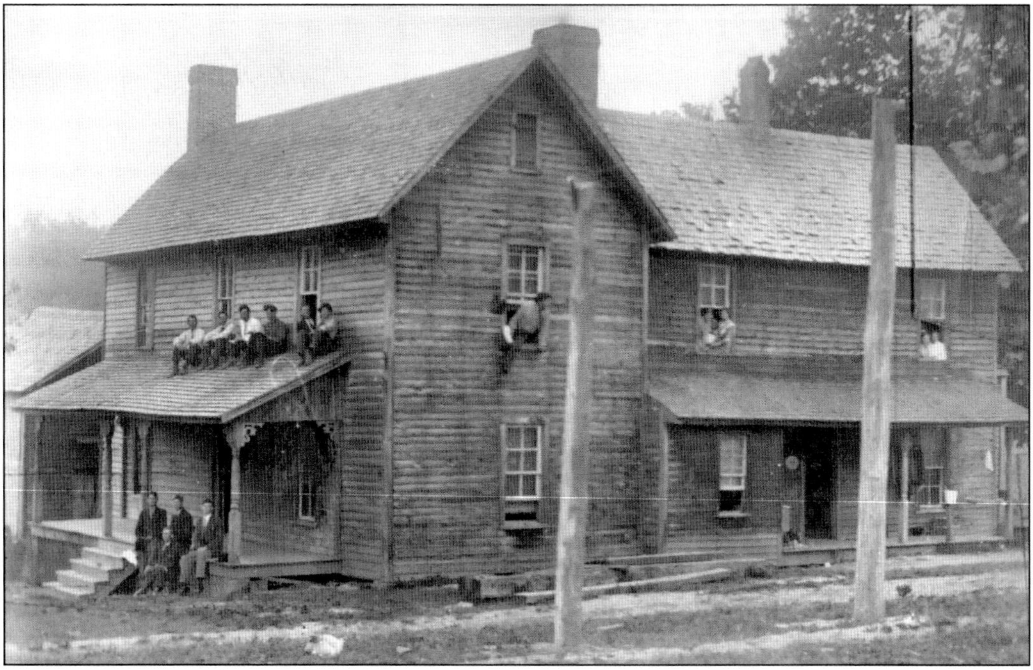

COMER SCHOOL. The Comer School was established by Will Comer at Shady Grove Baptist Church in the early 1900s. Comer's son Billy served as a teacher at the school, as did James Franklin Haynes. This photograph shows the Windy Gap home of Reverend Comer and a number of Comer School students who boarded there. (Courtesy of Wilkes Community College Library.)

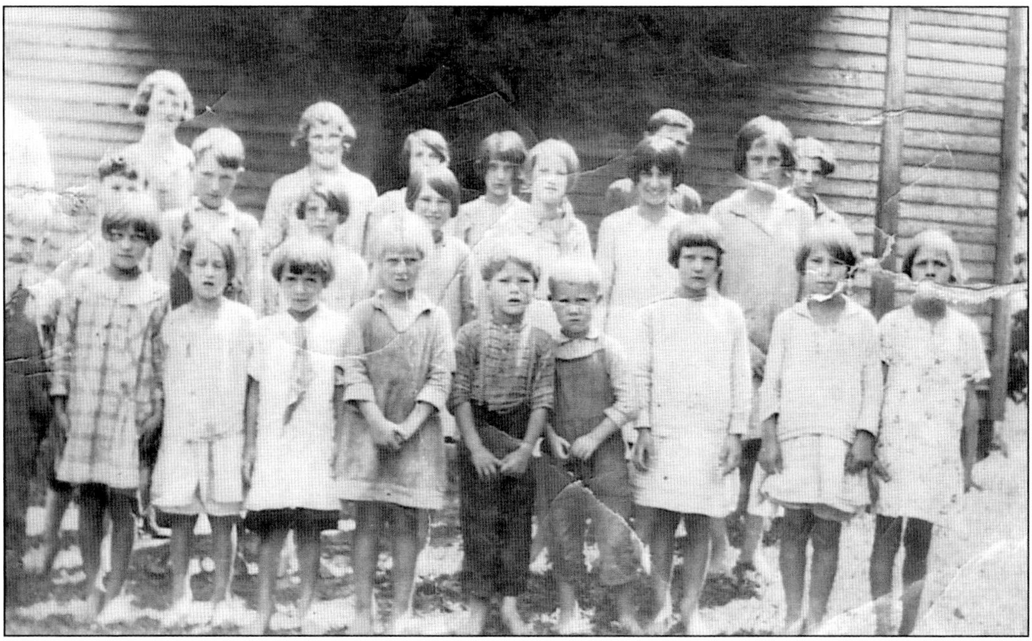

BIG IVY SCHOOL, 1930S. In 1933, Big Ivy School, located in Purlear, employed one teacher. Early teachers like Martisha Cordellia Roten Beshears could expect to earn from $7 to $10 a month. Big Ivy School was eventually consolidated into Mount Pleasant School. (Courtesy of Kathleen Calloway.)

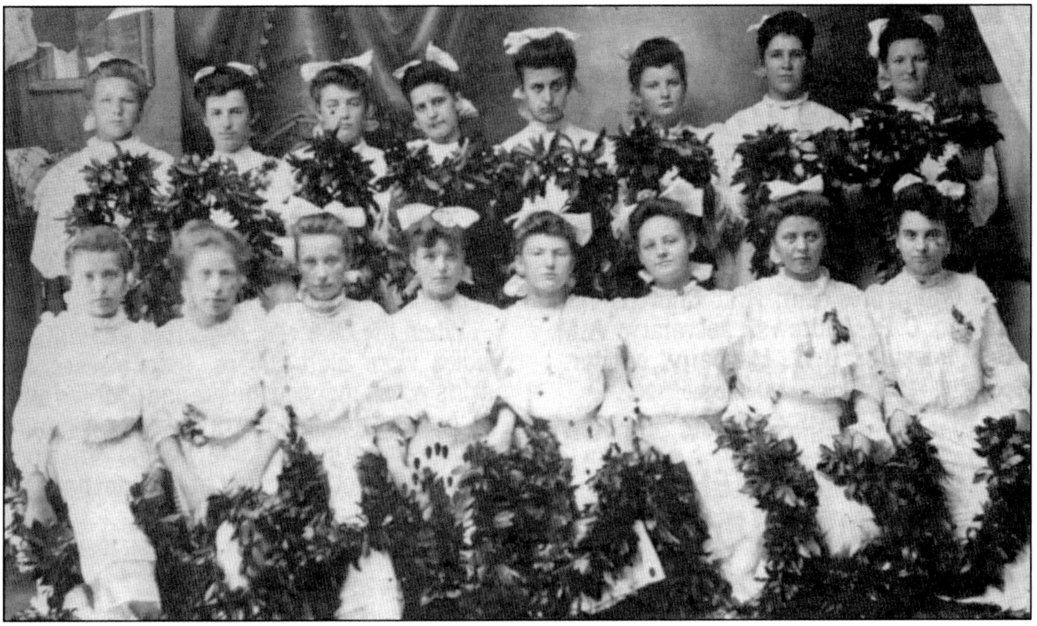

NORTH WILKESBORO GRADED SCHOOL, C. 1906. The North Wilkesboro Graded School children pictured from left to right are (first row) Mamie Williams, Nellie Hart, Mamie Jones, Mabel Hampton, Agnes Walter, Beatrice Myers, Della Brewer, and Hattie McLean; (second row) Annie Robinette, Hattie McNeil, Minnie Brown, Belle Faw, Minnie Turner, Willie Pardue, Flossie Hendren, and Estelle Myers. (Courtesy of Wilkes Genealogical Society.)

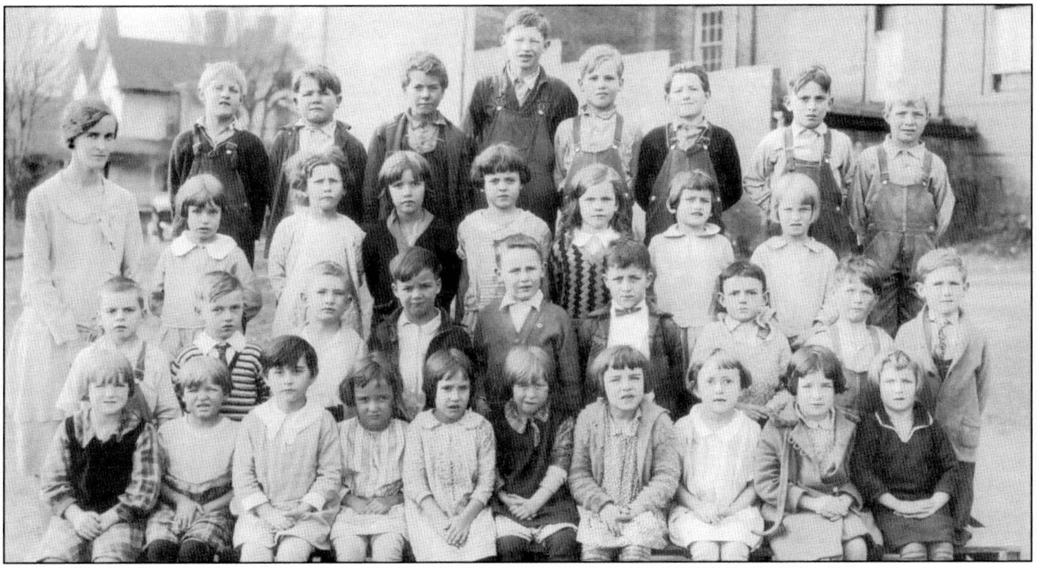

WILKESBORO ELEMENTARY SCHOOL, 1929. Pictured in this first grade class are, from left to right, (first row) Carolyn Linney, Oma Anderson, unidentified, Faye Wright, Frances Keyes, unidentified, Geraldine Johnson, Peggy Somers, Peggy Church, and unidentified; (second row) Percy Minton, Ray Stroud, Charles Foster, Bill Phillips, unidentified, James Hemphill, unidentified, Arnold Milam, and Wilson Warner; (third row) Mattie Pardue, Louise McLean, four unidentified, Elizabeth Welborn, and Lillie Crysel; (fourth row) Garfield Minton, two unidentified, David Keys, three unidentified, and Darrell Minton. (Courtesy of Laura Stroud.)

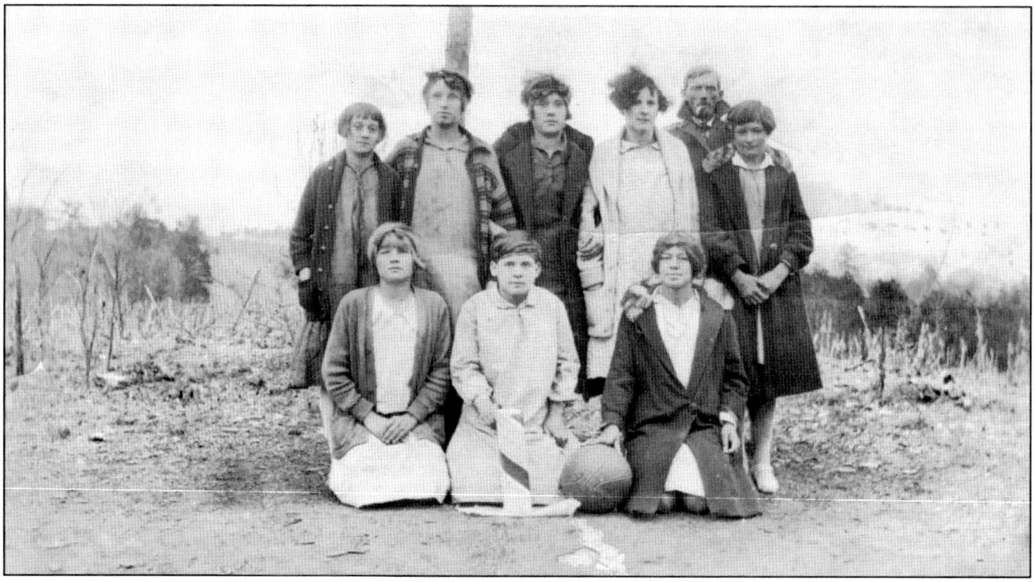

STONY RIDGE SCHOOL, c. 1927. Members of the girls' basketball team pictured from left to right are (first row) Maude Pruitt, Vallie Pruitt, and Lessie Billings; (second row) unidentified, Attis Pruitt Johnson Shepherd, Texie Richardson Alexander Jordan Wood, Alice Pruitt Blevins, Eugene Billings (teacher), and Inez Bauguess Crabb. (Courtesy of Jason Duncan.)

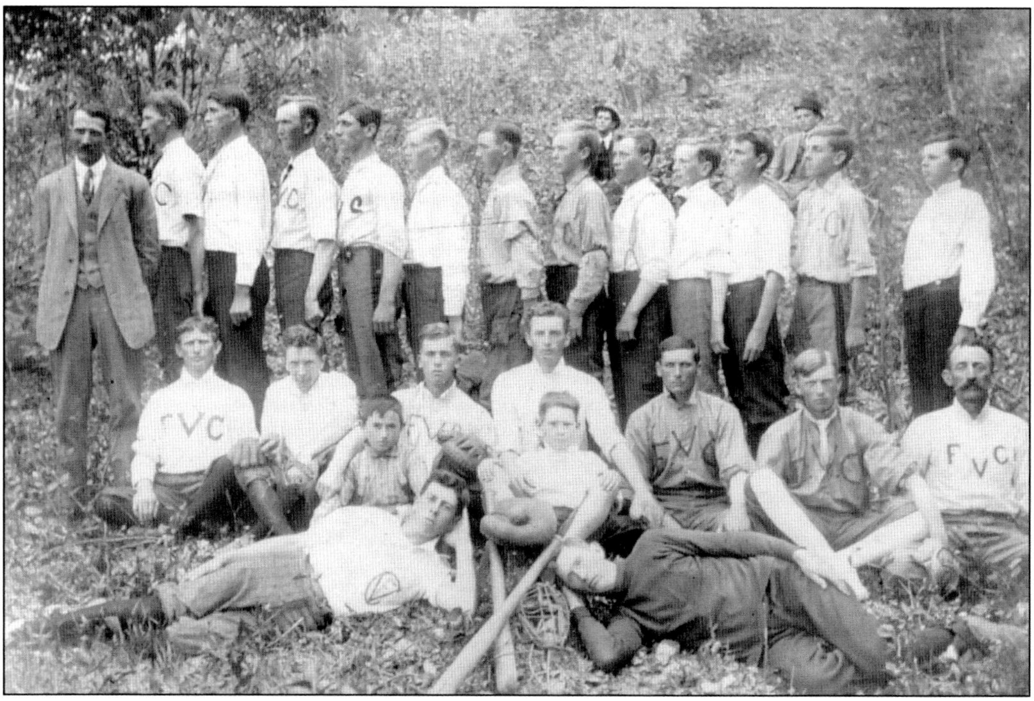

FAIRVIEW COLLEGE, c. 1911. Formerly Traphill Seminary and Traphill Academy, the school was officially chartered as Fairview in 1891, though earlier schools had been operating on-site since 1871. The college was closed from 1904 to 1909, reorganized and reopened c. 1910, and ultimately closed in 1918. The image shows the baseball team. (Courtesy of Wilkes Community College Library.)

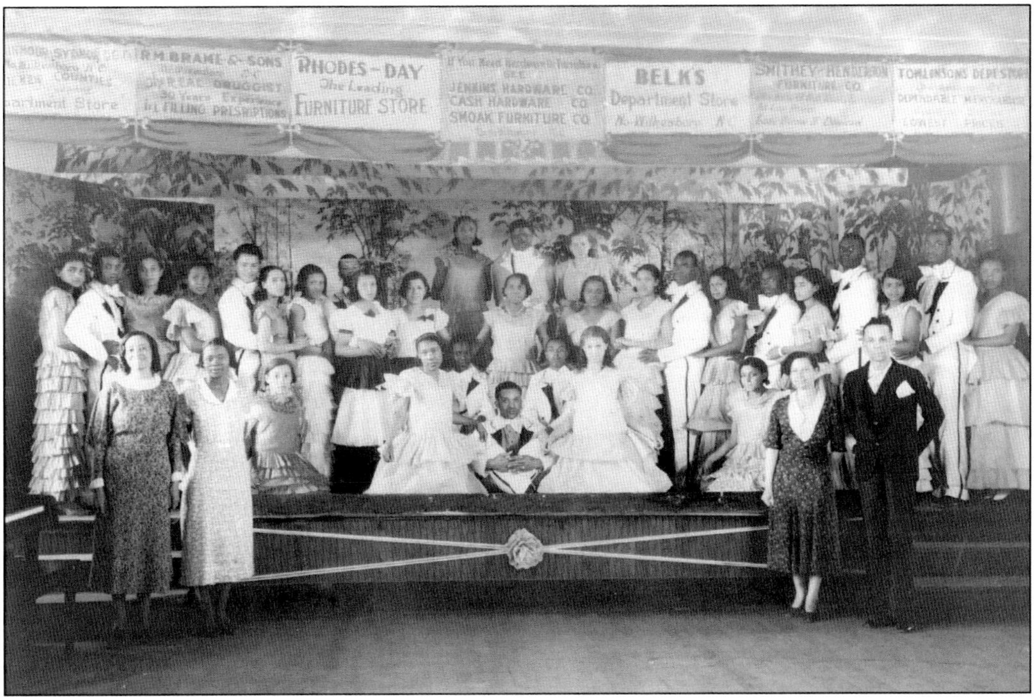

LINCOLN HEIGHTS. Lincoln Heights School was established in 1924. Prior to that, black students could only receive schooling through the seventh grade in local one-room schools. To remedy this, concerned citizens from across the county sold vegetables and cardboard bricks and engaged in other fund-raising activities to pay for a school with higher grades. The Julius A. Rosenwald Foundation contributed a 50-percent match to the cause. The original building had six classrooms and an auditorium. The name Lincoln Heights comes from a speech that sought to inspire children to reach the heights of Lincoln. The school closed in 1968, and students were integrated in other public schools. (Both courtesy of Wilkes Heritage Museum.)

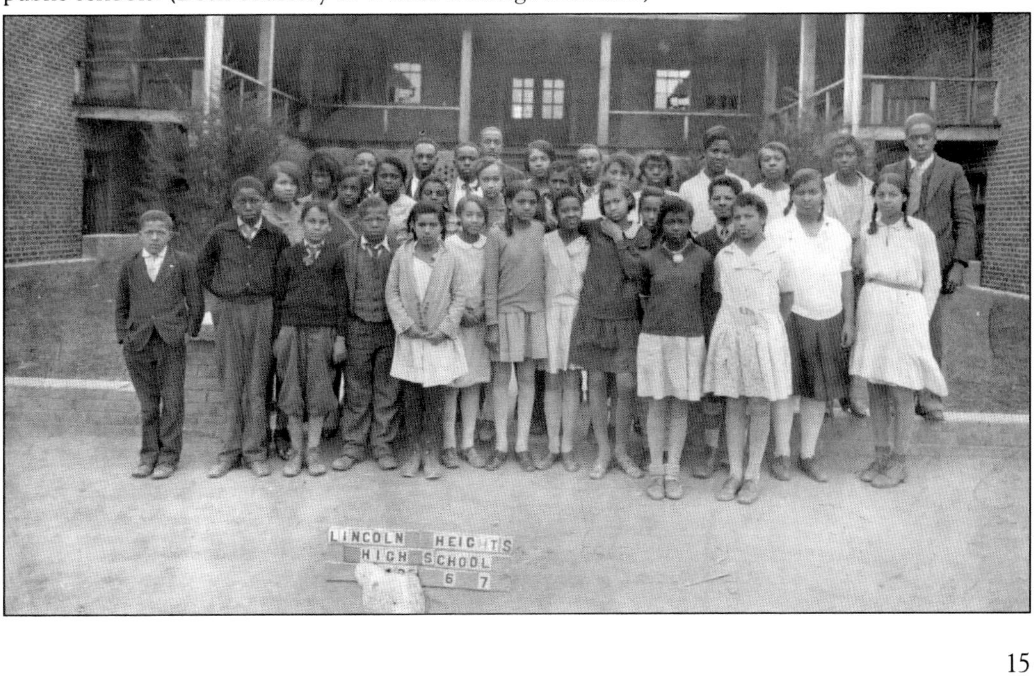

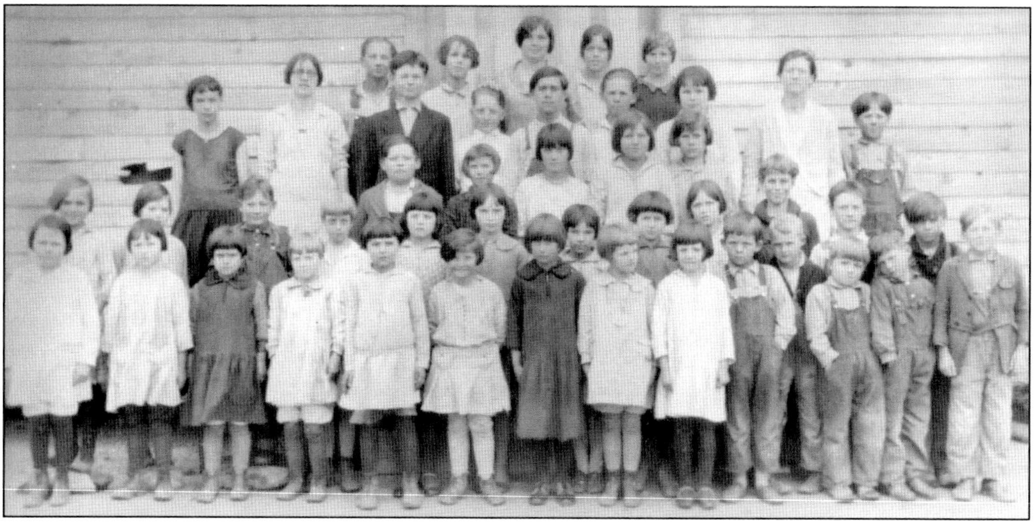

WHITE PLAINS SCHOOL, 1928. The students pictured here from left to right are (first row) Epsie Alexander, Mozelle Byrd, Ruth Parks, Marie Blackburn, Bertie Cothren, Lucille Harris, Mary Lucy Pardue, Opal Childress, Bruce Poplin, Guy Blevins, Elton Jordan, Ernest Dowell, and John White Truitt; (second row) Mary Nell Byrd, Bessie Jane Poplin, Junior Byrd, Lola Wood, Eloise Childress, Esther Johnson, Ruby Blackburn, Isabell Cothren, Vallie Byrd, Albert Wood, Charles Sparks, and Tom Bell; (third row) Roscoe Byrd, Hazel Jordan, Cordia Sparks, Lois Bell, Sadie Royal, and unidentified; (fourth row) Artie Blackburn, Buena Dowell (teacher), Jarvie Cothren, Eugene Pardue, Brett Parks, Clyde Jordan, Ina Blackburn, Minnie Pardue (teacher), and John Cothren; (fifth row) Con Bell, Ethel Truitt, Iva Caudill, Mae Wood, and Eva Caudill. (Courtesy of Wilkes Heritage Museum.)

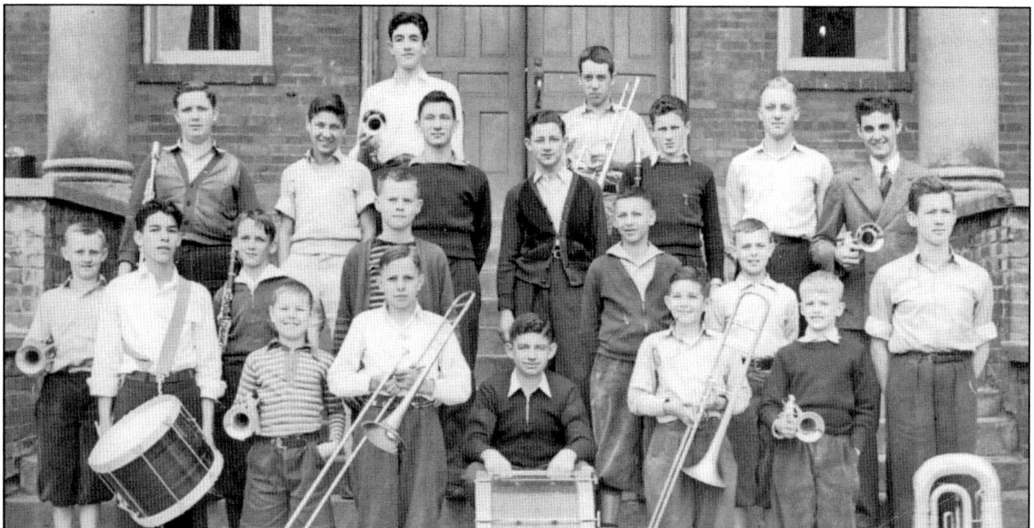

NORTH WILKESBORO SCHOOL BAND. The members of the band pictured here from left to right are (first row) Bruce Dyson, John E. Justice, Lomax Kilby, Malcolm Butner, Tal Barnes, Jay Johnson, and Walt Jones; (second row) Bill Gabriel, Genio Cardwell, Tom Eshelman, Mike Williams, and Andy Johnson; (third row) Mack Miller, Bob Day, Joe McCoy, Tommy Caudill, Joe Clements, Dwight Sebastian, and Bill Grier (leader); (fourth row) John I. Myers and Bob McCoy. (Courtesy of North Wilkesboro High School Alumni Association.)

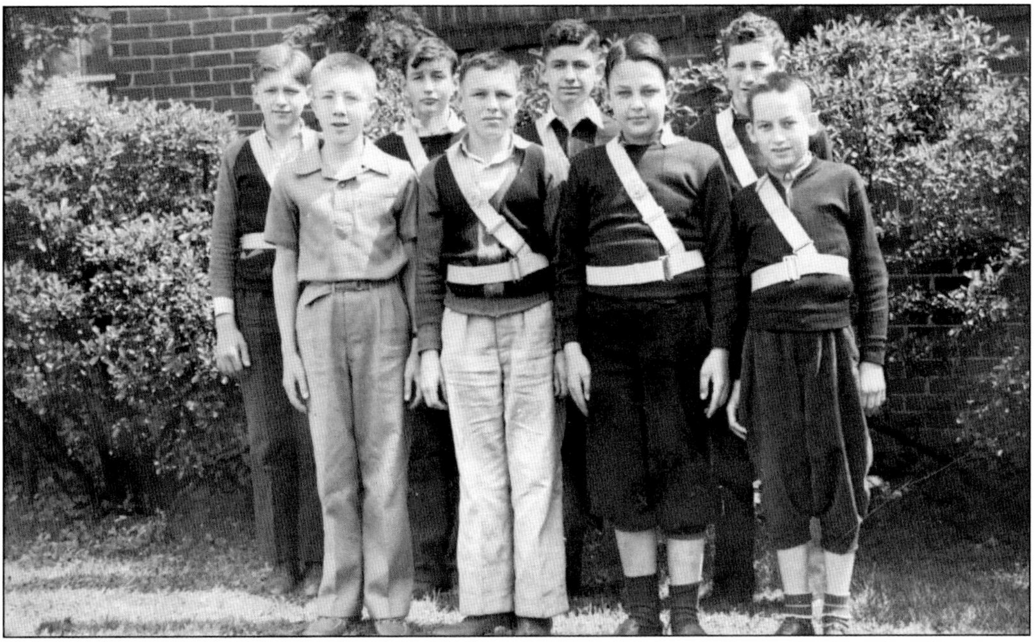

NORTH WILKESBORO SAFETY PATROL. Children wearing orange belts across their shoulders were familiar sights in areas where school children crossed traffic. Members of the North Wilkesboro Safety Patrol pictured from left to right are (first row) Ike Coffey, Bill Estes, "Punk" Stewart, and Lynn Kerbaugh; (second row) Jay Joines, Bill Hudson, Malcolm Butner, and Joe Clements. (Courtesy of North Wilkesboro High School Alumni Association.)

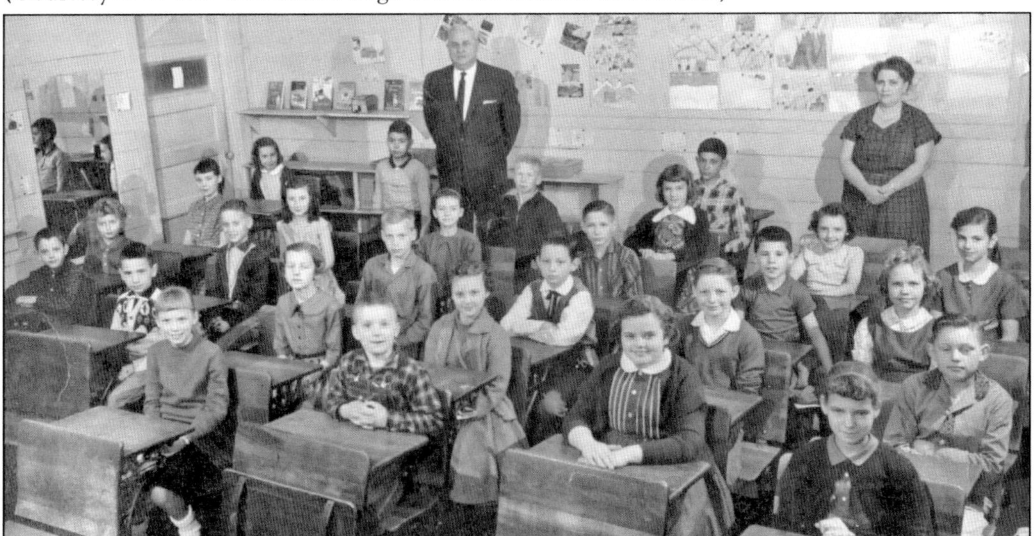

WILKESBORO SCHOOL, 1959. Included in this picture are Judy Ann Anderson, Susan Anderson, Laura Stroud, David Church, Donnie Hogan, Helen Minton, Robert Trivette, Jay Thomas Jones, Bruce Blevins, Linda Mae Davidson, Jeremy Lee Howell, Wanda Blevins, Barbara Gail Bauguess, Danny Beachboard, Shirley Jewel Russell, Jody Johnson, Roger Dale Hendren, Faye Williams, Fred Canter, Carolyn Walker, Warner Minton, Michael Parker, Nancy Susan Whittington, Deloris Carlton, Terry Johnson, Christine Weaver, and Rebecca Louise Waugh. (Courtesy of Laura Stroud.)

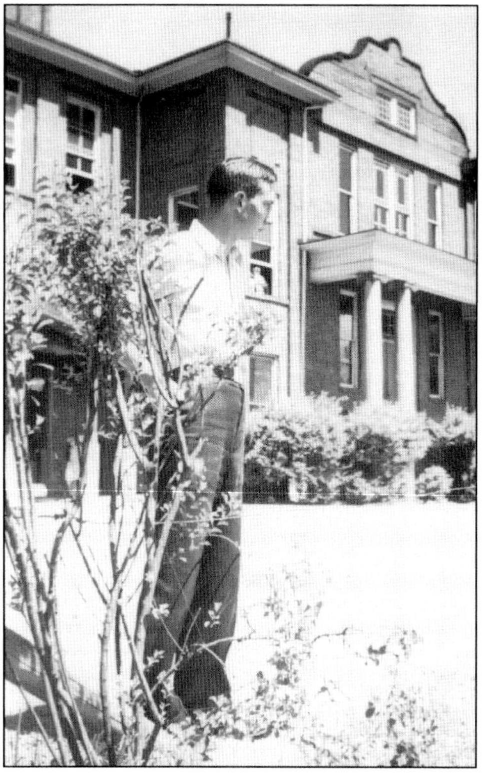

NORTH WILKESBORO SCHOOL. This structure was completed in 1914. A building for upper grades was constructed in 1924 and used until North Wilkesboro High School consolidated into Wilkes Central in 1952. The building, now called Benton Hall in memory of Lucille Rhodes Benton, has been home to the Wilkes Playmakers since 1994. Walter Martin stands in front of the building. (Courtesy of North Wilkesboro High School Alumni Association.)

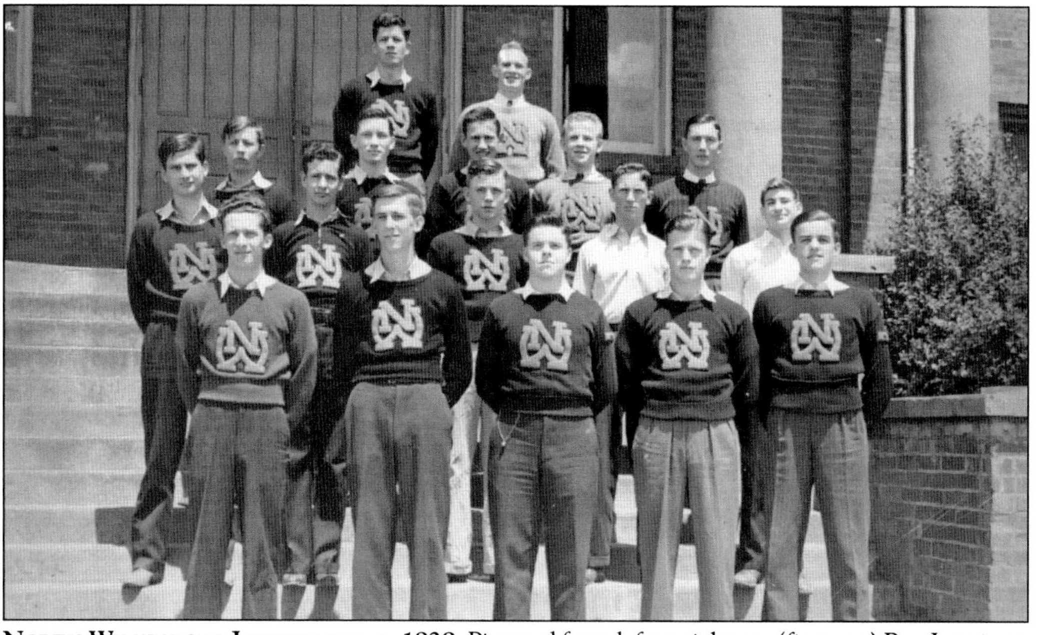

NORTH WILKESBORO LETTERMEN, C. 1939. Pictured from left to right are (first row) Ray Jennings, Ben Harrison, Paul Haigwood, Don Craven, and Lomax Crook; (second row) Jay Grayson, George Campbell, Ward Kenerly, Charles Shatley, and Buck Faw; (third row) Royal Johnson, Joe McCoy, Houston Steelman, Russell Pearson, and Walter Martin; (fourth row) Walter Call and W. J. Hudson. (Courtesy of North Wilkesboro High School Alumni Association.)

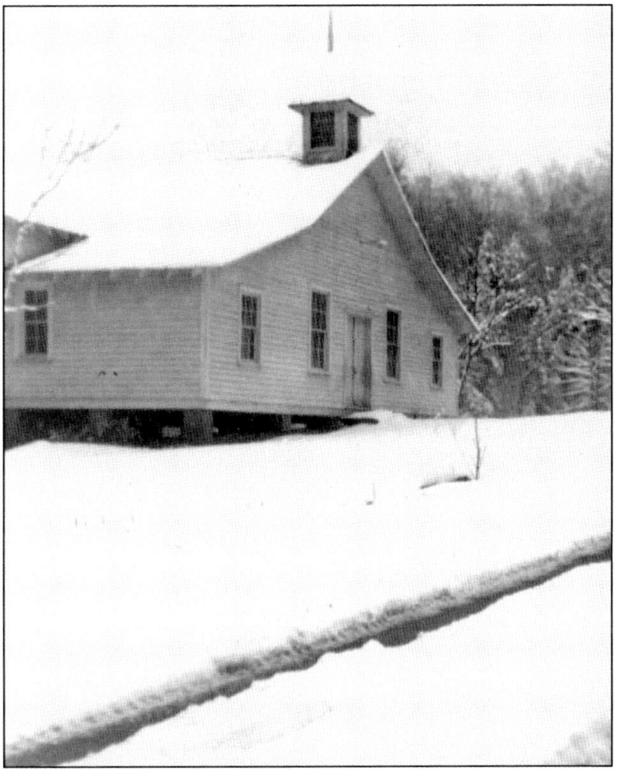

HENDRIX SCHOOL, 1964. The Hendrix School was located in the Mount Zion community of western Wilkes County. In 1933, the school had two teachers. Hendrix School was consolidated into Mount Pleasant School in the 1950s. John Barnett served as a teacher and principal at the school for 20 years. (Courtesy of Linda Triplett.)

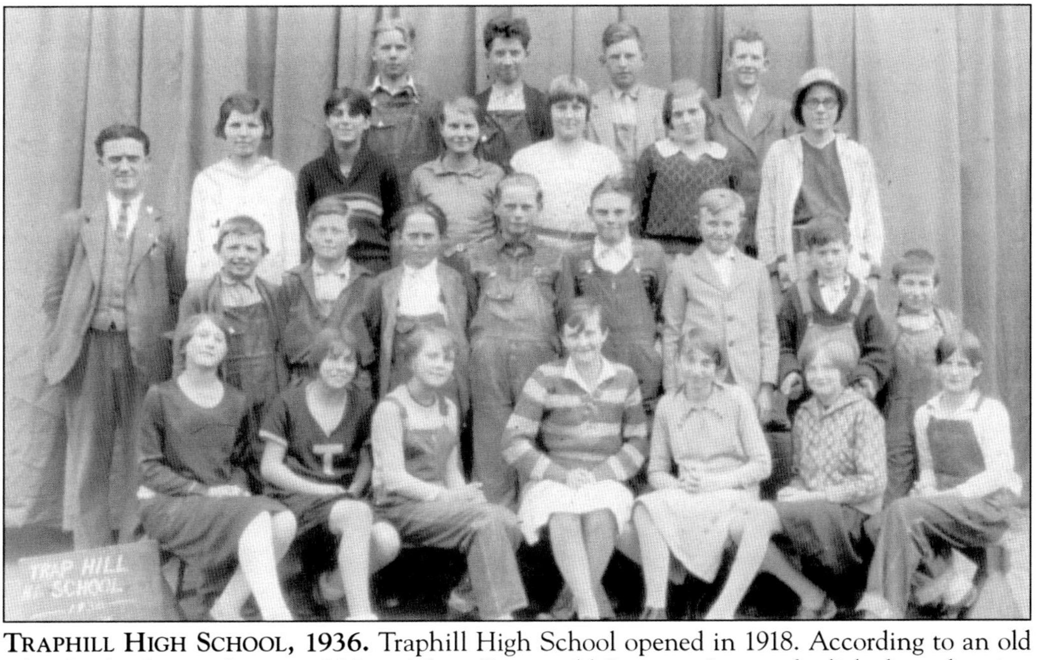

TRAPHILL HIGH SCHOOL, 1936. Traphill High School opened in 1918. According to an old school calendar, students could board for a "reasonable" rate or "rooms for light housekeeping may be secured." Students studied math, science, athletics, history, English, and Latin. For an extra $3 a month, students could also take music classes. This photograph shows fifth, sixth, and seventh graders. (Courtesy of Wilkes Community College Library.)

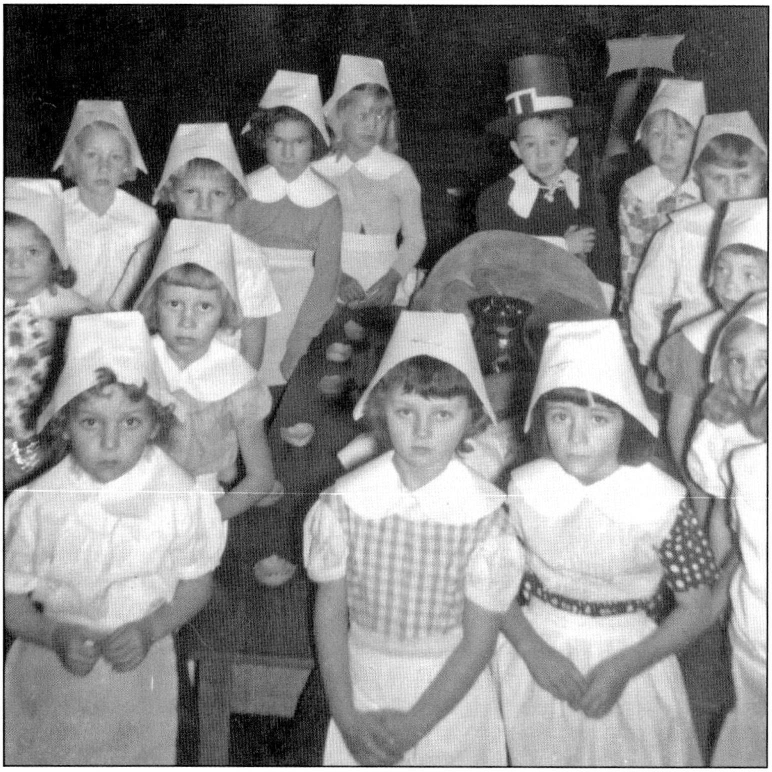

WILKESBORO SCHOOL, C. 1956. School pageants were a common practice at elementary schools, particularly in the 1950s. Christmas pageants were especially popular, complete with handmade costumes and piano accompaniments provided by music teachers. Pictured here are first-grade students from Wilkesboro Elementary School dressed as pilgrims for Thanksgiving festivities. (Courtesy of Gail Haynes.)

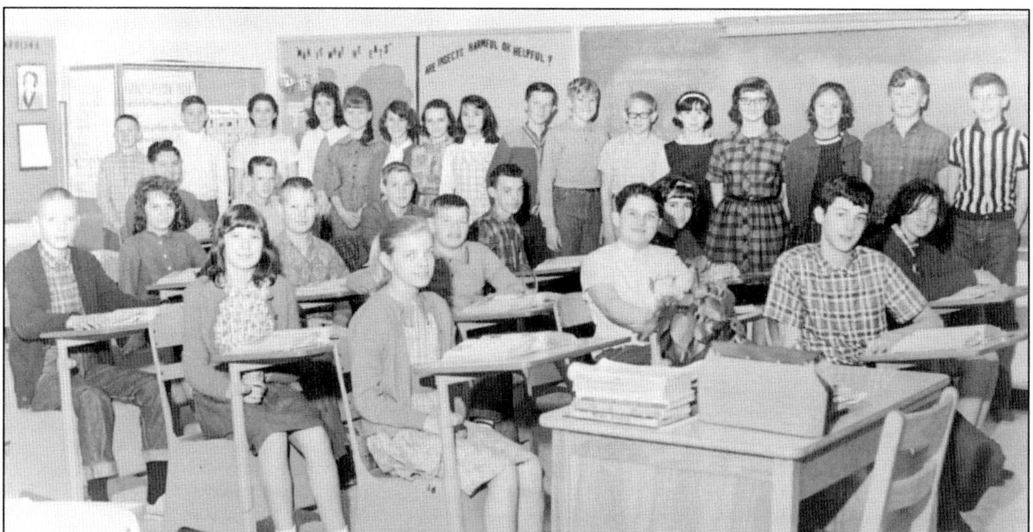

WILKESBORO SCHOOL, C. 1962. Blanche McNeill's seventh-grade class included, from left to right, (sitting) Tommy Johnson, Betina Ball, Johnny Mac Brown, Wanda Absher, David Smithey, Lee Edward Anderson, Robert Laws, Rebecca Call, Rickey McLain, Robert Hamby, Barry Foster, Gail Pardue, Larry Christenbury, and Evelyn Younce; (standing) Thomas Hayes, Terry Love, Cathy Triplett, Nancy Gentle, Ray Ann Carlton, Patricia Jones, Wanda Anderson, Diana Joines, Quincy Michael, Doug Williams, Jay Martin, Carolyn Goodman, Patricia Stamey, Billie Culler, Tommy Waddell, and Bill Warden. (Courtesy of Gail Haynes.)

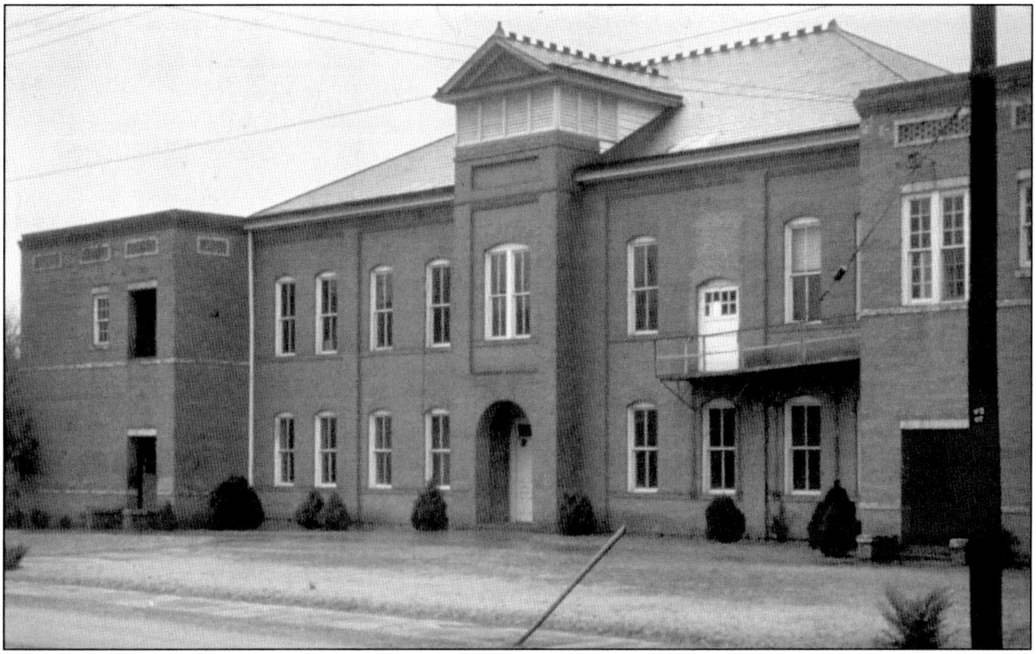

Wilkesboro High School. Wilkesboro High School's first permanent building was completed in 1908. Additional wings for classrooms were added in 1922, and in 1949, an agricultural building made of cinder blocks was built. After Wilkesboro consolidated with Ferguson High School and North Wilkesboro High School to form Wilkes Central High School in 1952, the Wilkesboro gymnasium and lot were traded for the old Wilkesboro post office building that for a number of years housed the Wilkes County Board of Education. The school building was torn down, and the Johnson J. Hayes Federal Building was constructed on the spot of the old school. Pictured below is the Wilkesboro High School class of 1930. (Both courtesy of Vergie Foster.)

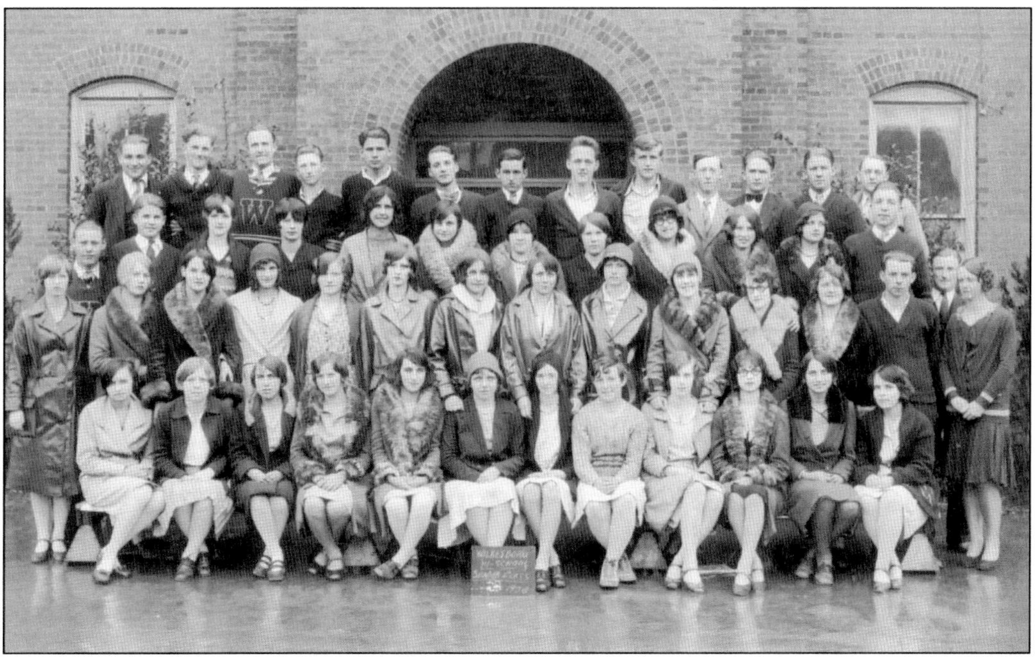

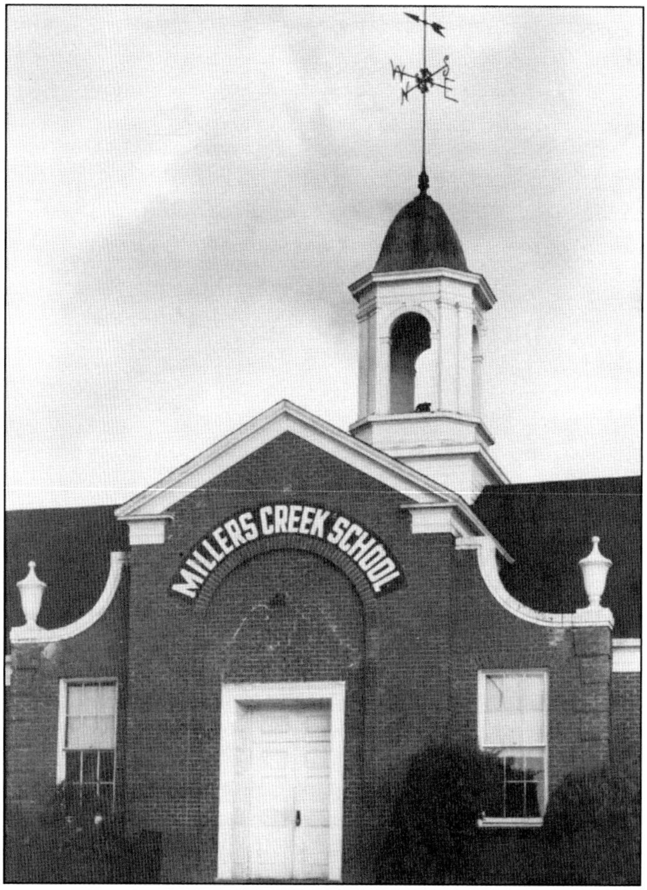

MILLERS CREEK SCHOOL. The first brick structure housing Millers Creek School was built in 1936. The structure, which included 15 rooms, a lounge, and an office, replaced earlier wood buildings that had probably operated since the 1820s. In the early years, the school served both elementary and high school students and graduated its first class in 1930. In the upper grades, young ladies learned domestic arts. Young men and war veterans learned about agriculture and woodworking, including how to dehorn cattle, plant trees, improve mailboxes, and other practical tasks. Millers Creek High School and Mount Pleasant High School were consolidated to form West Wilkes High School in 1956. Pictured below are members of the first-grade class *c.* 1951. (Both courtesy of Sheri Hayes.)

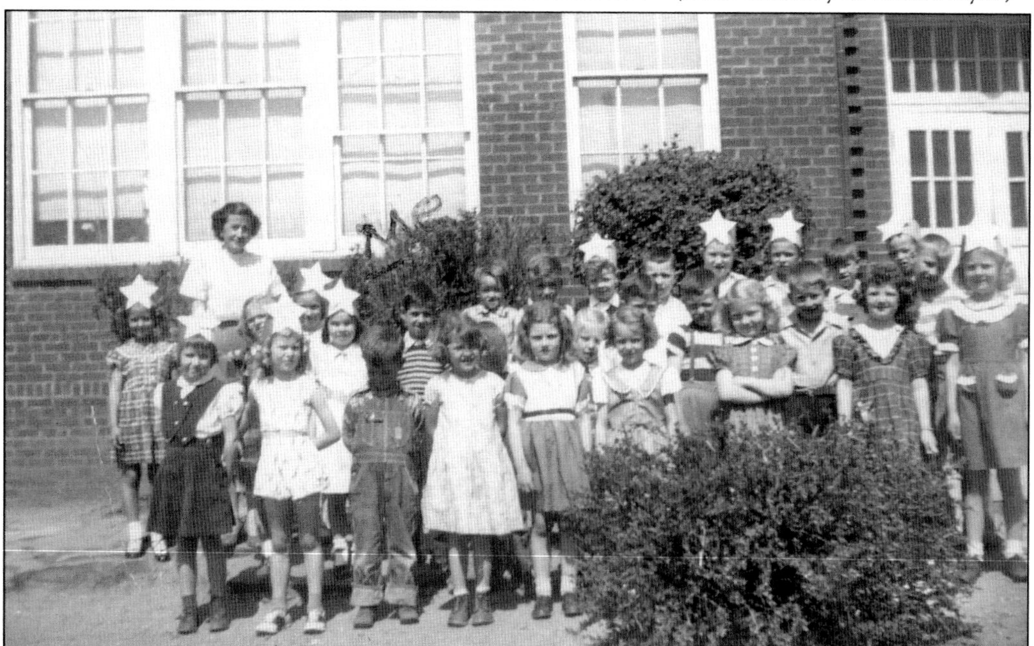

HOMECOMING QUEENS. Annual homecoming games most likely evolved from alumni football games held at colleges and universities. In September or October, Wilkes County high schools celebrated the return of former residents and alumni with football games, parades, bonfires, and pep rallies. Reunions were designed to renew old friendships and revive school spirit. One of the most popular festivities has been the coronation of the homecoming queen. Pictured at right is the crowning of Maxine Nichols as Millers Creek High School homecoming queen in 1955. Pictured below are members of the West Wilkes court in the homecoming parade in downtown North Wilkesboro in 1960. (Right, courtesy of the *Chieftain*; below, courtesy of the *Hawkeye*.)

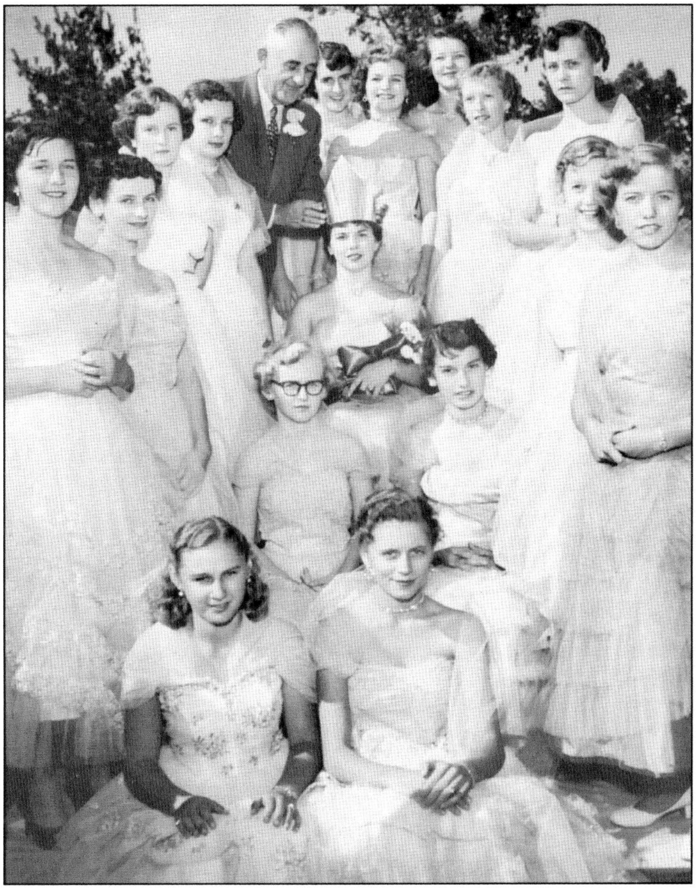

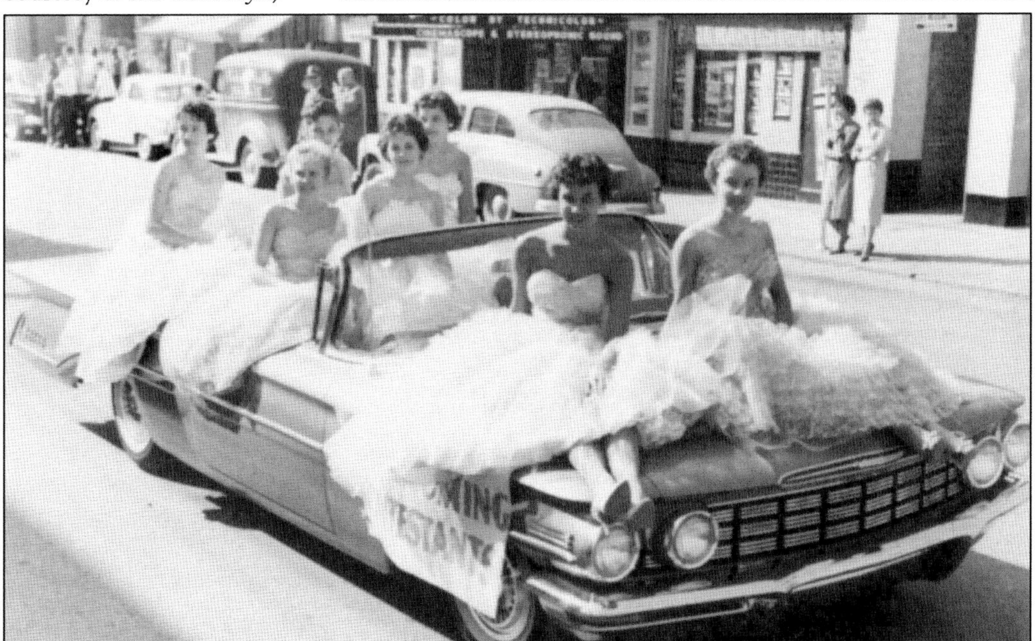

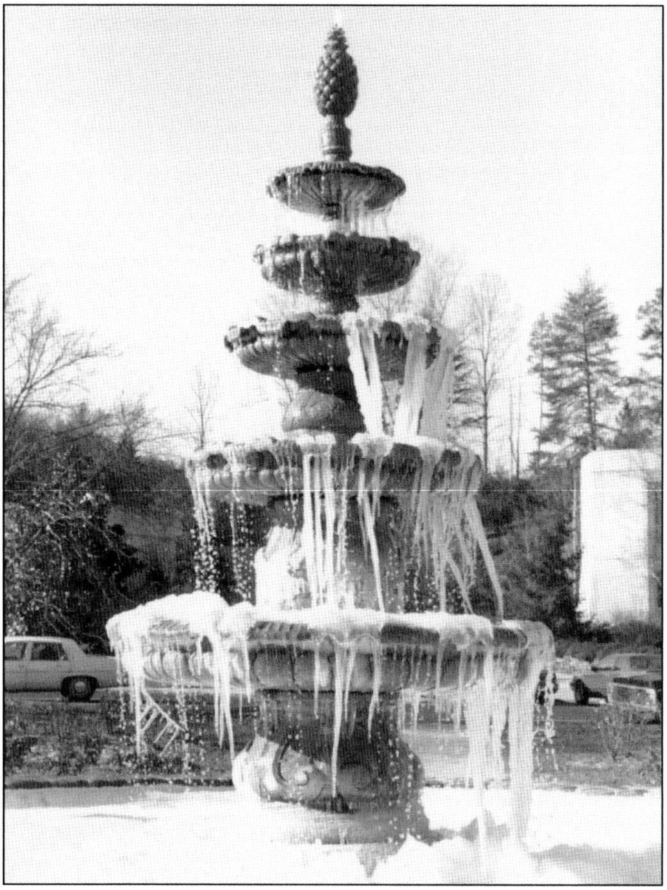

WILKES COMMUNITY COLLEGE. Wilkes Community College (WCC) was established in 1964 to serve Wilkes, Ashe, and Alleghany Counties. Enrollment for the first year at WCC was 68 students. The first one-year program awarded diplomas to practical nurses that had begun classes in 1965. The Associate in Arts and Associate in Applied Science programs began admitting full-time students in 1966. The actual college facilities, covering 75 acres and including three buildings, were not completed until 1969. Prior to that, classes were held in businesses, schools, and churches in Wilkesboro. Pictured at left is the Colvard fountain; pictured below is an aerial view of the college campus, home of the annual Americana music festival MerleFest. (Both courtesy of Wilkes Community College Library.)

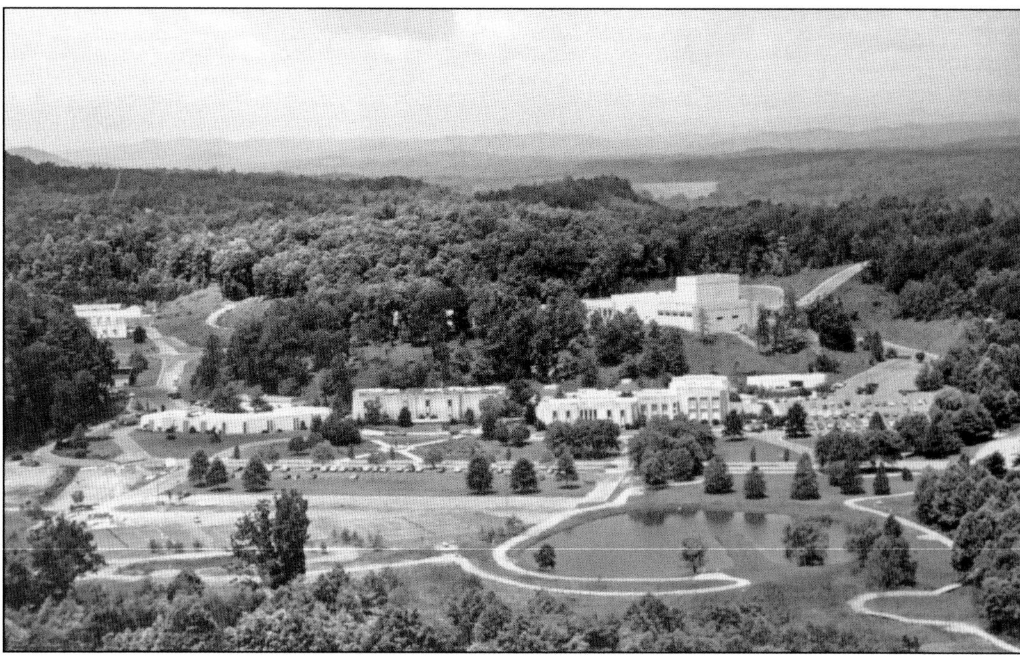

Two

Praising the Lord

Though Moravians considered settling here in the late 1700s, Wilkes County has always been a predominantly Baptist county. From the earliest meetings at Mulberry Fields Meeting House, the Baptist faith proved well suited to the area. Fiercely independent and personal in their relationship with God, Baptists were strict disciplinarians that chastised members for playing cards, drinking, and dancing. They debated issues like Sunday school, missions, foot washing, and inerrancy. And they celebrated together at camp meetings, river baptisms, and prayer meetings.

Methodists, Presbyterians, and Episcopalians gained popularity in the mid-1800s. Methodist circuit riders on horseback served remote areas. Presbyterians and Episcopalians often ministered under trying conditions as well. Other groups developed over the years, each with unique traditions, rituals, and doctrinal interpretations. Each church, no matter how large or small, has played a crucial role in the spiritual life of Wilkes County.

Regardless of denomination, similar practices developed. Ministers promised the rewards of Heaven and threatened the fires of Hell to unrepentant sinners. Hymns reinforced the messages of the Scriptures. Revivals were preached, often loudly and dramatically, so that people within the church could experience renewal and people without could experience conversion. Most churches practiced some form of baptism, either immersion or sprinkling, to symbolize rebirth. People turned out in their finery to worship together and thank God for the blessings in their lives.

Churches have always been central to the social and cultural life in Wilkes County. Religion has provided comfort, a belief system, a means for understanding the inexplicable, and a course for enduring the hardships of life. People gained strength from their faith when nothing else seemed to sustain them. Funerals, wakes, poundings, and sympathetic church families guided them through times of sorrow and need. Just as importantly, covered-dish suppers, Christmas pageants, homecomings, old-fashioned days, picnics, and gospel sings provided opportunities for people to come together and enjoy hospitality and camaraderie. Wilkes County is truly a good and well-blessed land.

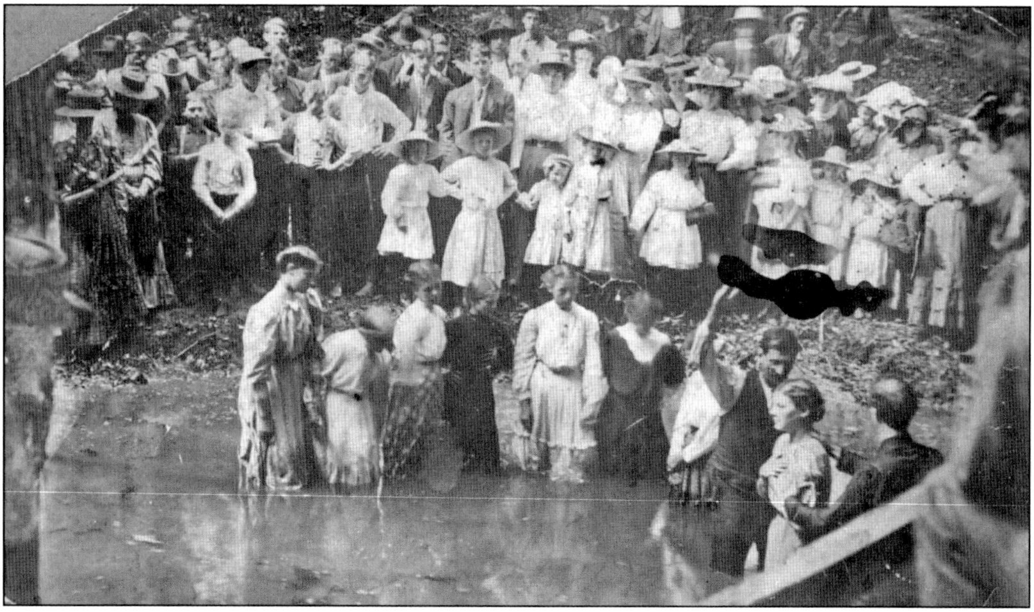

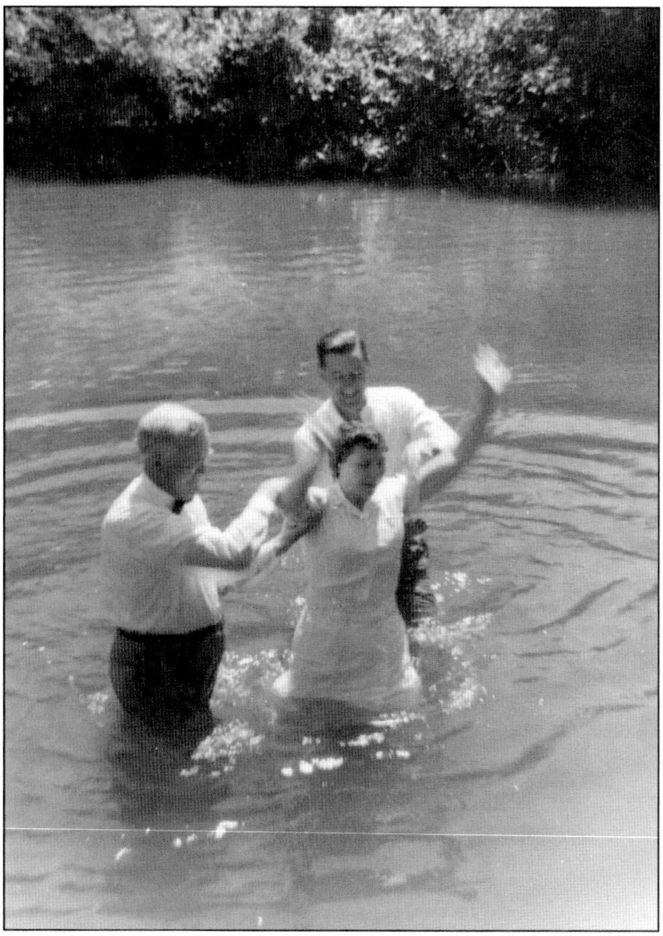

RIVER BAPTISMS. Baptists were the leading denomination in Wilkes County for years. As the Baptist faith is characterized in part by the act of immersion as a ritual of purification, it was not uncommon to see church members being baptized in the river in the days before indoor baptismal wells were common. Often entire families would be baptized at the same time. Some churches still perform river baptisms periodically. These images were made in the Mount Zion community (above) near the Lewis Fork creek in the late 1800s and in the Grandin community (left) near Caldwell County in the 1910s. (Above, courtesy of Linda Triplett; left, courtesy of Wilkes Community College Library.)

CENTER BAPTIST CHURCH. Center Baptist Church in the Mulberry community was established in 1886 as an offshoot of Liberty Grove Baptist Church. The charter members wanted a church of their own in which they could worship as they chose with Sunday school, revivals, and musical instruments. This building was rebuilt in 1922 and incorporated into a newer building in 1956. (Courtesy of Sheri Hayes.)

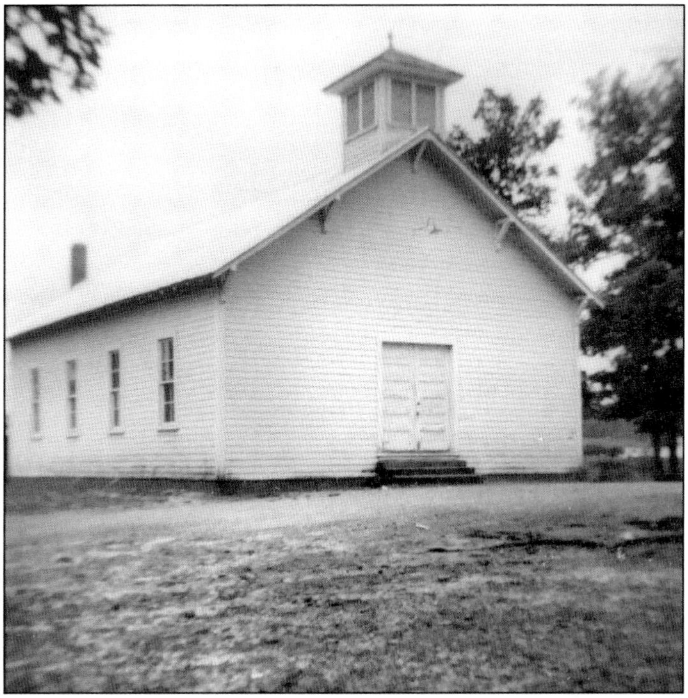

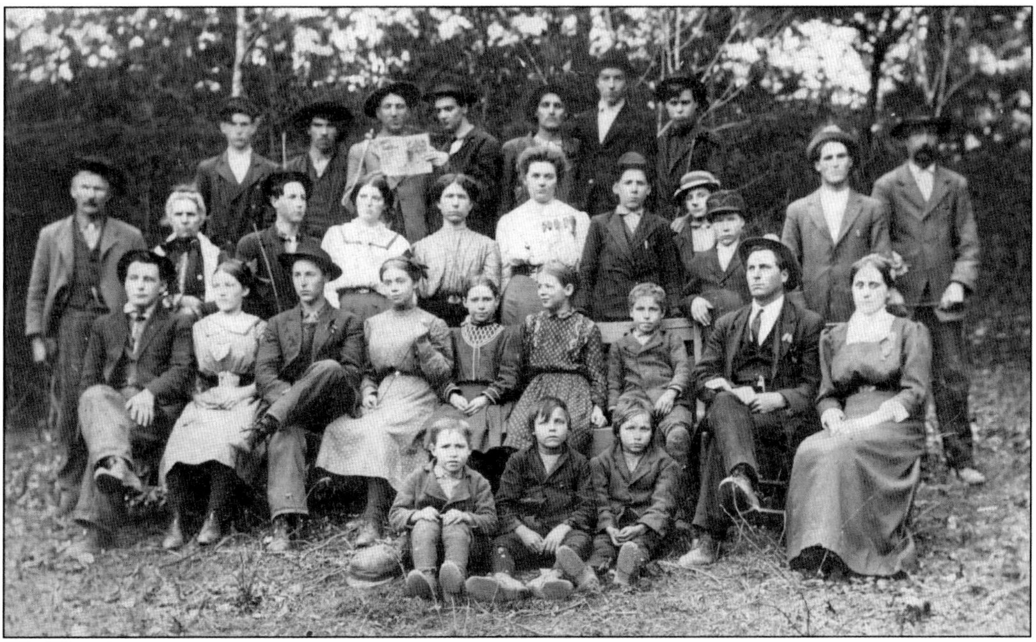

MOUNT ZION SINGING SCHOOL, C. 1912. Pictured from left to right are (first row) Dewitt Barnett, Esau Hodges, and Dewey Hodges; (second row) Izzard Barnett, Della Hendrix, Grady Triplett, Lettie Welch, Vivian Barnett, Viola Welch, Verlin Barnett, Amos Hampton, and Gertie Hampton; (third row) Will Minton, Eliza Minton, Dallas Triplett, Lottie Hall, Ada Minton, Minnie Welch, Willard Welch, Mont Wellborn, Robert Minton, Jake Wellborn, and Joe Triplett: (fourth row) Isaac Minton, Iredell Minton, Hort Jones, Jack Welch, Jeff Hodges, Mathie Triplett, and Job Triplett. (Courtesy of Linda Triplett.)

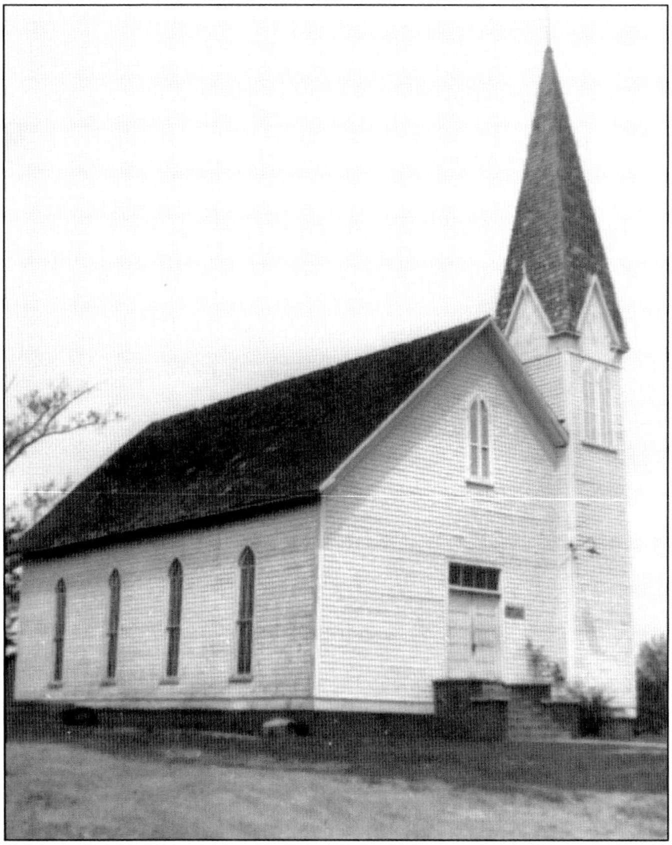

MORAVIAN FALLS BAPTIST CHURCH. Moravian Falls Baptist Church was established *c.* 1886 with 17 charter members, some of whom were baptized in the cool waters of the falls. This first church building was replaced in 1950. Included in the cornerstone of this building, laid in 1949, were a Bible, a history of the church, and a church roll. (Courtesy of Wilkes Community College Library.)

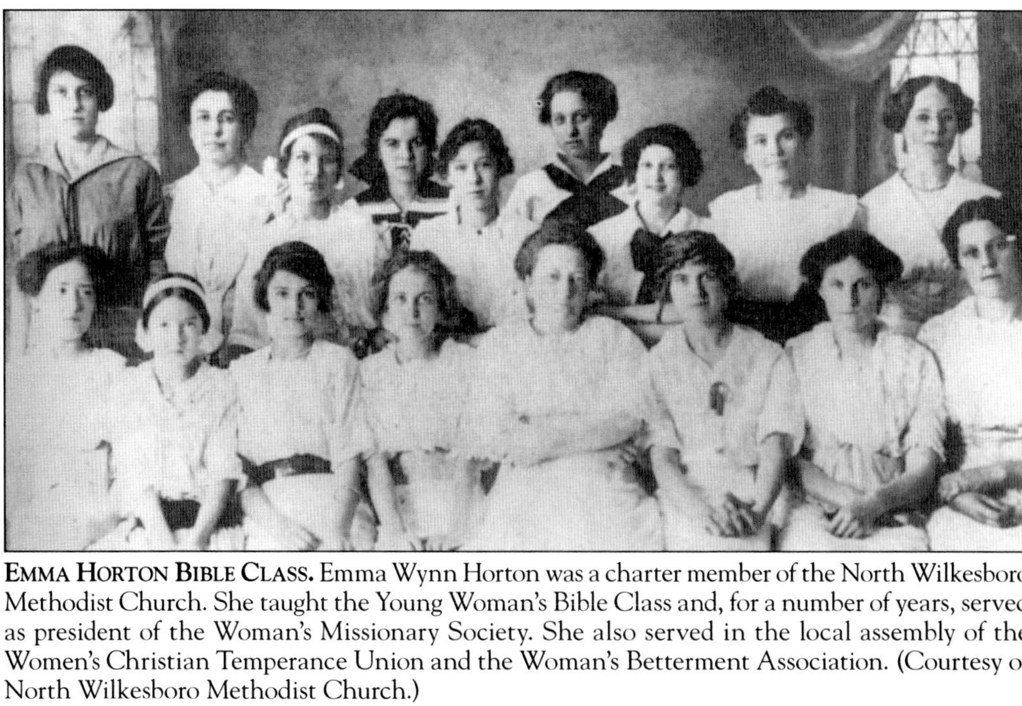

EMMA HORTON BIBLE CLASS. Emma Wynn Horton was a charter member of the North Wilkesboro Methodist Church. She taught the Young Woman's Bible Class and, for a number of years, served as president of the Woman's Missionary Society. She also served in the local assembly of the Women's Christian Temperance Union and the Woman's Betterment Association. (Courtesy of North Wilkesboro Methodist Church.)

BEULAH METHODIST CHURCH. Beulah Methodist Church was formed in 1875 when Shiloh Methodist on old Boomer Road and Sharon Methodist Church northeast of Moravian Falls were combined. Soon after, this white frame building was constructed. One of the earliest pastors was James Purvis. Sunday school rooms were added in 1954, and the church was bricked in the early 1960s. (Courtesy of Wilkes Community College Library.)

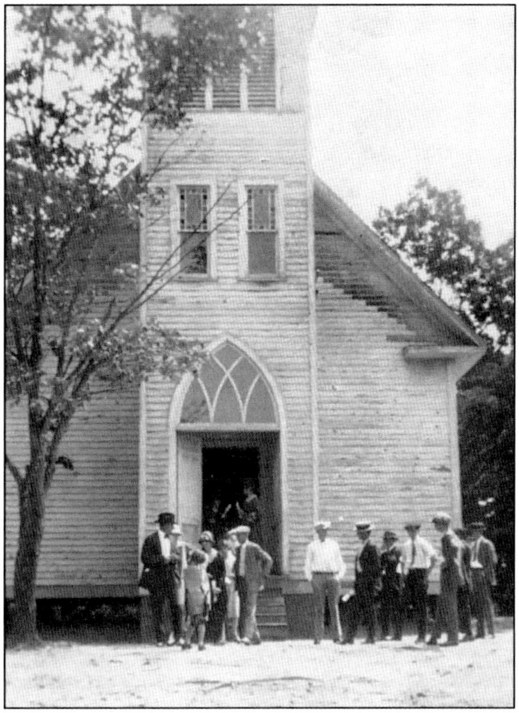

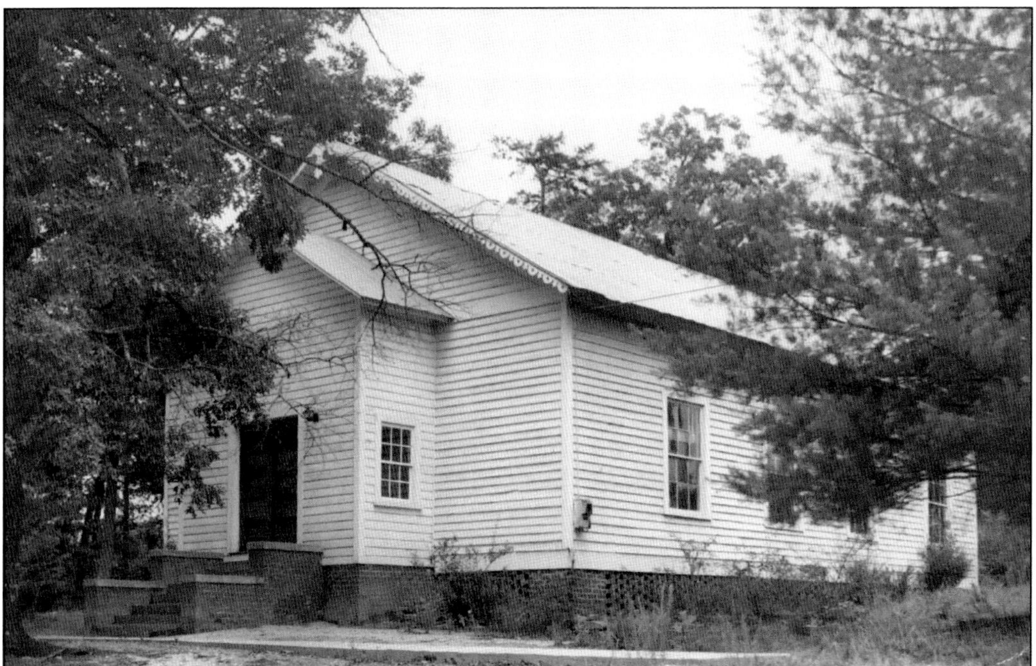

BEAVER CREEK ADVENT CHRISTIAN CHURCH, 1947. Beaver Creek Advent Christian Church in Ferguson was organized in 1879 with 19 charter members. The first wooden-frame church had two front doors, one for ladies to enter and another for men to use. Seating in the church was segregated as well. The church did not have a full-time pastor until 1981. (Courtesy of Wilkes Community College Library.)

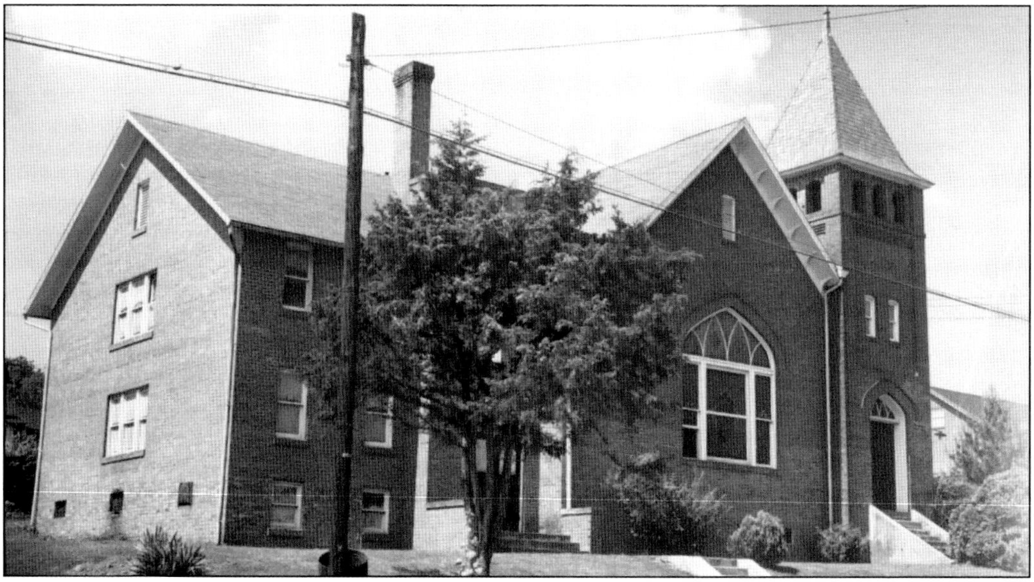

WILKESBORO BAPTIST CHURCH. Wilkesboro Baptist Church was established in 1880 with 20 charter members. The first church building was a white frame structure located on West Street at Henderson Drive. This building stood on the present location at Woodland Boulevard until 1959. In 1959, the present sanctuary was dedicated, and numerous additions have been constructed to accommodate the growth of the congregation. (Courtesy of Wilkesboro Baptist Church.)

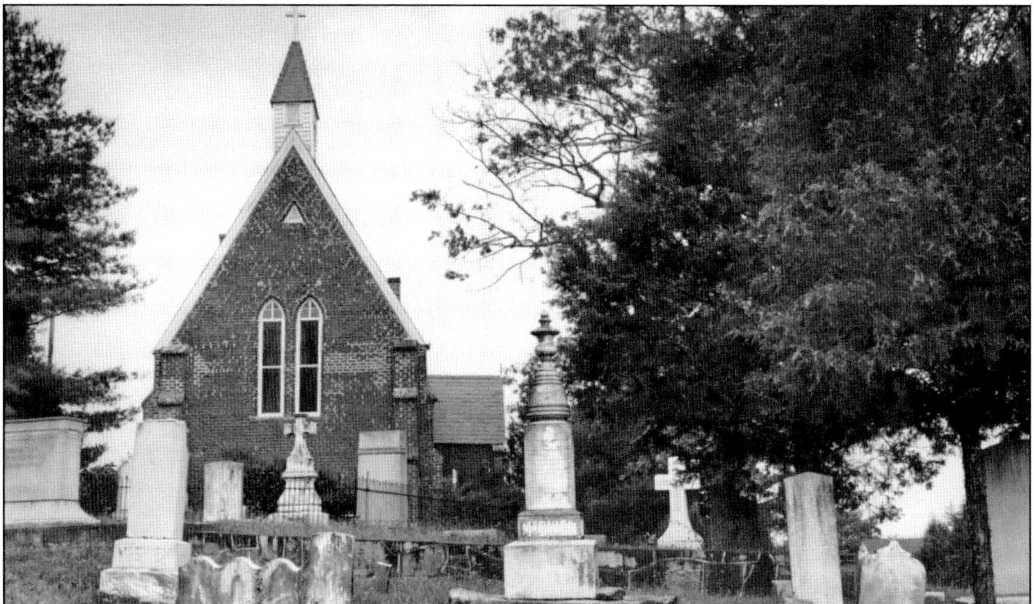

ST. PAUL'S EPISCOPAL CHURCH. St. Paul's Episcopal Church was completed in 1849. Civil War general James B. Gordon, rector and early school superintendent Richard Wainwright Barber, and novelist Kathleen Morehouse are interred here. The chapel houses two frescoes by noted artist Benjamin Long, the grounds include the Coventry Chapel and the Labyrinth, and the church is included on the National Register of Historic Places. (Courtesy of Wilkes Community College Library.)

GAYLE AND TERESA FOSTER. Easter in Wilkes County is traditionally an occasion for new pastel dresses and Sunday suits, bonnets, gloves, sunrise service, and egg hunts. Dinner typically includes baked ham, deviled eggs, and coconut cake. Ready for church and pictured here in handmade dresses are Gayle and Teresa Foster, daughters of Jim and Vergie Foster of Millers Creek. (Courtesy of Vergie Foster.)

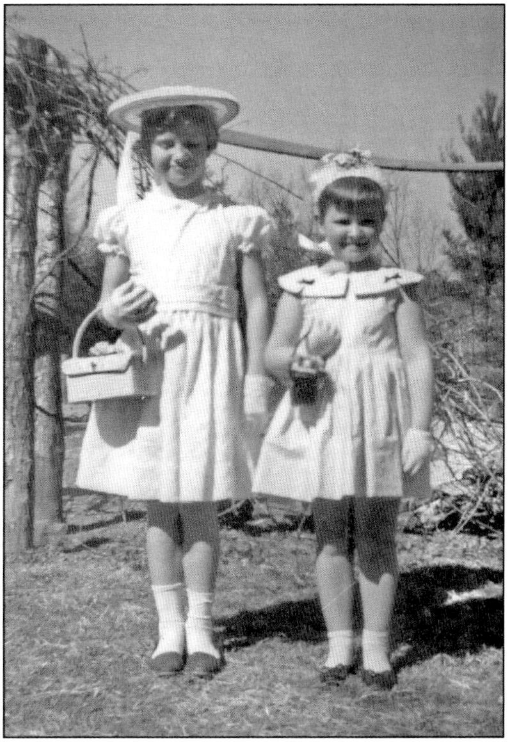

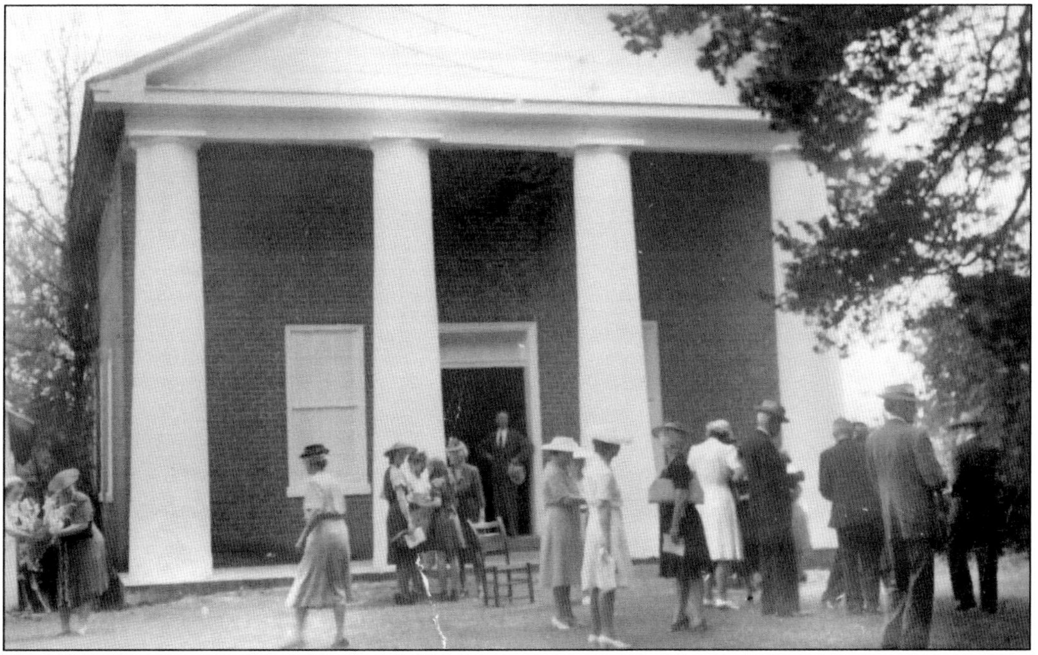

WILKESBORO PRESBYTERIAN CHURCH. Wilkesboro Presbyterian Church, established in 1837, is one of the oldest Presbyterian churches in western North Carolina. There were six charter members, with two additional members joining days later. This distinctive building was built in 1849 and originally included a gallery for slaves. This gallery was later removed during a renovation. Pictured is a celebration from the 1930s. (Courtesy of Wilkes Community College Library.)

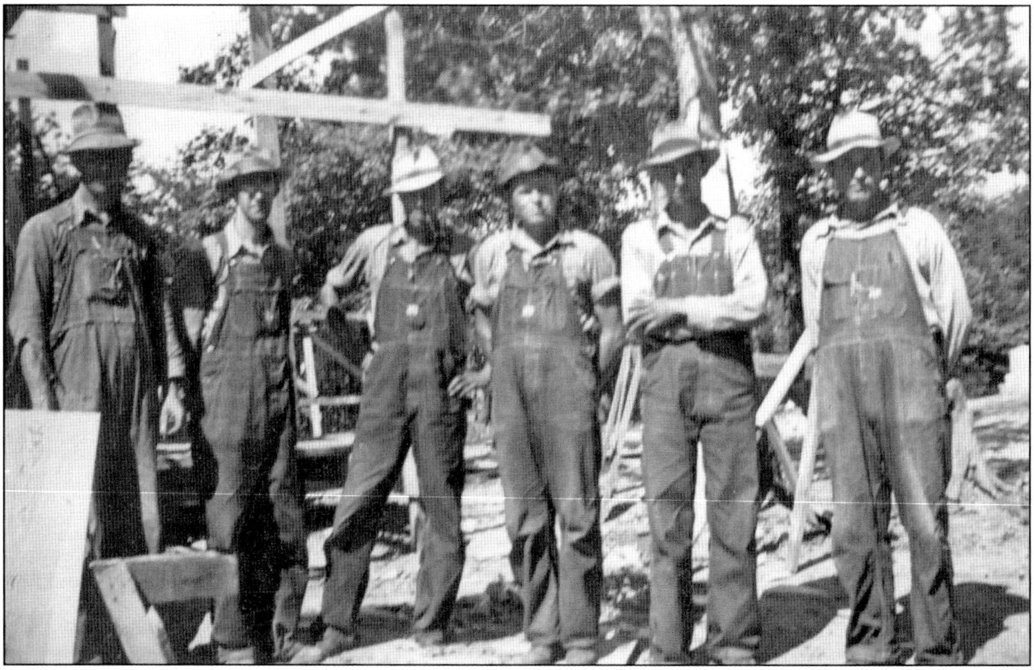

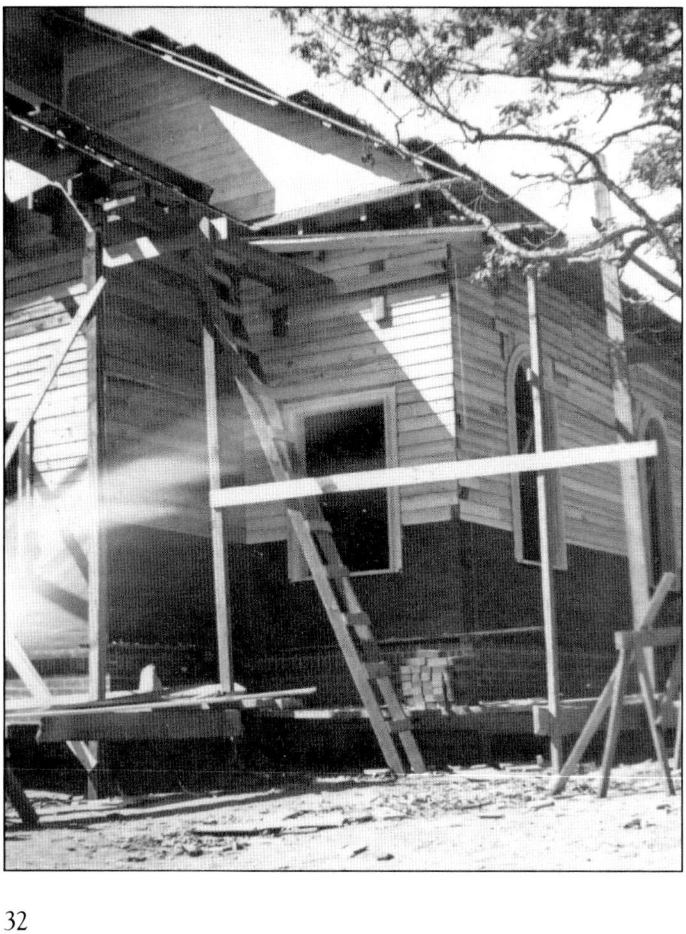

LEWIS FORK BAPTIST CHURCH. Lewis Fork Baptist Church, like many early rural churches, often called upon members to build and maintain church buildings. The church was organized in 1792 under the leadership of George McNeil. The first mention of a Sunday school at Lewis Fork appears in the church minutes for 1879, when a Sabbath school superintendent was appointed. The first church building was 35 feet long and 24 feet wide with one window. Several subsequent churches were built, including buildings in 1829, 1875, and 1909. Renovations were made in 1947. Pictured church members who worked on this c. 1943 building are, from left to right, four unidentified, Jim Triplett, and Osco Triplett. (Both courtesy of Sheri Hayes.)

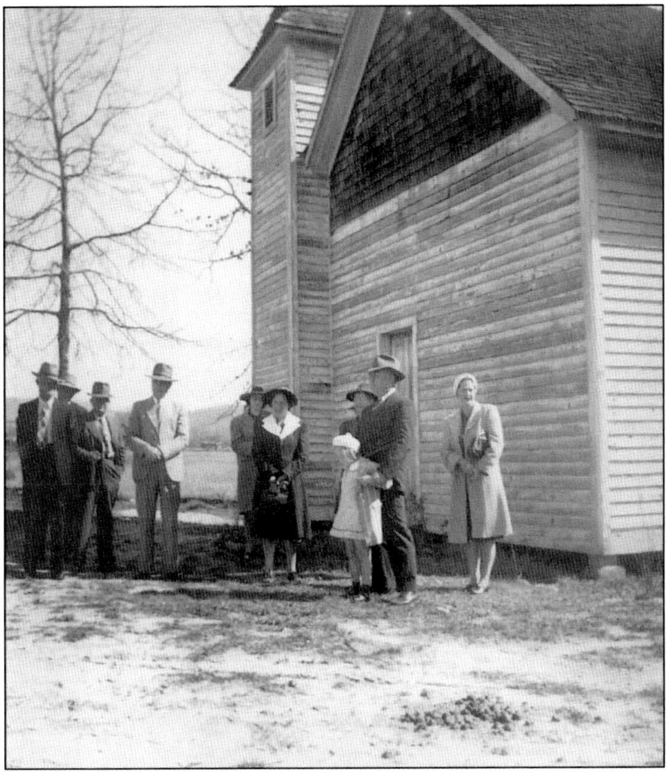

BOOMER ADVENT CHRISTIAN CHURCH. Boomer Advent Christian Church was organized on January 22, 1895, under the leadership of John A. Cargile and W. R. Cottrell and accepted into the Piedmont Advent Christian Conference on May 12, 1895. The "Second Advent Church," as it was called, often shared members with the local Methodist church and Zion Hill Baptist Church. (Courtesy of Boomer Advent Christian Church.)

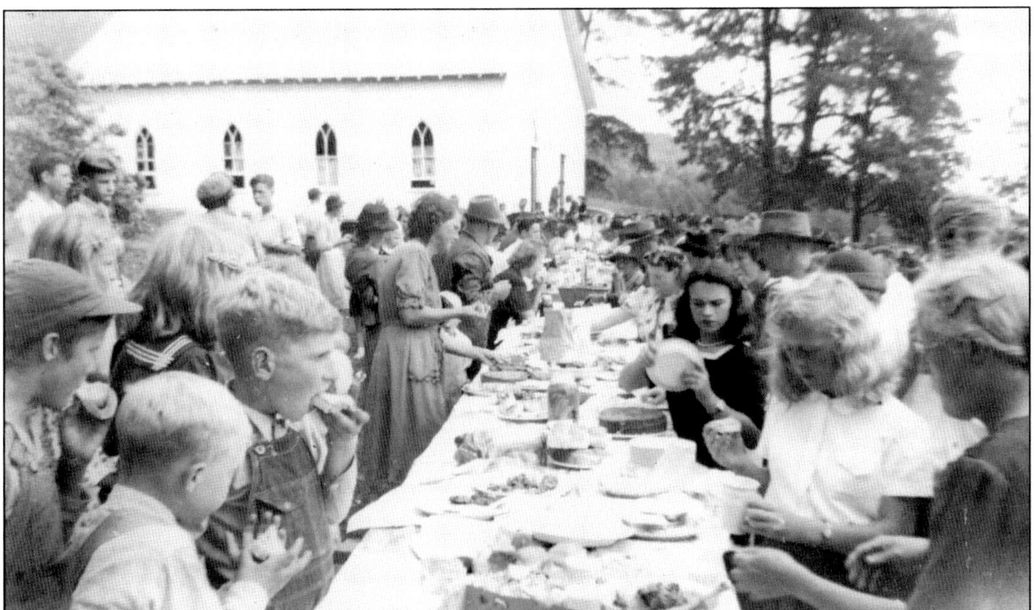

MOUNT ZION BAPTIST CHURCH, 1949. Mount Zion Baptist Church was established in 1849 with about a dozen charter members. They met in an old schoolhouse until they built a log church in 1924. The Sunday school classrooms were added, and the church was bricked in 1956. This photograph shows members celebrating Mount Zion's centennial with dinner on the grounds. (Courtesy of Linda Triplett.)

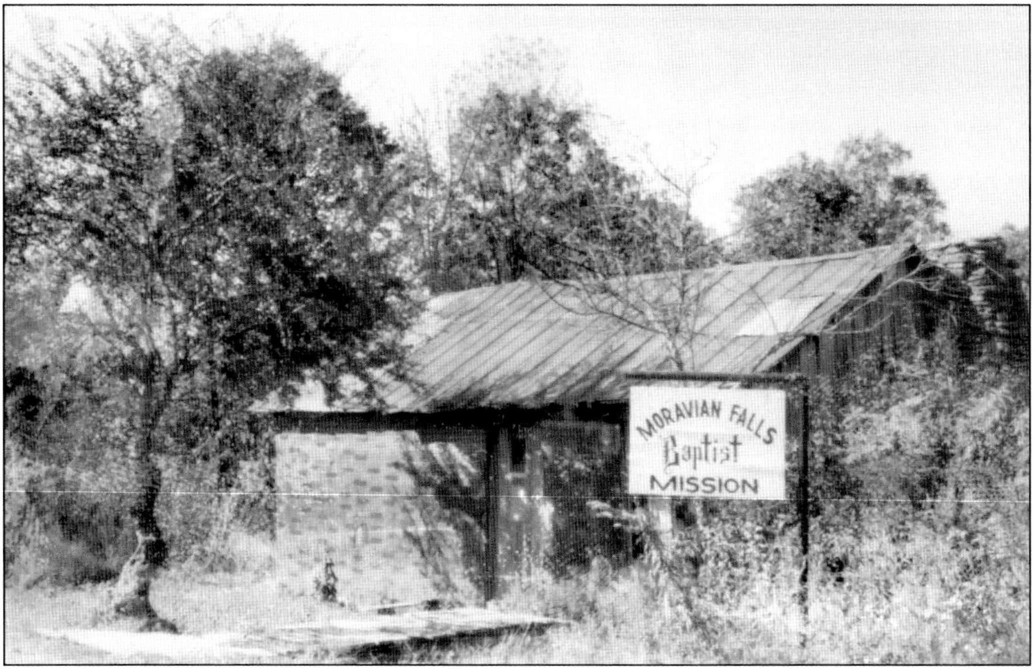

MORAVIAN FALLS BAPTIST MISSION, C. 1958. In the late 1950s, Moravian Falls Baptist Church addressed the spiritual needs of families who wanted to worship closer to their homes by establishing the Moravian Falls Baptist Mission Church three miles from the site of the existing church. Early meetings were held in a tent, and Sunday school and worship services were held once a month with revival held twice a year. The group later moved to this building. Community members donated land and more than 500 hours of labor toward the completion of a more modern church in 1961. Pictured below are children of the Moravian Falls Baptist Mission. (Both courtesy of Wilkes Community College Library.)

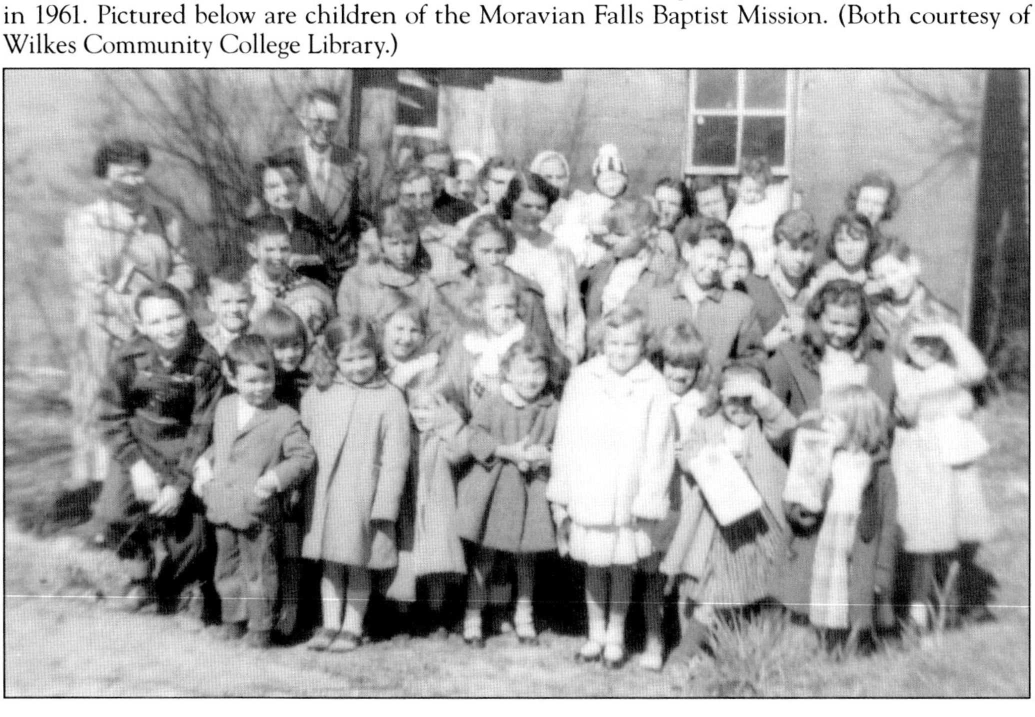

Three

A Roof over Our Heads

From early settlements on the frontier to homes, buildings, and industrial structures of the early 20th century, much of the history of Wilkes County is spoken through its design. Few reminders of settlers in an area tell a story better than their homes. Architecture contributes to a sense of time and place, particularly in the case of Wilkes County when this construction is juxtaposed with the splendor of the North Carolina landscape.

Upon arrival, most settlers used log construction for dwellings. Axes, saws, and froes helped clear timber and craft logs to build cabins. Some structures, like the log home of folk legend Daniel Boone, have long since been razed. Others, like the Robert Cleveland log home built in 1779, remain as evidence of times long forgotten. As sawmills became more common during the late 19th century, frame dwellings gradually replaced log buildings. Home construction kept pace with merchant and industrial growth around the beginning of the 20th century. Late Victorian, Queen Anne, and Colonial Revival homes were constructed in the Wilkesboros. Bungalows were also popular during the 1920s. Churches were typically situated on knolls and hills. They were gable-fronted buildings that were later rebuilt or refaced with brick. Notable exceptions are the Gothic Revival structures that house the St. Paul's Episcopal Church in Wilkesboro and the North Wilkesboro Presbyterian Church.

Like many North Carolina railroad towns, North Wilkesboro spreads out from a commercial district near the railroad depot. It is remarkably uniform in character, especially on Main Street, as most of the buildings were constructed around the same time to replace early frame buildings hastily constructed during the first years of the town's history. One noteworthy exception is the former Bank of North Wilkesboro building that currently serves as the town hall. Wilkesboro centers on the courthouse square around the 1902 neoclassical revival building. Residential districts in both municipalities spread up the nearby hillsides. Big, functional frame factories remain in North Wilkesboro and Ronda. Further out, country stores, barns, and rural crossroads dot the Wilkes County countryside.

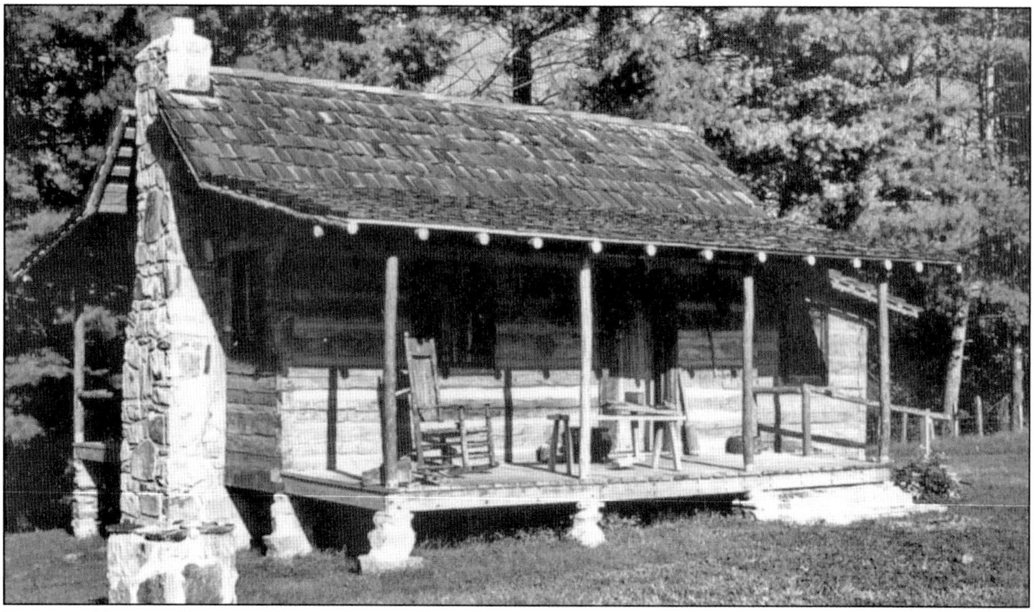

DANIEL BOONE REPLICA CABIN. Legendary pioneer Daniel Boone married Wilkes County native Rebecca Bryan and lived in Wilkes County in two locations along the Yadkin River *c.* 1760. This replica cabin was constructed on the site of the Whippoorwill Academy and Village in the Ferguson community, and the chimney contains rocks from Boone's original cabin. (Courtesy of Wilkes Heritage Museum.)

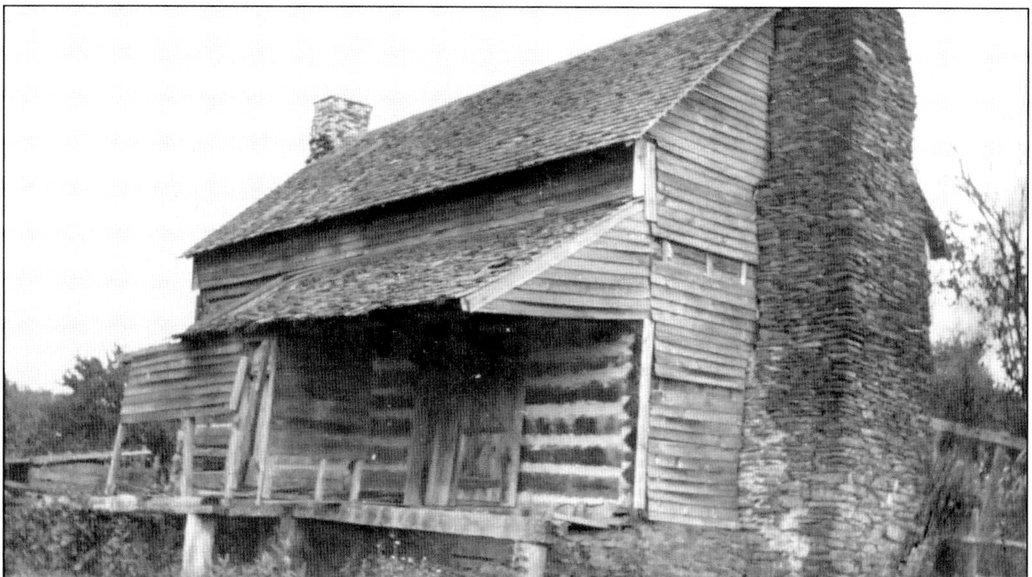

ROBERT CLEVELAND LOG HOME. Cleveland was a militia captain during the Revolutionary War. His home, originally located on Parsonsville Road, is believed to be the oldest still standing in Wilkes County. Old Wilkes purchased the home in 1987, dismantled it, and reassembled it behind the Wilkes Heritage Museum. The original logs were used, and the mountain rocks that formed the chimney were washed and stacked to form the chimneys and fireplaces. (Courtesy of Wilkes Heritage Museum.)

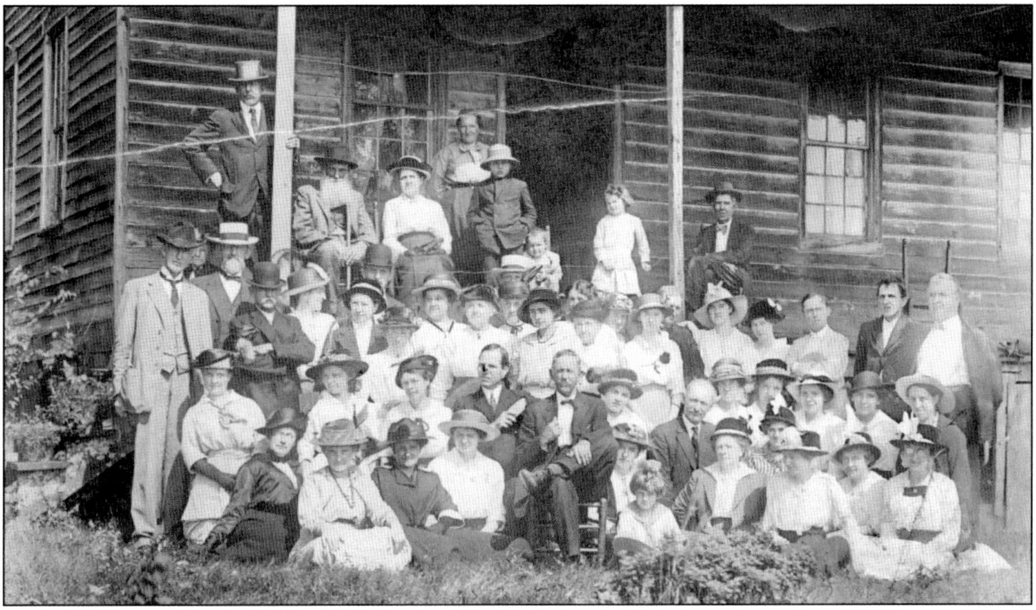

STOKES HOMESTEAD. Former governor Montford Stokes settled on his Mourne Rouge plantation at Brown's Ford, west of Wilkesboro. The home was built in Wilkes County prior to 1779 by Hugh Montgomery. Mourne Rouge was destroyed by fire in 1972 on the day it was listed on the National Register of Historic Places. Pictured is a gathering at the Stokes homestead *c.* 1910. (Courtesy of Wilkes Community College Library.)

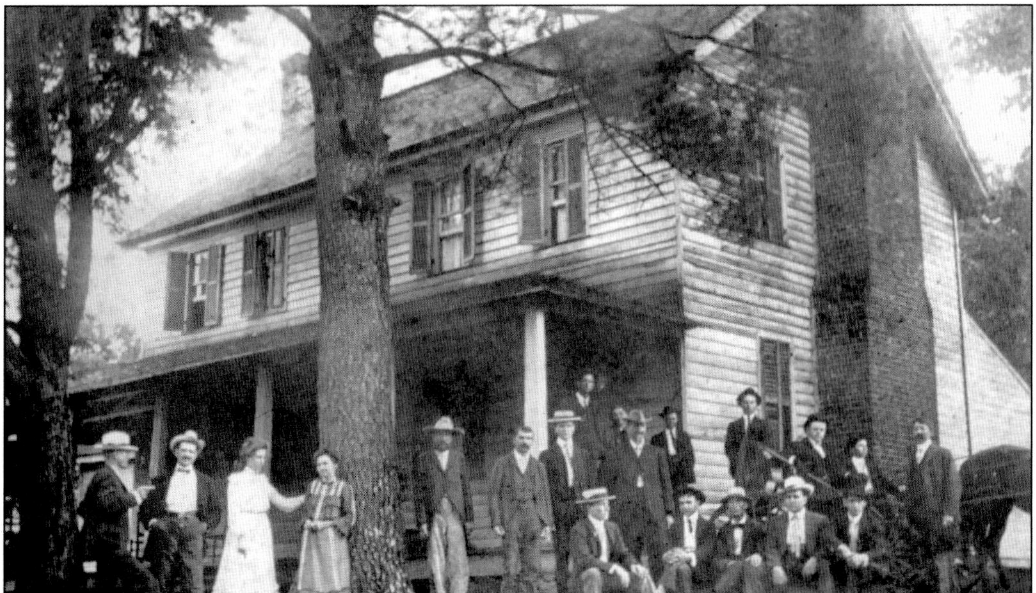

FAIRMONT. According to legend, Fairmont was built on the site of a fort called the Red House. Situated in Kensington Heights, Fairmont was home to Augustus Finley. Finley was eventually persuaded to sell his property to the Winston Salem Land and Improvement Company for the construction of a railway spur. The house was moved to a nearby location and still serves as a residence. (Courtesy of Wilkes Heritage Museum.)

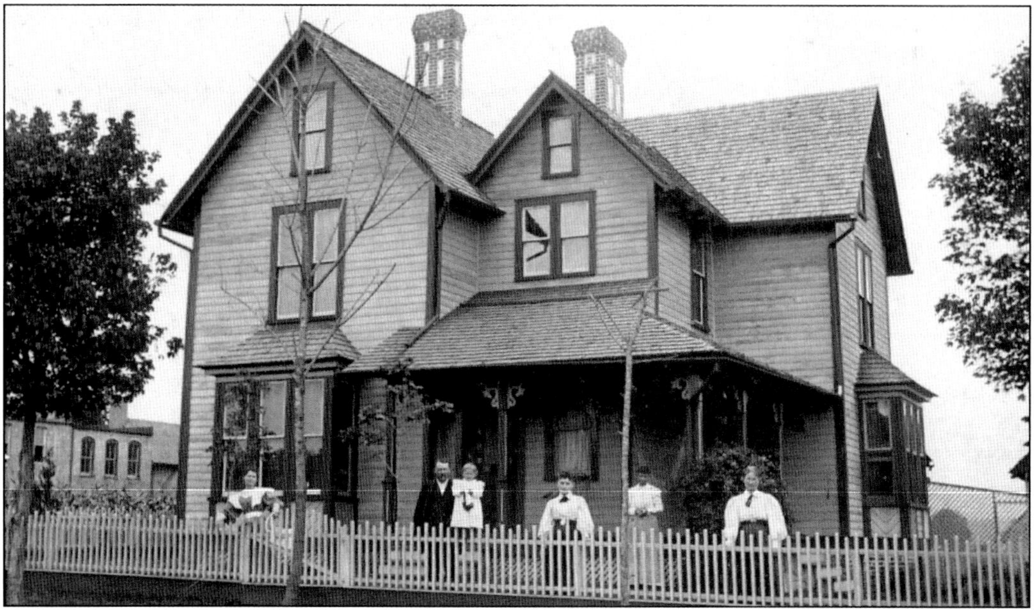

WINKLER HOME. This home, built in 1892 by Carter Winkler, stands one block from the 1902 courthouse in Wilkesboro. In front of the house are, from left to right, Mamie Wallace Deal, Carter Winkler, Annie Winkler, Lou Bower Winkler, Mary Brown, and Matilda Ward Wallace. Carter was a farmer and at one time manufactured locust pins. (Courtesy of Wilkes Heritage Museum.)

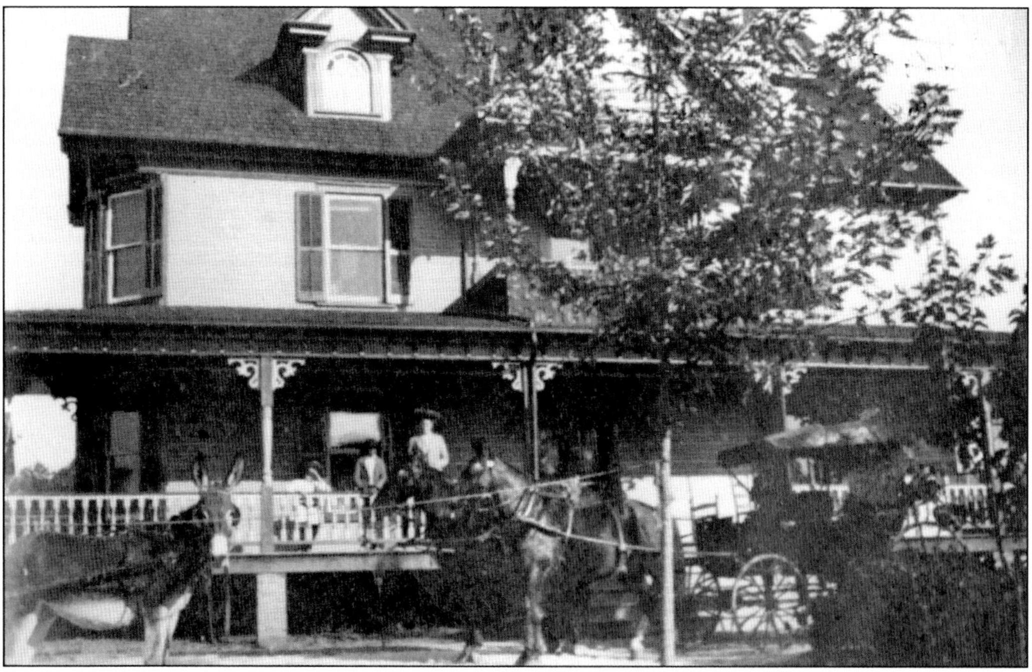

TANNER'S REST, C. 1903. Tanner's Rest was the home of J. C. Smoot, the proprietor of Smoot Tannery. The grove of his stately home (no longer standing) would later be the site of a municipal park in North Wilkesboro named in Smoot's honor. Smoot Park opened in 1943 with swings, benches, picnic tables, barbecue pits, and facilities for croquet, tennis, horseshoe pitching, and archery. (Courtesy of Wilkes Community College Library.)

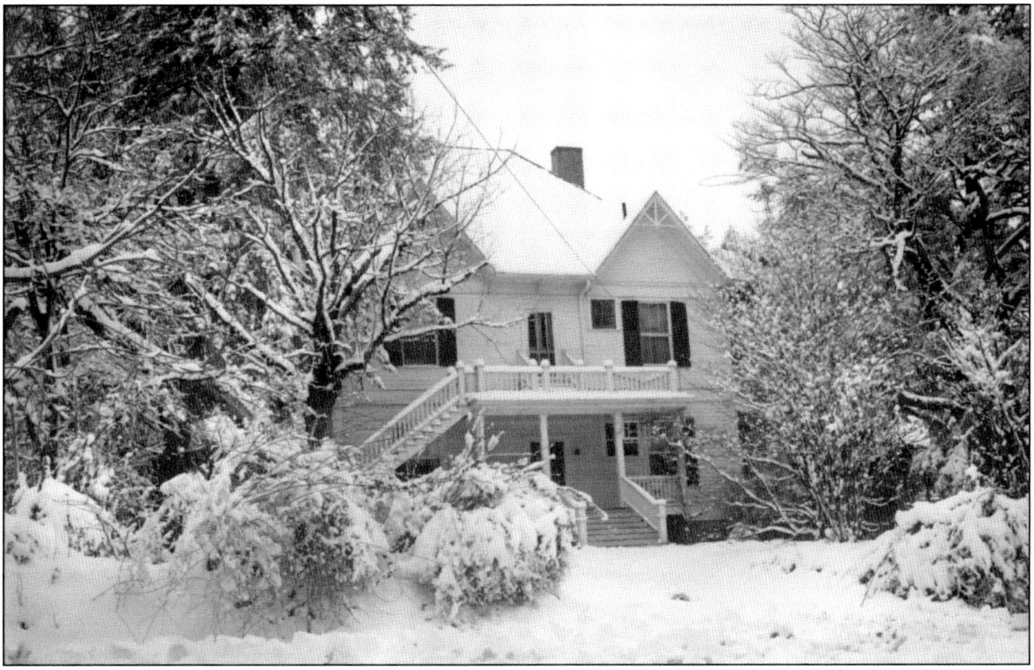

Greene Home. William Greene was a Confederate veteran who practiced medicine in Wilkesboro during the Civil War. Later in his career he became interested in dentistry, which he practiced until he retired. This colonial home was built prior to 1900. In Dr. Greene's lifetime, there was a dental office situated near the front gate. (Courtesy of Wilkes Community College Library.)

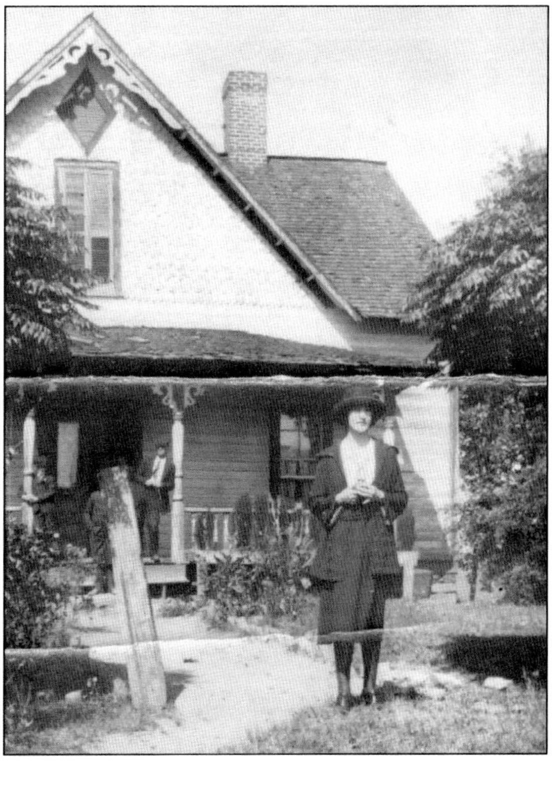

Dellaplane Home, c. 1930. Dellaplane, located in the eastern section of Wilkes County, was named for Della Cooper, the niece of the local postmaster. Dellaplane had a school, a post office, and a church prior to the 1910s. R. A. Spainhour opened a store here *c.* 1870 that grew into the Spainhour department stores chain. Pictured here in front of a Dellaplane home is Zelma Grubbs. (Courtesy of Vergie Foster.)

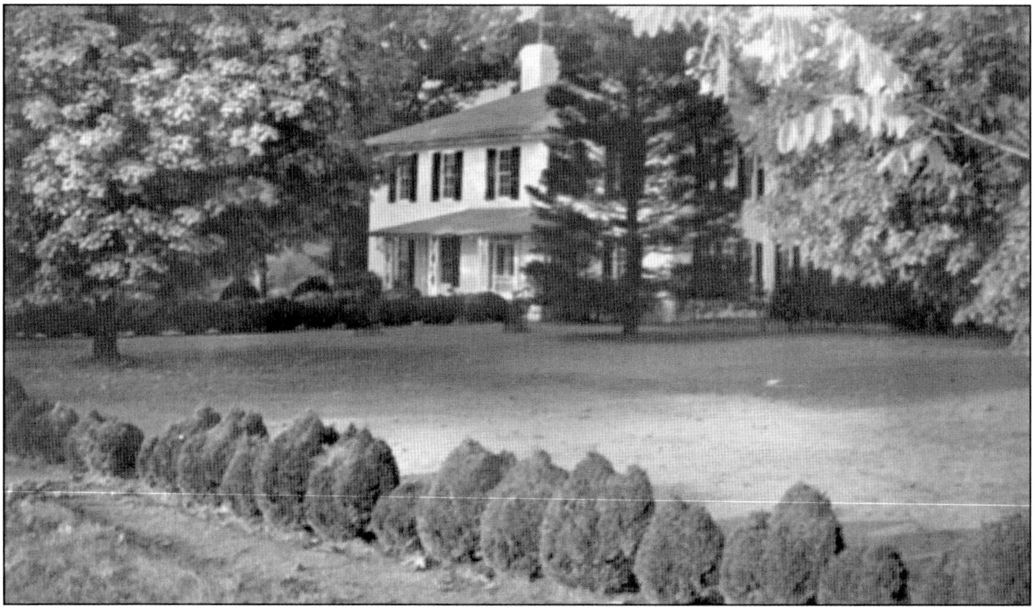

ROUNDABOUT. This Roundabout farmhouse was built c. 1855 in Ronda on the site of the home of Benjamin "Old Roundabout" Cleveland. Cleveland, a colonel in the Revolutionary War, was infamous for hanging Tories on the Tory Oak in Wilkesboro. At least two structures preceded this 10-room building, one of which was struck by lightning that cracked the walls, rendering the house unsafe. (Courtesy of Wilkes County Public Library.)

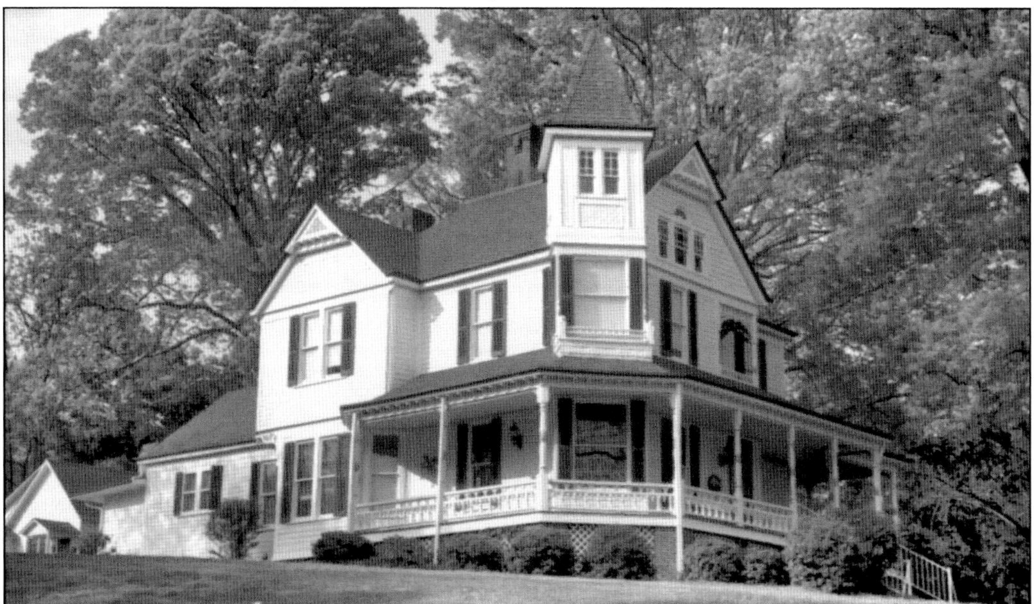

FINLEY HOUSE. The Thomas Finley House, located on E Street in North Wilkesboro, is a Queen Anne–style structure with inviting porches, balconies, and a corner tower. It was built in 1893 for Finley, a lawyer and superior court judge. At one time, there was a tennis court located behind the house that served as a meeting spot for his children and their friends. (Courtesy of the North Carolina State Archives.)

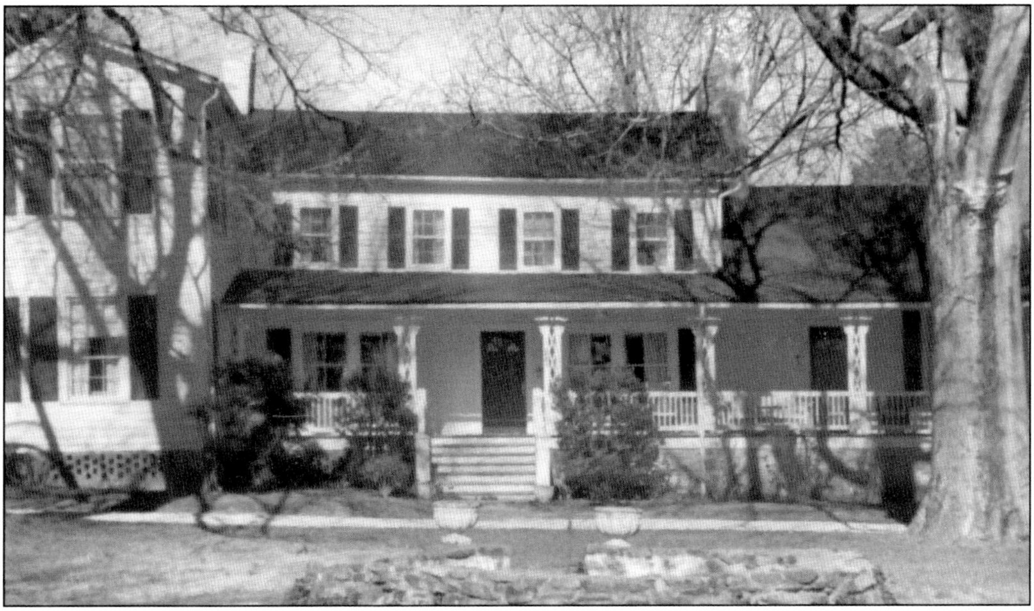

Brown-Cowles House. This house in Wilkesboro was built for sheriff Hamilton Brown *c.* 1830 and later was home to William H. H. Cowles, a Confederate veteran, lawyer, and politician. Some of the old outbuildings are still in evidence at the rear of the house. Both this home and the law office that stands in front of it are listed on the National Register of Historic Places. (Courtesy of Wilkes Heritage Museum.)

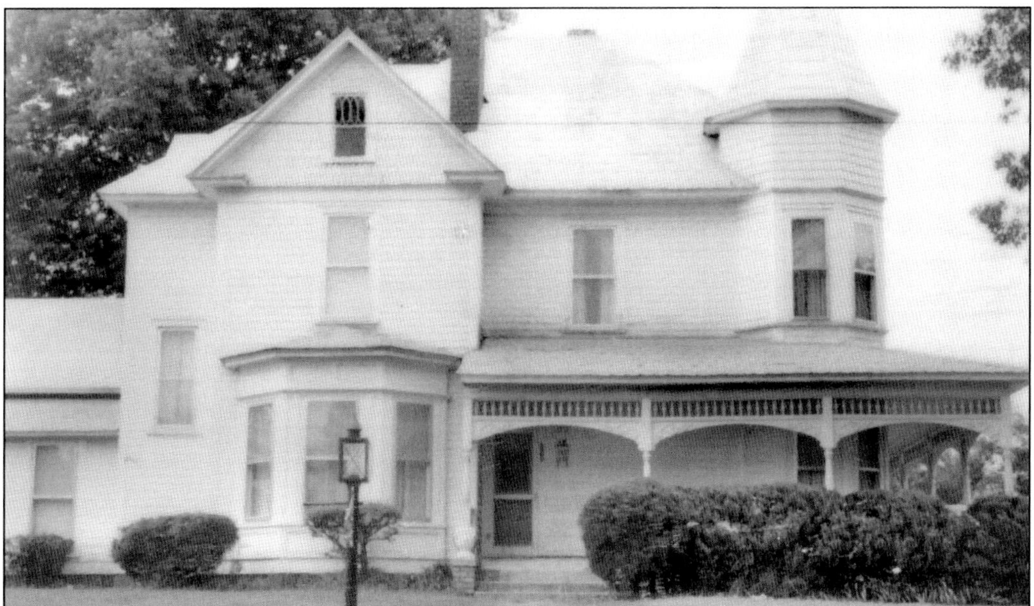

Lowe-Hemphill House. The Lowe-Hemphill House in Wilkesboro was built in 1899 by J. L. Hemphill, a prominent North Wilkesboro businessman. The 11-room home was one of the county's finest when it was built. A kitchen and dining area were added in the early 1900s. Carl Lowe bought the home *c.* 1922. The home is listed on the National Register of Historic Places. (Courtesy of Wilkes Heritage Museum.)

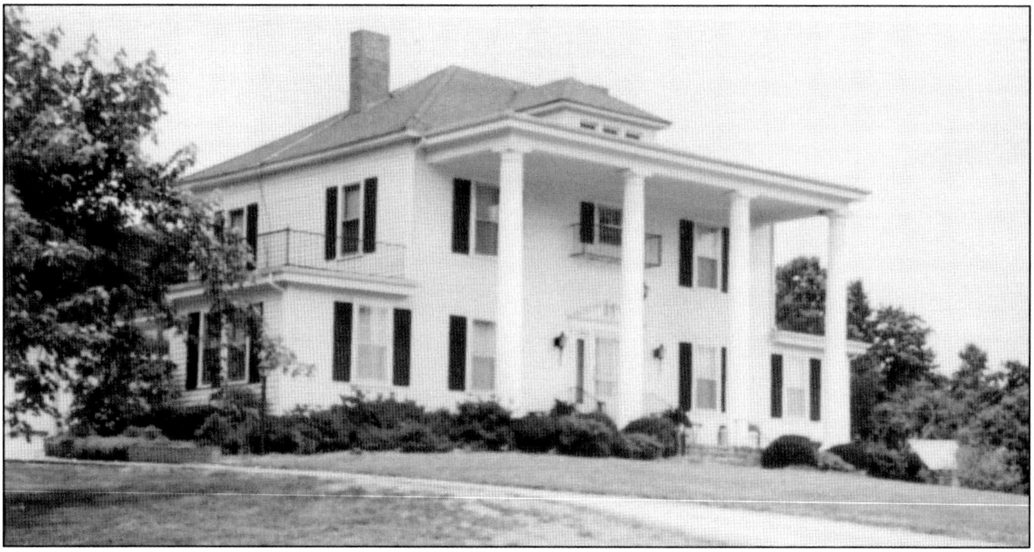

MINTON HOME. This house, located in the Mount Pleasant community, was home to Thomas Otto and Belva Eller Minton. Minton raised two children here, and Belva Minton cooked meals for 40 farm hands daily on their Champion Poultry Farm. In addition to his contributions to the poultry industry, T. O. Minton was instrumental in getting telephone service to rural communities in Wilkes. (Courtesy of Eloise Church.)

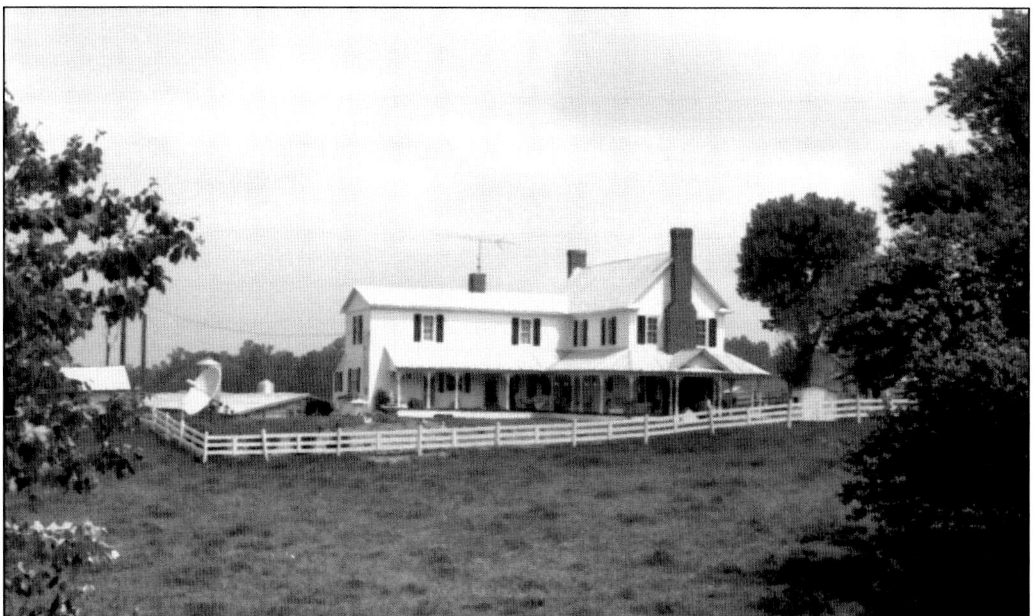

MARTIN-PARDUE FARM. Willie and Dicie Martin built the original log portion of this house c. 1865. Located near the Brushy Mountains, the main portion of the home was added in 1910. The Martins raised corn, wheat, and oats. When James and Nellie Pardue acquired the farm in the 1950s, they built long chicken houses on the land and began chicken farming. (Courtesy of the North Carolina State Archives.)

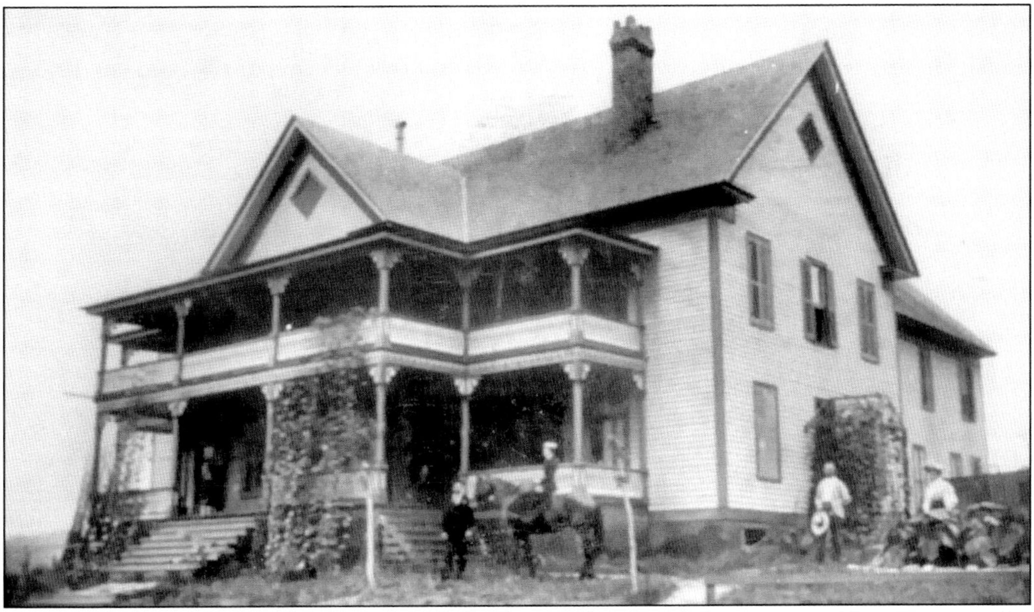

HOTEL GORDON. Hotel Gordon was built by the Gordon Hotel Company *c.* 1904. Directors for the company were T. B. Finley, J. C. Smoot, S. V. Tomlinson, J. R. Finley, and J. E. Finley. The Hotel Gordon building was razed in 1937, although the Hotel Wilkes had long since displaced the Hotel Gordon as the lodging of choice in North Wilkesboro. (Courtesy of Wilkes Community College Library.)

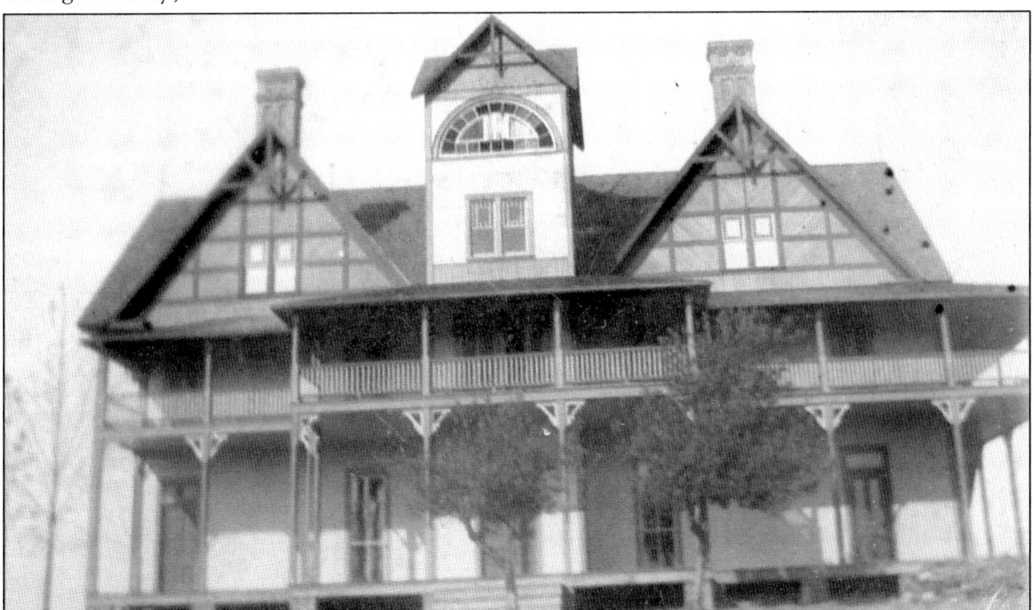

HOTEL LITHIA. The Hotel Lithia was located in the Brushy Mountain community. The primary attraction in the area was a mineral spring a short walk from the hotel. Opening in 1898, the hotel operated for four years before it burned to the ground in 1902. A local reporter noted "all was lost except the trunks and clothing of the guests." (Courtesy of Wilkes Community College Library.)

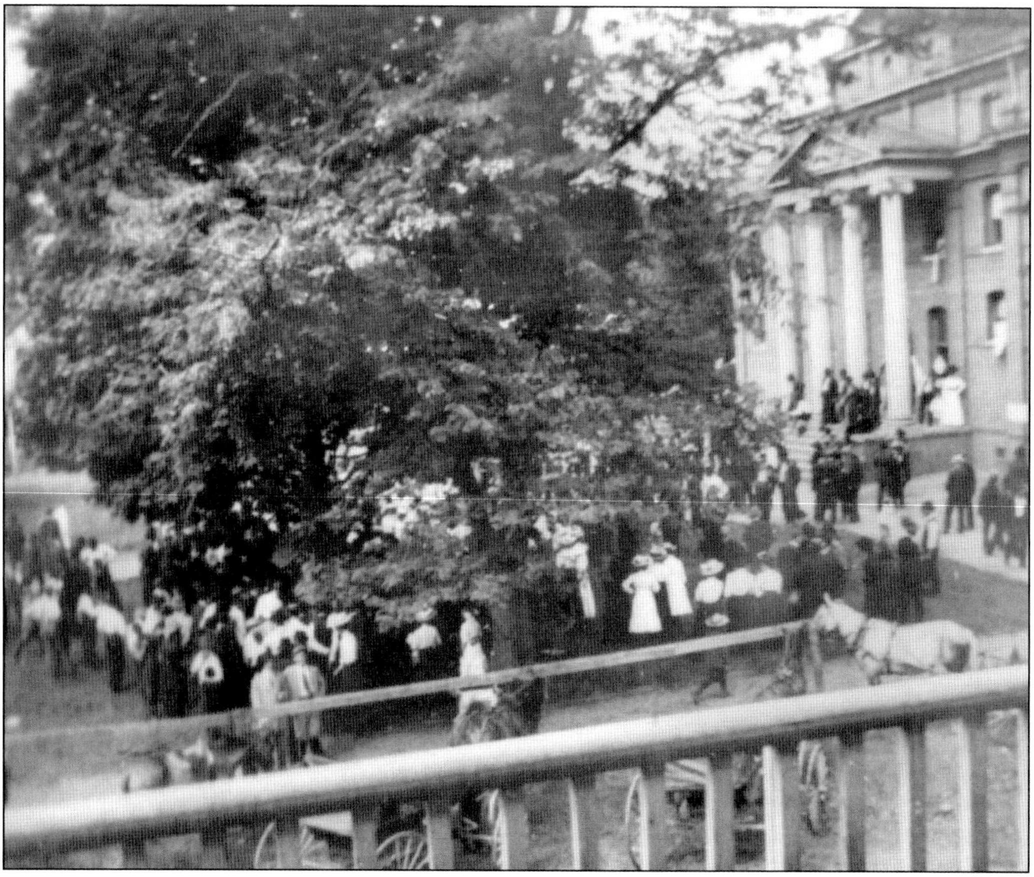

WILKES COUNTY COURTHOUSE. In the 1770s, county court proceedings were held in the Mulberry Fields Meeting House. A second courthouse was erected in the 1820s; both early structures were constructed of wood. Court days were social events where people gathered on the courthouse lawn to hear proceedings and verdicts. Civil and criminal cases provided entertainment to the spectators, and ambitious salesmen like Nike Smithey sold their wares to the assembled masses. The photograph above shows a scene on the lawn during court day taken from the balcony of the Smithey Hotel (where many lawyers and judges found lodging during court appearances). In the photograph below, Chap Minton and his son, Lundy, pose in their family vehicle on the courthouse square around 1905. This shot looks south across Main Street from the courthouse lawn. (Both courtesy of Wilkes Heritage Museum.)

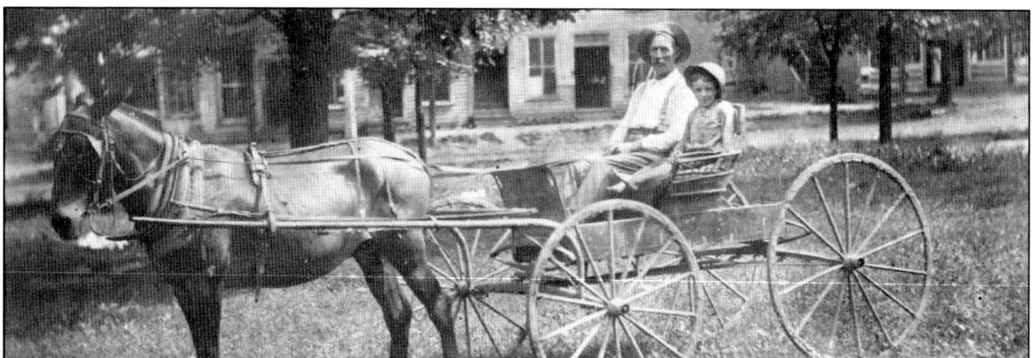

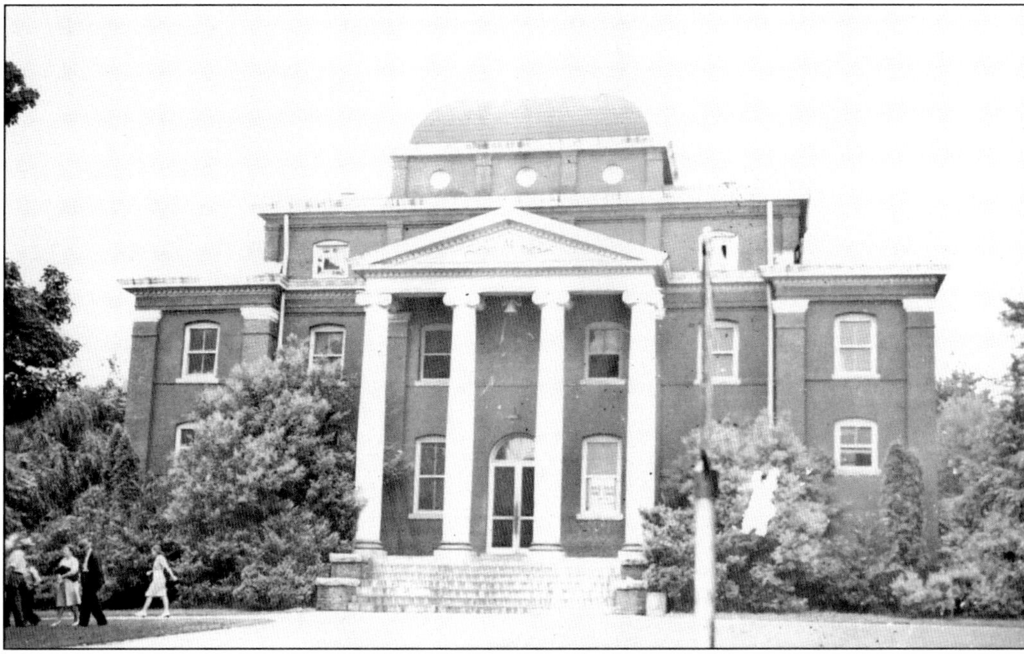

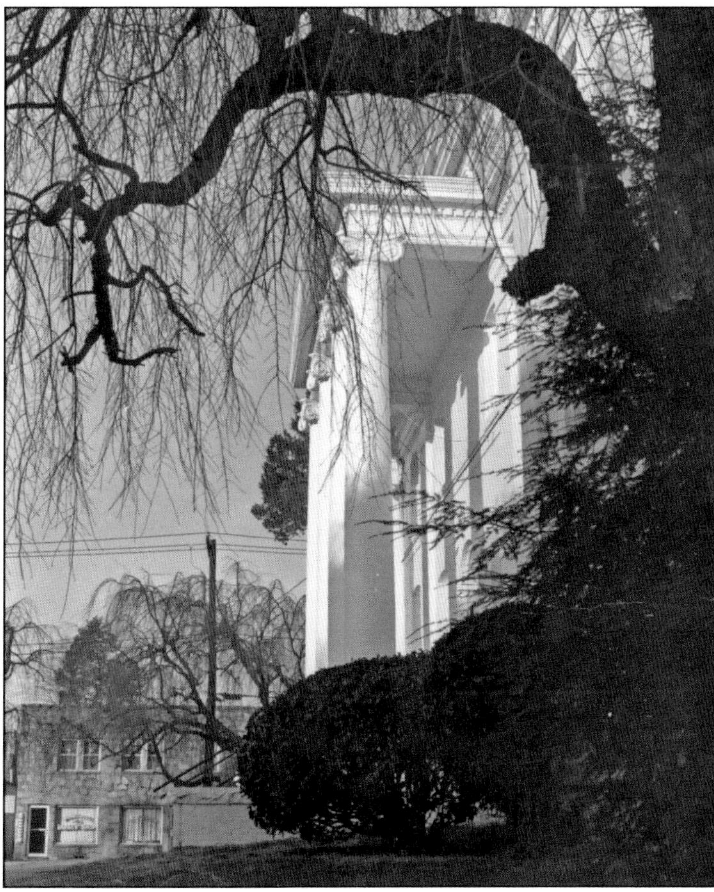

WILKES COUNTY COURTHOUSE. This courthouse, the third of four to date in Wilkes County, is one of six remaining courthouses designed in the neoclassical style by architect Oliver Wheeler and his associates. It was constructed in 1902 at a cost of $42,000. A rear entrance was added in 1937 as part of a North Carolina Works Progress Administration project. Wings on the sides of the building were later added. Because these wings did not match the original brick, the entire structure was painted white. Standing on the courthouse square in downtown Wilkesboro, the former courthouse is now the home of the Wilkes Heritage Museum. (Both courtesy of Wilkes Heritage Museum.)

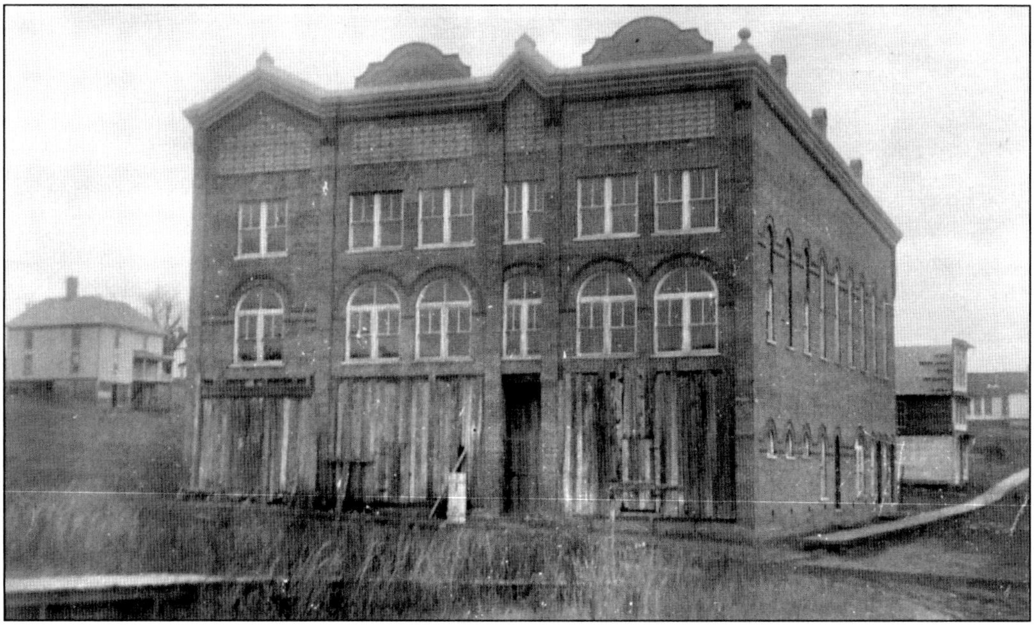

OPERA HOUSE. The Opera House was built in 1906 on the corner of Fifth and D Streets in North Wilkesboro. It was an entertainment venue that also housed business offices, a bank, and an athletic underwear factory. Though it had once been conceived as a hotel, no records confirm that it ever served in this capacity. The building burned in January 1921. (Courtesy of Wilkes Community College Library.)

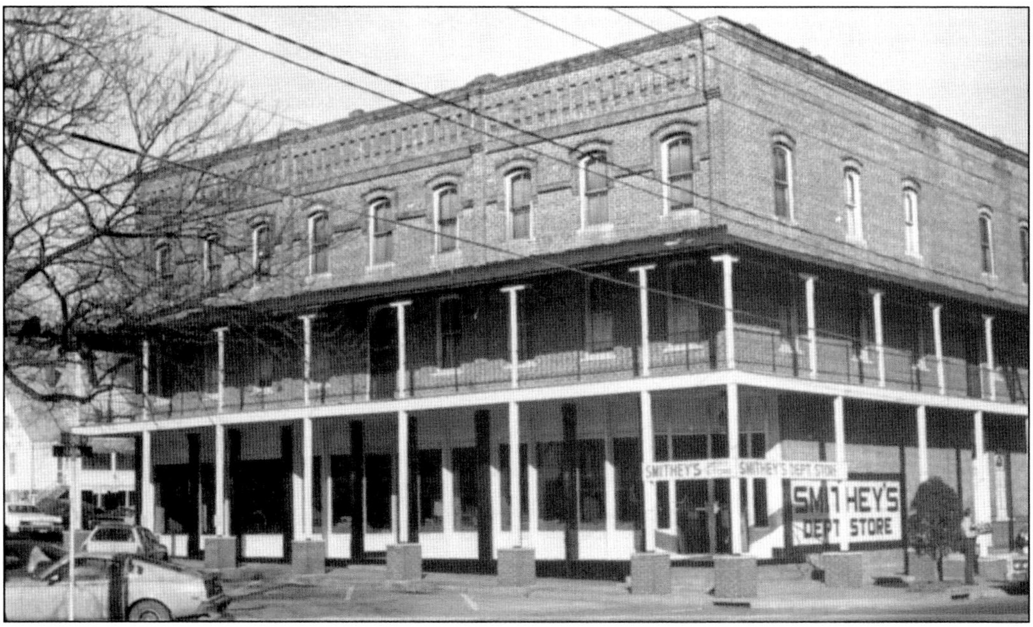

SMITHEY HOTEL. The Smithey Hotel was built by the Wilkesborough Hotel Company in 1891. It replaced the wooden Wilkesborough Hotel, which predated the Civil War. Nike Smithey bought the hotel in 1906 for $3,800. He opened Smithey's Department Store on the first floor and operated a hotel on the second and third floors. He lived there with his wife, Hattie, for 49 years. (Courtesy of Wilkes Heritage Museum.)

Four

Living off the Land

Bounded by the Blue Ridge and Brushy Mountains, Wilkes County possesses a wealth of natural resources. European settlers arrived in the 18th century, finding an area well suited to agriculture. Isothermal ridges in the Brushy Mountains provided the perfect climate for apple, peach, and cherry trees. Farmers grew vegetables, wheat, rye, and corn. Cows, sheep, and horses were raised here, as were pigs and chickens. Local mills ground wheat for flour and corn for meal for the farmers of each community. Lush forests provided timber and tan bark for tanneries, lumber mills, and furniture factories. Man-made flumes along the Yadkin and Reddies Rivers provided transportation for lumber until floodwaters washed them away.

Hunting, fishing, and trapping have long been a part of Wilkes County's economy and sporting life. In fact, the community of Traphill was named for the hundreds of wild turkeys that were trapped in its forests during the 1800s. Native Americans and settlers alike hunted game for meat, clothing, and trading. The most well known of these hunters was legendary Daniel Boone, who settled for a time on the banks of the Yadkin River. Extensive hunting and deforestation over the years brought deer to the brink of extinction. Then from 1930 to 1960, state and federal governments successfully revived the deer population by enacting game laws, reserving lands for national and state forests, and restocking whitetails.

Fishing in rivers and streams provided opportunities for sport and added variety to rural diets. Disastrous floods in 1899, 1916, and 1940 destroyed homes, crops, businesses, and industries, and took many lives along the Yadkin and Reddies Rivers and their tributaries. The W. Kerr Scott Reservoir, opened in 1963, put an end to such disastrous floods. It also gave Wilkes County a recreational lake to add to its array of beautiful natural resources, many of which farmers and sportsmen still enjoy much as their forebears did centuries ago.

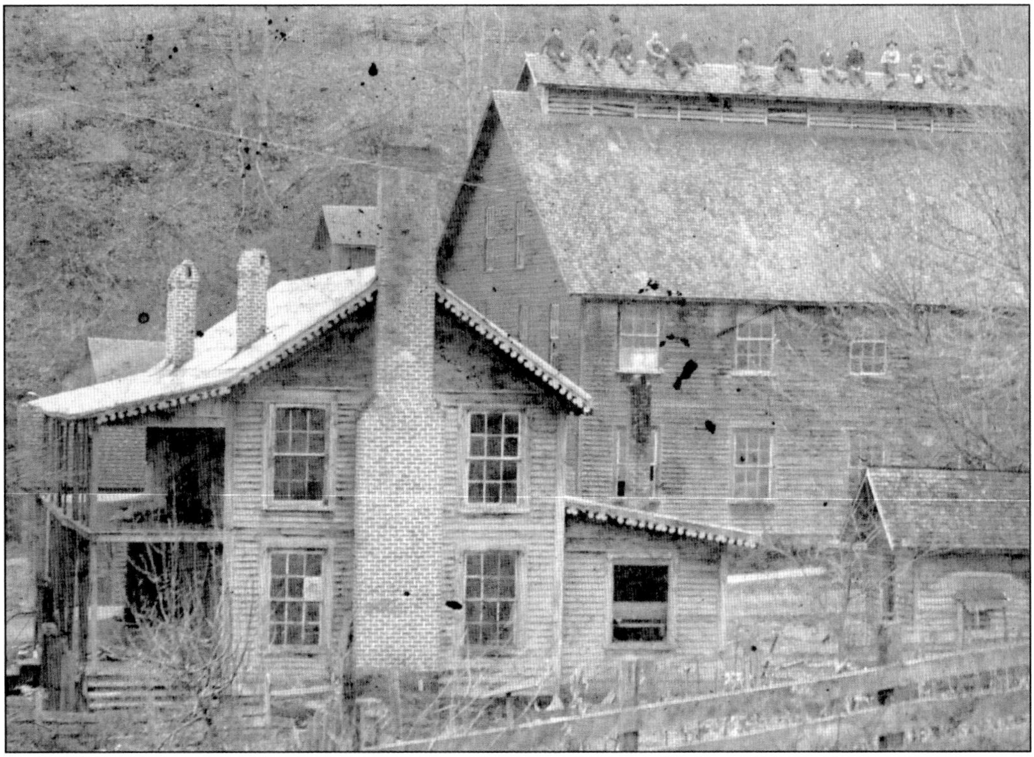

STANTON TANNERY. Stanton Tannery, located near Purlear, began operating *c.* 1900. This location was chosen for its proximity to chestnut oak bark used in processing leather. The community included not only the tannery, but also the houses of the workers, several general stores with merchandise for workers, and a large boardinghouse for tannery employees. According to tradition, the tannery closed *c.* 1906 as a result of financial liabilities that stemmed from a defective batch of leather. Most of the remnants of the operation were washed away with the flood of 1940. Pictured above are workers sitting atop a tannery building. Pictured below are employees of the Stanton Tannery. (Both courtesy of Wilkes Community College Library.)

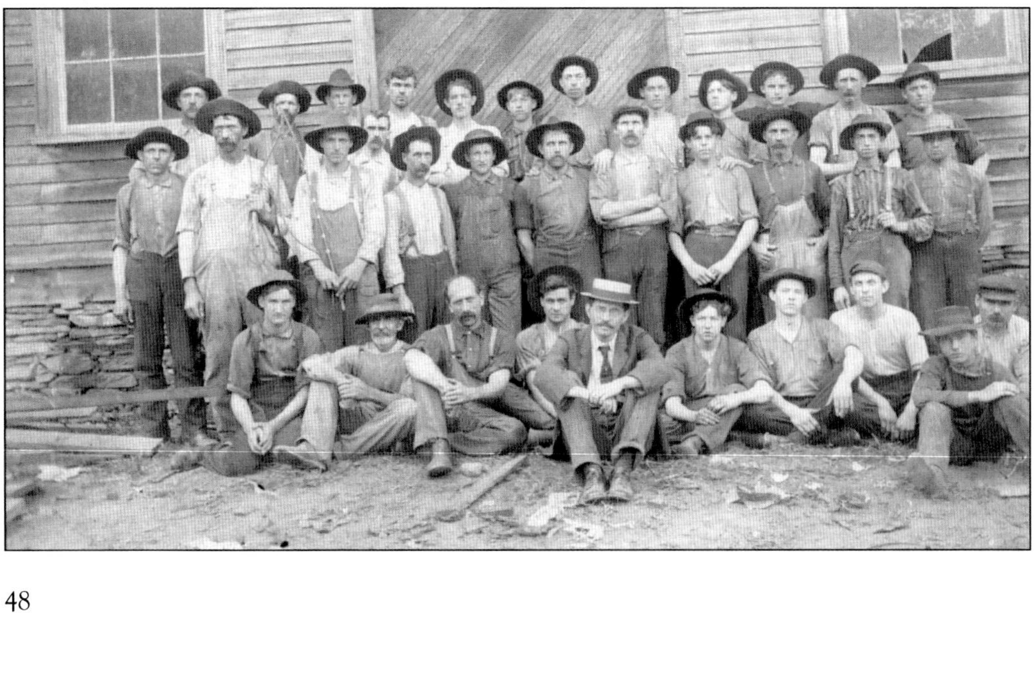

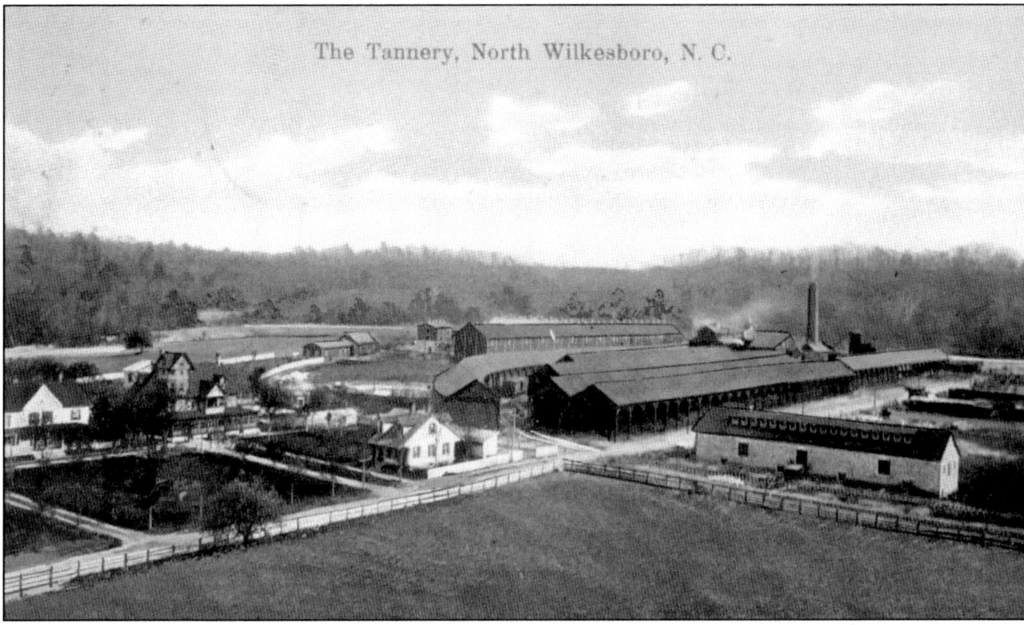

SMOOT TANNERY. Smoot Tannery was established in North Wilkesboro in 1895. In *c.* 1906, the tannery was believed to be the largest steam tannery in the South and provided a market for local chestnut oak bark. In 1925, International Shoe Company purchased the tannery. Proprietors elected not to rebuild after fire destroyed the facility during the 1940 flood, though extract manufacturing continued until 1945. (Courtesy of Wilkes County Public Library.)

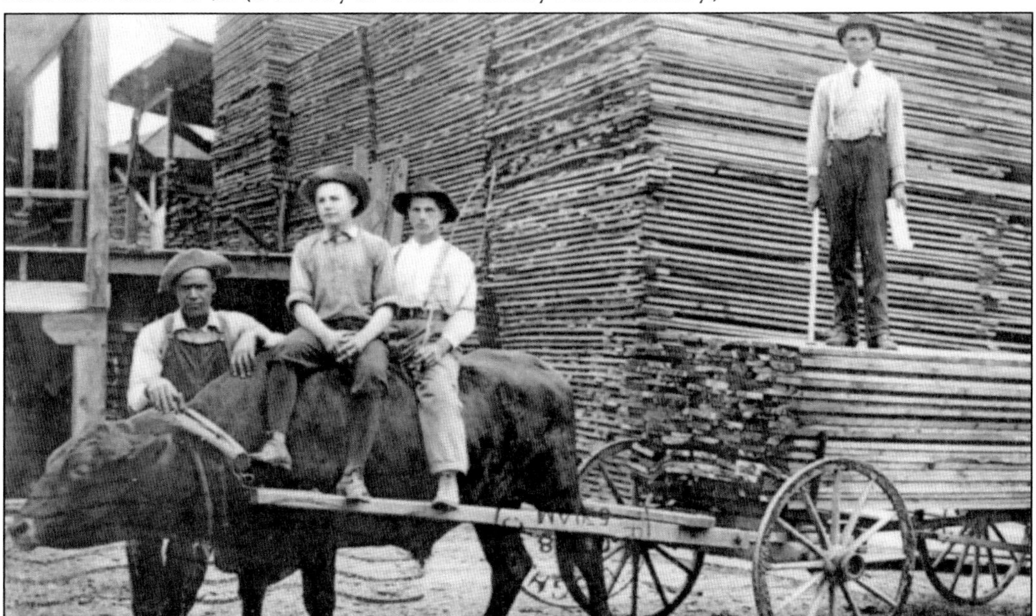

LUMBERYARD. In the early 1900s, a boom in development created a need for men to log wood, mill it, and cut it to specifications. After the introduction of the railroad in North Wilkesboro, there was a strong demand for building supplies and service that provided employment for men like those pictured in the photograph above, taken in North Wilkesboro. (Courtesy of Wilkes County Public Library.)

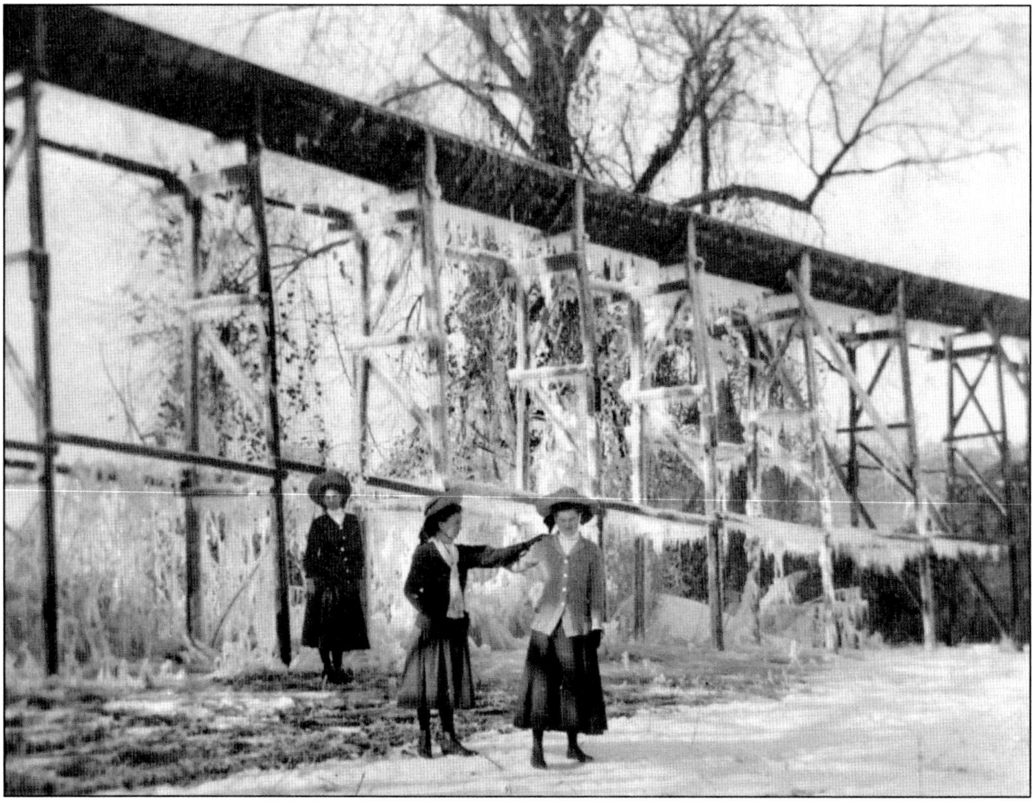

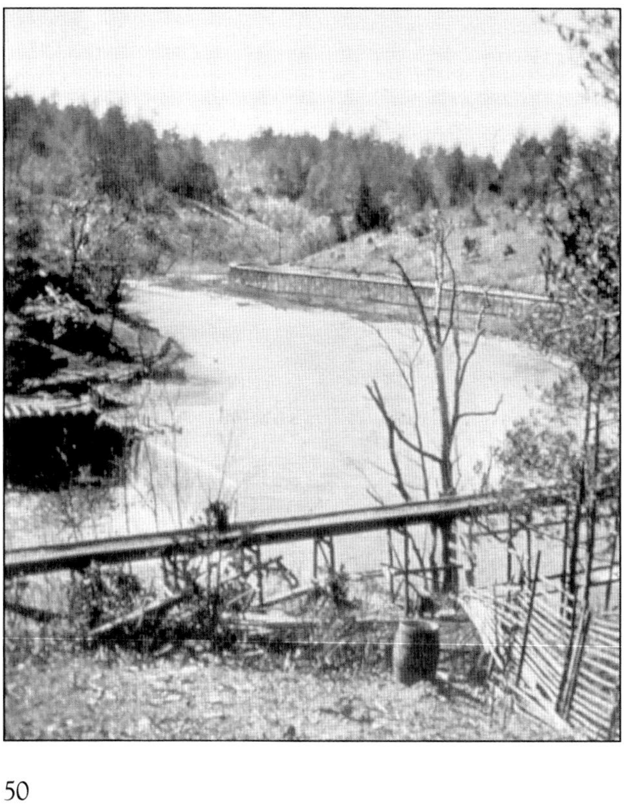

The Flume. This flume, built in the early 1900s by the Giant Lumber Company, transported timber along the Reddies River 20 miles to the finishing mill in North Wilkesboro. The trough was made of hemlock lumber, and the supporting structure was locust. Men began putting lumber in the flume around midnight to have it arrive in North Wilkesboro around 8:00 a.m. To keep lumber from jamming, ends were nailed together with nails designed to allow the boards to pivot as they rounded the curves in the flume. When the boards arrived in North Wilkesboro, the nails were pulled and shipped back up to the beginning of the flume to be used again. The flume operated until the 1916 flood washed away most of the structure. (Both courtesy of Wilkes Community College Library.)

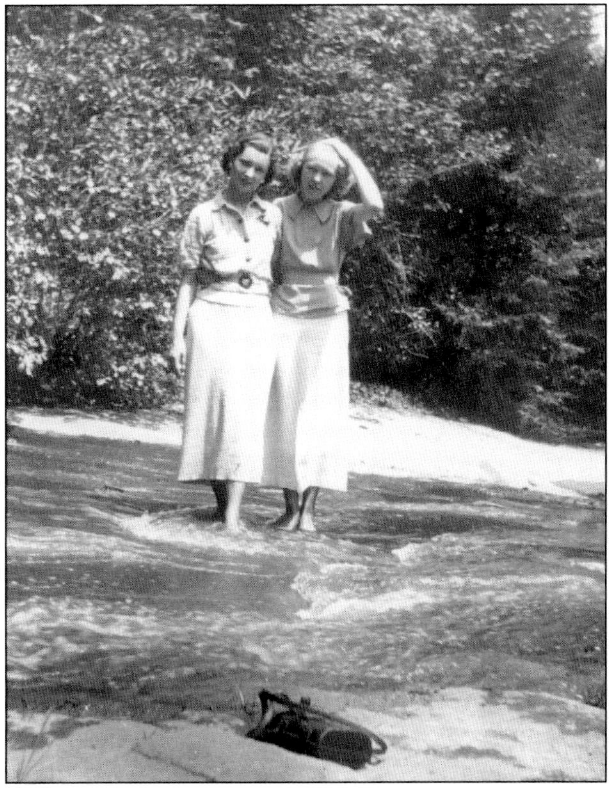

Moravian Falls. Moravian Falls was named for surveyors granted land in Wilkes County, though Moravians never settled the area. The first burr flour mill in Wilkes County was built here in the early 1800s. In 1911, an electric power plant was constructed, generating power from a dam on the falls that provided light for citizens in Wilkesboro. The mill building was torn down in 1927, and business activities at the falls ceased. After that, the falls drew people who enjoyed the recreational opportunities the spot afforded. The photograph at right shows Gustia Kilby (right) and Irene McNeil at the falls *c.* 1930. The photograph below depicts the falls prior to the removal of the mill. (Right, courtesy of Nicole Brown de Bruijn; below, courtesy of Wilkes Heritage Museum.)

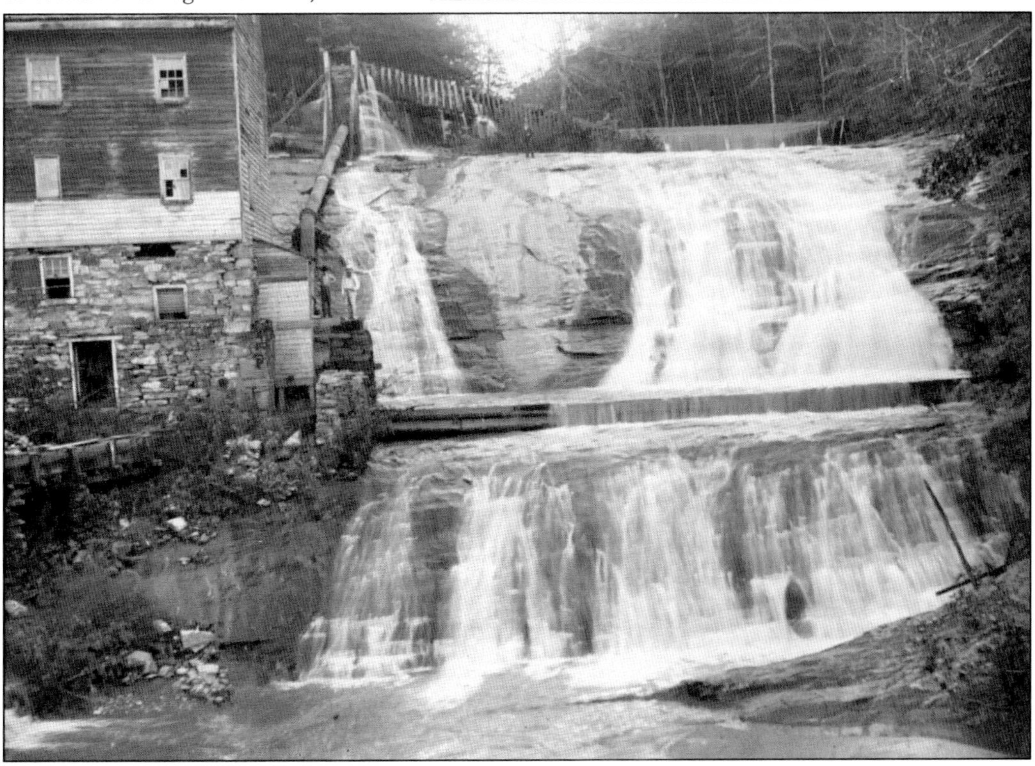

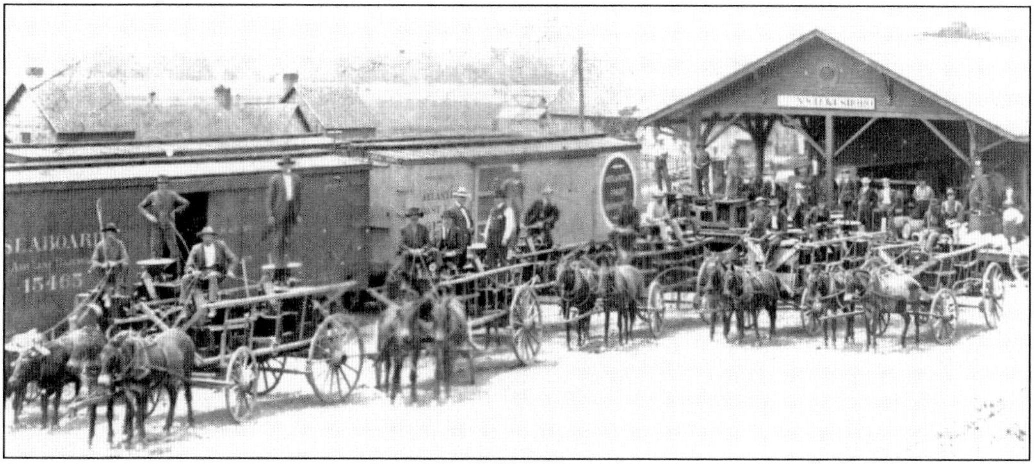

TRAIN DEPOT. Pictured are wagons containing gristmills being brought to the rail depot in North Wilkesboro. The railroad not only led to the establishment of the town of North Wilkesboro but also provided a better means of transporting goods to larger markets. Companies such as Meadows Mills, a local gristmill manufacturer, prospered at the beginning of the 20th century in part because of the new railroad. (Courtesy of Wilkes County Public Library.)

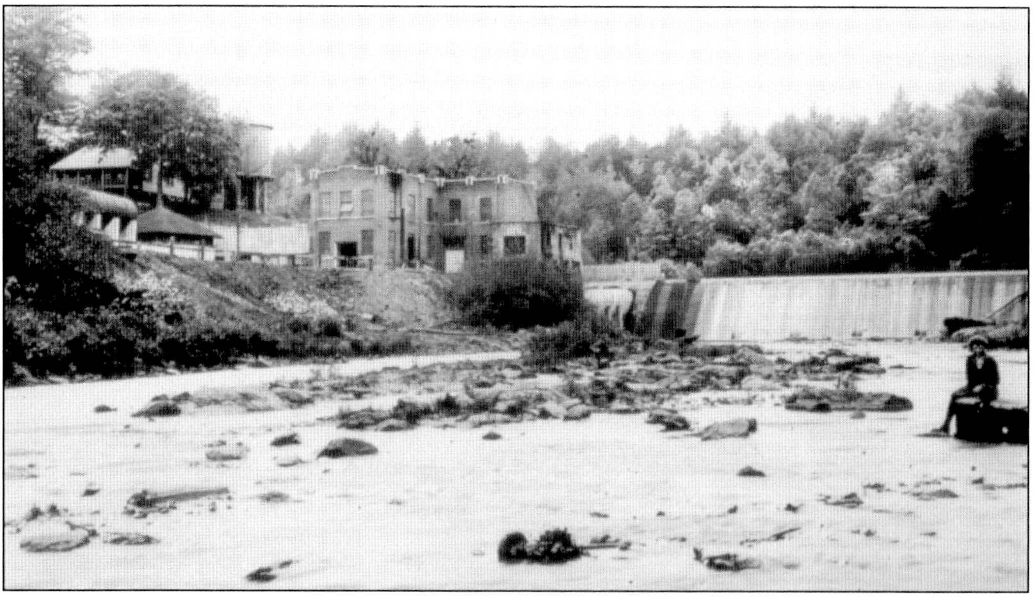

REDDIES RIVER. The Reddies River Dam was used by the North Wilkesboro City Water Works Pumping Station. It was located on the former site of a wooden dam and Hackett's Mill, which was owned by brothers James Gordon and Richard Nathaniel Hackett. The Hackett brothers' mill was the "grindingest institution" ever seen in this section of the state, said the *Wilkes Journal-Patriot*. It had the capacity to grind 50 bushels of corn per hour. (Courtesy of Wilkes Community College Library.)

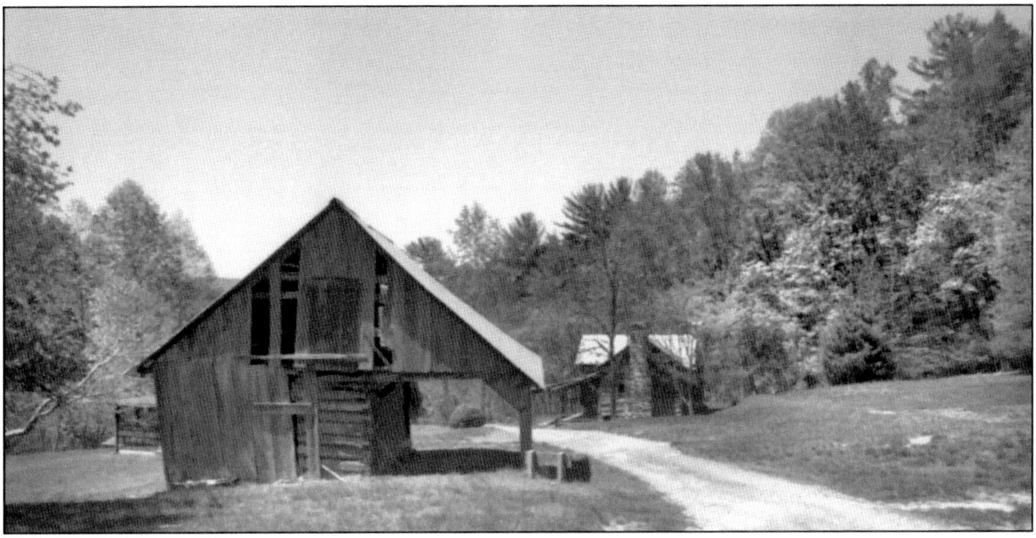

HUTCHINSON FARMSTEAD. The oldest part of the Hutchinson homestead, located at the base of Stone Mountain, was built *c.* 1852 by John and Sidney Brown Hutchinson. Later their son John Ely added a section to the eastern side of the building. The property was acquired by the state in 1977 and exemplifies life in rural farmsteads of the Blue Ridge Mountains. (Courtesy of the North Carolina State Archives.)

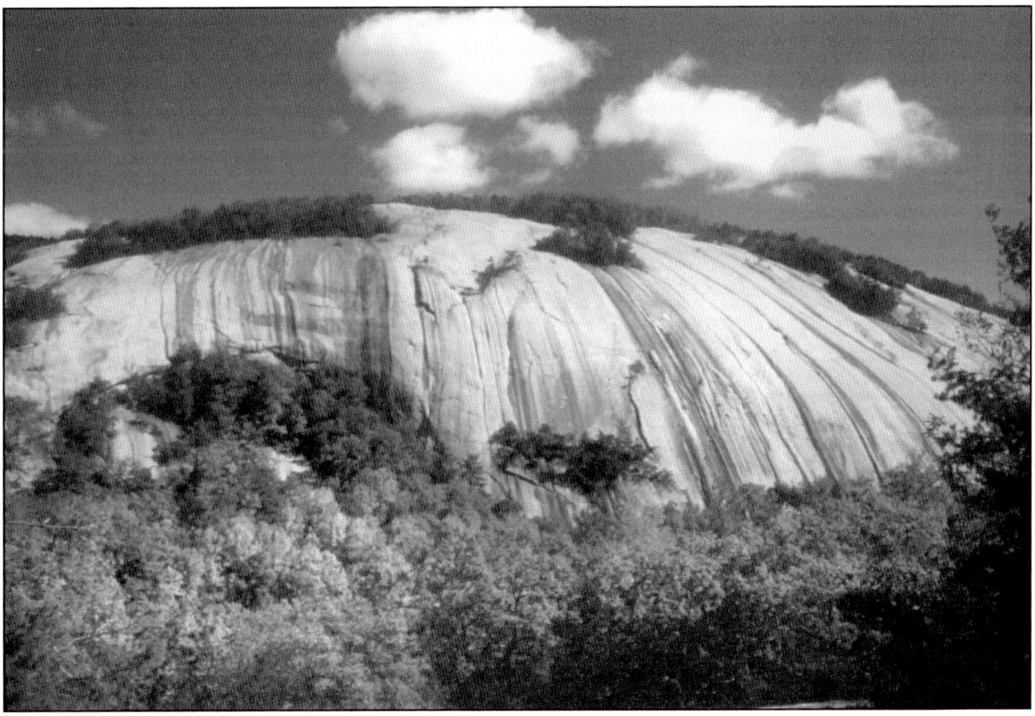

STONE MOUNTAIN. Stone Mountain State Park is topped by a 600-foot granite dome surrounded by 14,000 acres of parkland. The park was established in 1969, and the mountain was designated a National Natural Landmark in 1975. Prior to becoming a state park, settlers in the area around Stone Mountain built log homes, farms, mills, churches, and schools in their community. (Courtesy of Wilkes Heritage Museum.)

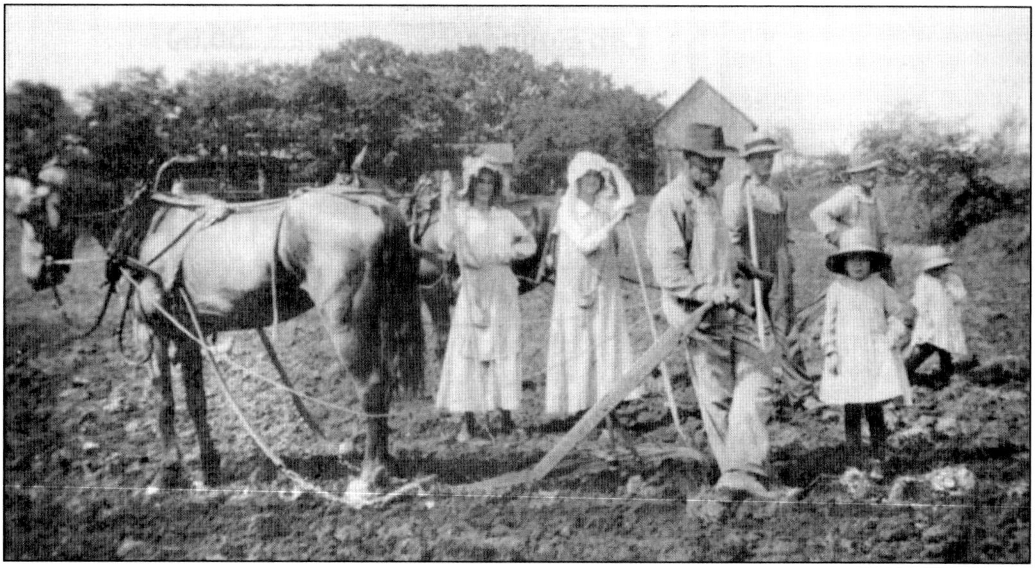

JESSE BYRD FAMILY, C. 1900. Jesse Byrd leans against the plow as he and members of his family take a break from work on their farm in the Lomax community. With Byrd are, from left to right, Hallie Byrd Couch, Hallie's sister Blanche Byrd Burcham, Hallie's brothers Marvin Byrd and Tom Byrd, and Marvin's children Mary Jane Byrd and Charlotte Byrd. (Courtesy of the *Wilkes Journal-Patriot*.)

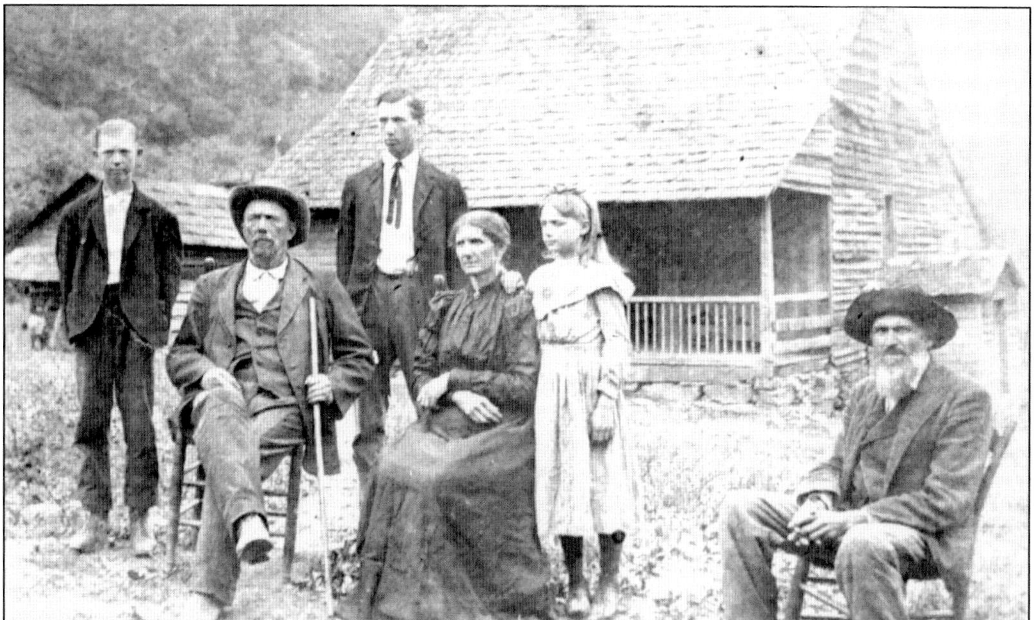

ALEXANDER FAMILY. Freel Alexander's farm in the Long Bottom area produced apples, grapes, peaches, cherries, Irish potatoes, beans, corn, rye, and wheat, and included a dairy barn. Sheep and cattle grazed on ridges above the farm. Alexander was elected sheriff of Wilkes County. Pictured from left to right are (seated) Freel and Sarah Spicer Alexander and their neighbor John Adams; (standing) the Alexanders' children, John, Cleve, and Fay. (Courtesy of Wilkes Community College Library.)

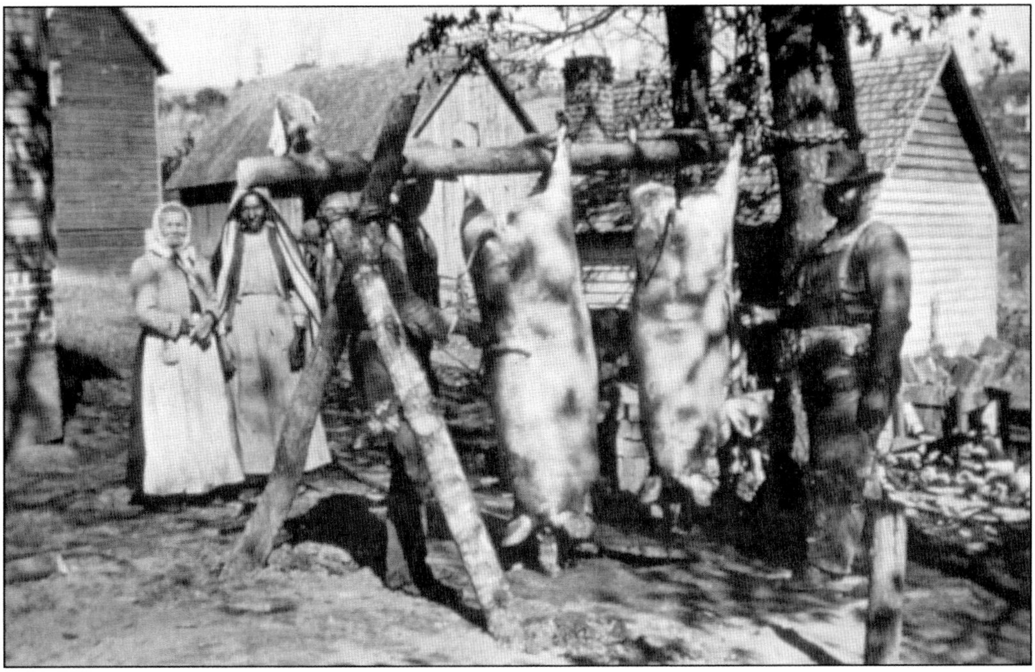

HOG-KILLING TIME. Hogs were slaughtered to provide meat through the winter, usually after the first cold spell of the year because meat would store better during colder weather. Hogs were hung and scalded repeatedly so that bacon and ham could cure with the skin left on. Other parts of the hog went into sausage, lard, cracklings, and lye soap. (Courtesy of Wilkes Community College Library.)

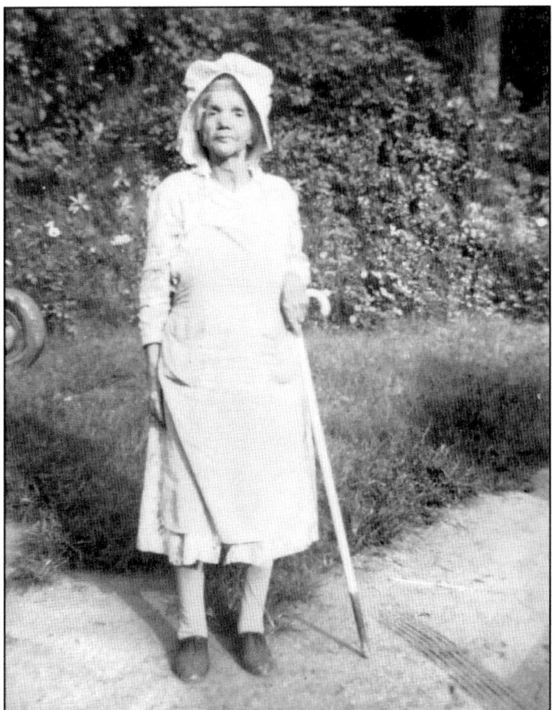

IDA CHURCH. Ida stayed with Estelle Triplett in the western section of Wilkes County to help her take care of her children. Like many women in Wilkes County, she spent time employed in the sewing trade. (Courtesy of Sheri Hayes.)

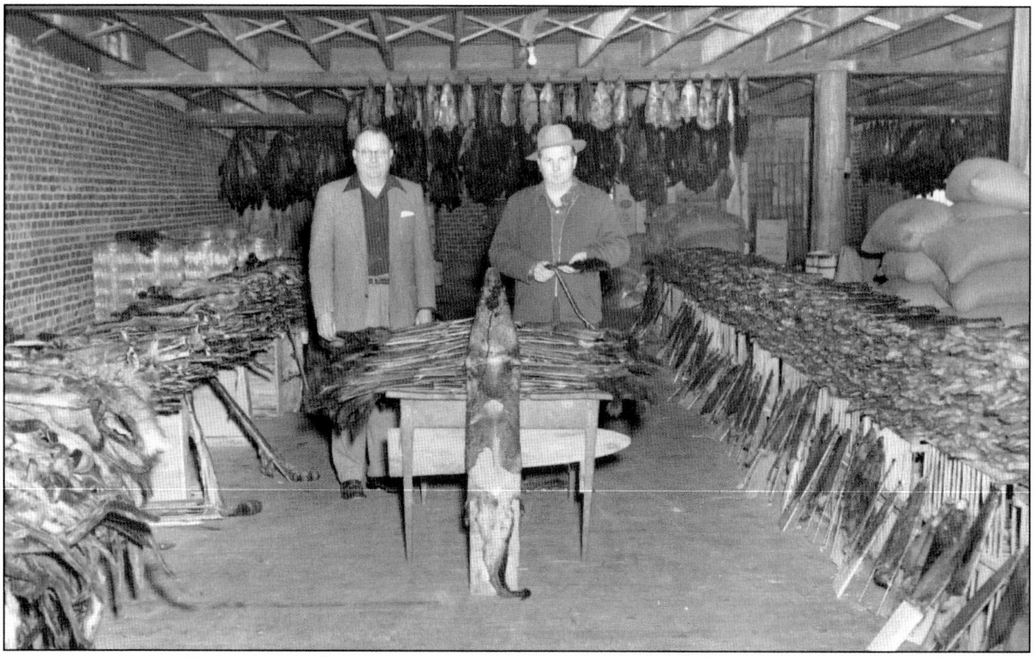

LOWE FUR AND HERB. C. A. Lowe founded the Lowe Fur and Herb Company in the early 1900s. The company's warehouse held more than 30,000 furs along with numerous herbs, including ginseng, blackberry root, peppermint leaves, poke root, and wild cherry bark. (Courtesy of Wilkes Community College Library.)

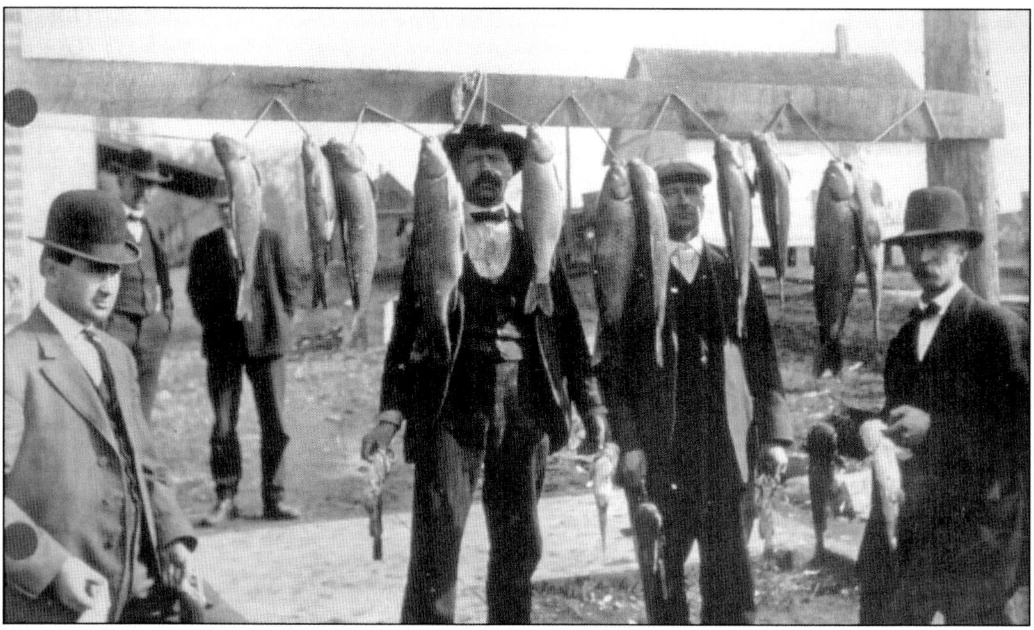

YADKIN RIVER. The Yadkin River has long been used for recreation, including fishing for sunfish, catfish, and bass. People made fishing poles from bamboo, creek cane, alder bushes, or sourwood; lines from horsehair or strings; and sinkers from lead beaten thin and wrapped around the line. Pictured here are fish caught in the Yadkin River. (Courtesy of Wilkes Community College Library.)

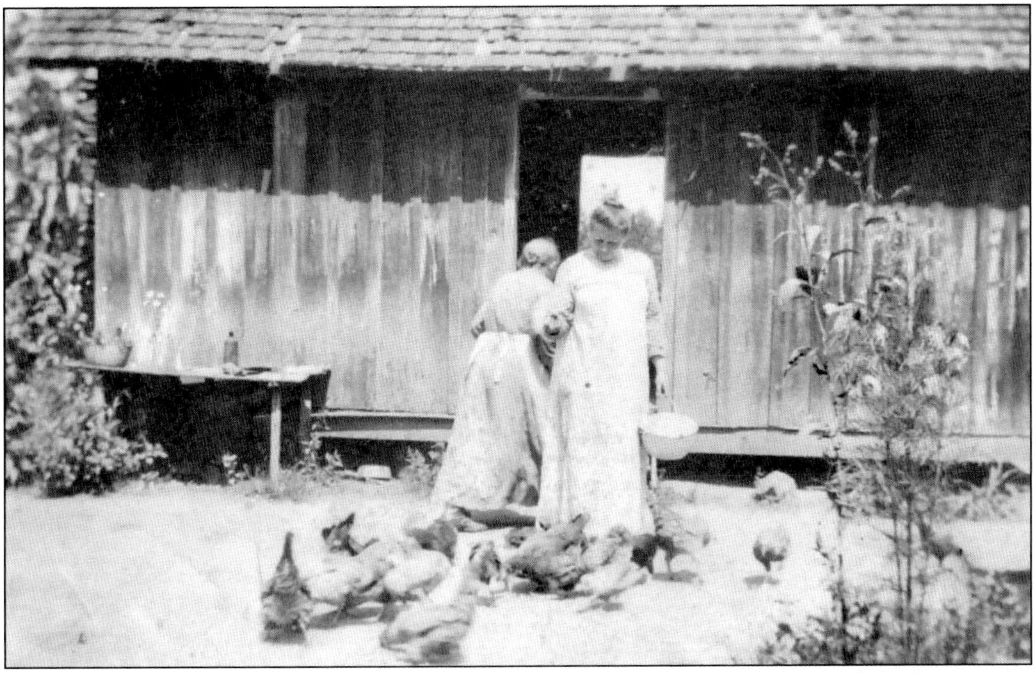

FEEDING CHICKENS. In this photograph, Nancy Foster and Neelie Haynes feed chickens at the Haynes home. The separate kitchen was built away from the home in case of fire. Another reason for keeping the kitchen separate in the rural South was the fact that the sultry climate of the region made cooking an unpleasant task, particularly in the summer. (Courtesy of Vergie Foster.)

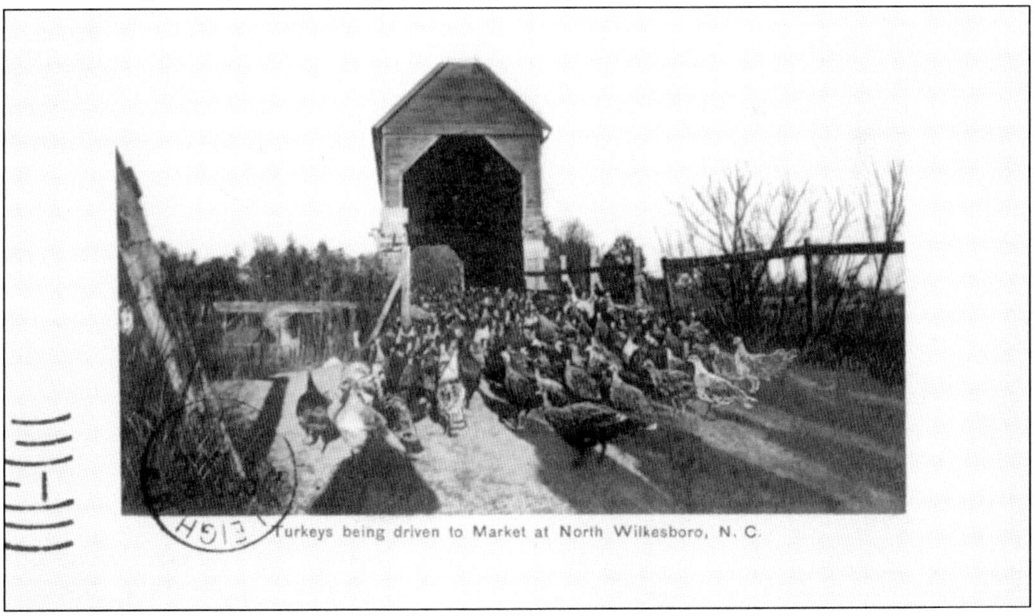

DRIVING TURKEYS TO MARKET. William Blackburn settled in Wilkes County around 1775 and devised a rail-pen trap to catch wild turkeys. He placed traps on a hill, and the name Traphill was born. Catching turkeys became a thriving industry. Trappers herded hundreds of wild turkeys 13 miles to the depot to ship them out to larger markets. Turkey herding ended during the 1920s. (Courtesy of Wilkes County Public Library.)

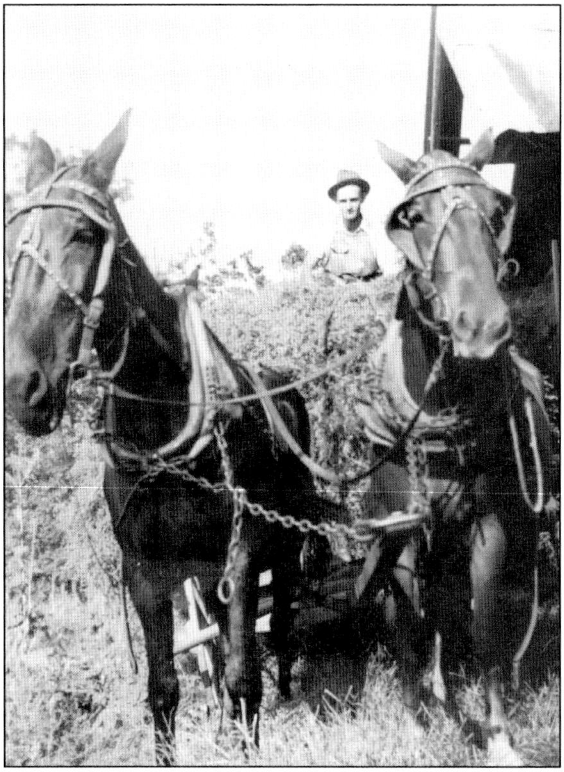

PLOW MULES. Some Wilkes County farmers preferred mules to horses for plowing on their farms because mules endure heat better, eat less, have less hoof problems, are more physically durable, and live longer on average than horses. Pictured is Paul Pardue working on the family farm in the Fishing Creek community. (Courtesy of Gail Haynes.)

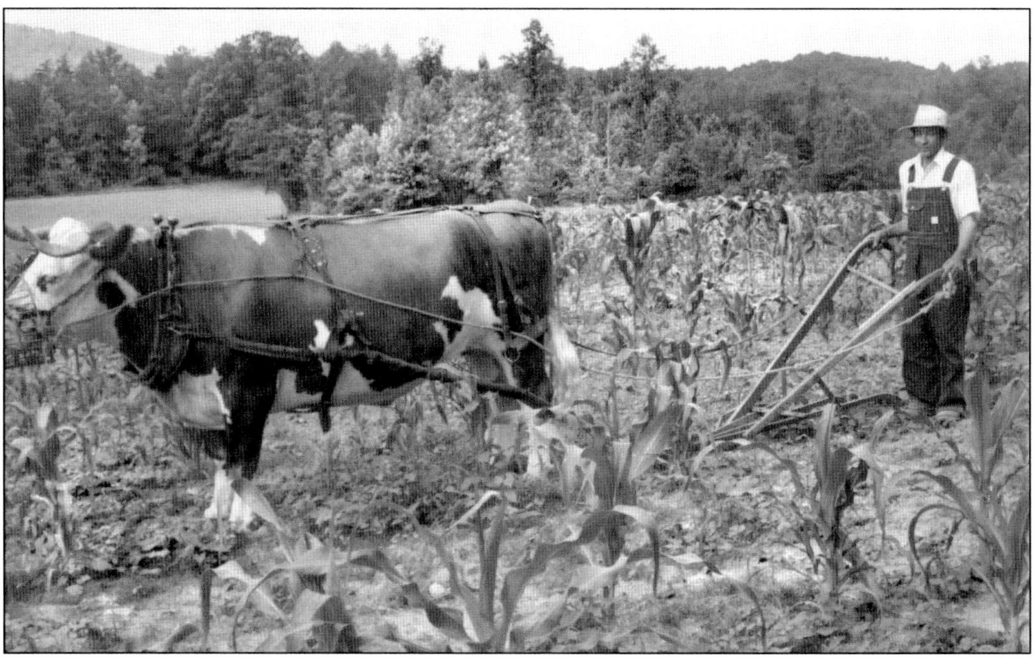

HUGHEY HARRIS. Farmer Hughey Harris graduated from Lincoln Heights High School in 1956 and spent his life working on the family farm of his father, Camie Harris. Camie was a hospital orderly, farmer, and deacon of New Damascus Baptist Church. Hughey is shown plowing Camie's garden with an ox. (Courtesy of Wilkes Community College Library.)

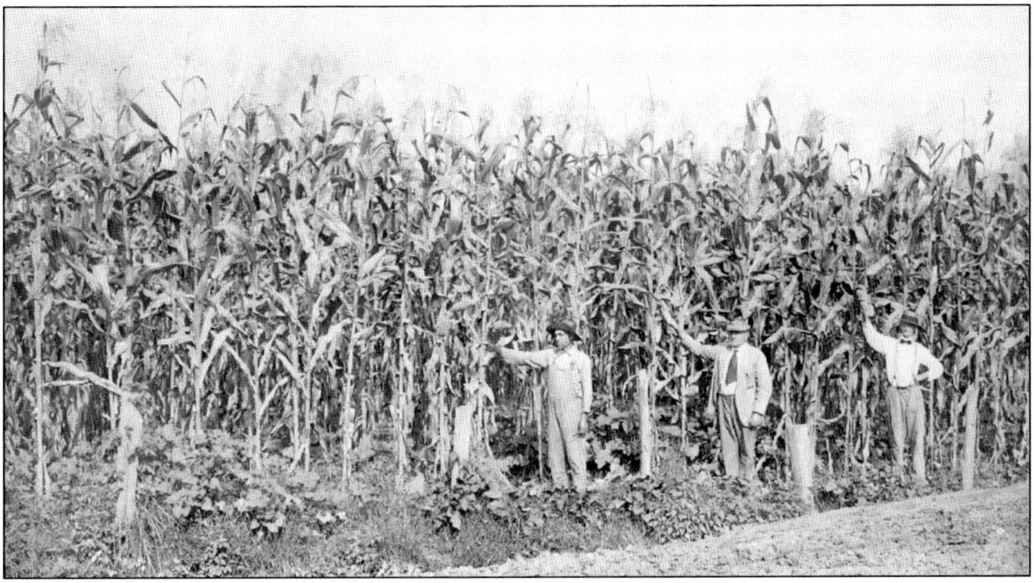

WILKES COUNTY CORN CLUB. Under the guidance of farm agents, farmers employed crop rotation, soil conservation, and other techniques to boost corn production. For members of the Wilkes County Corn Club, pictured below, production of 75 to 130 barrels an acre was not uncommon. The club had more than 400 members *c.* 1914, the largest membership of any county in the South. Members took numerous prizes for their produce, including honors for the best 10 ears of corn in 1910 at the state fair in Raleigh, earning a cash prize of $100. Other winners received prizes at the South Atlantic Corn Exposition, such as a ton of fertilizer. In 1917, the Wilkes County Corn Club swept the competition at the 4-H Corn Show. The corn club had a sister organization in the Girls Tomato Club. (Both courtesy of Wilkes Heritage Museum.)

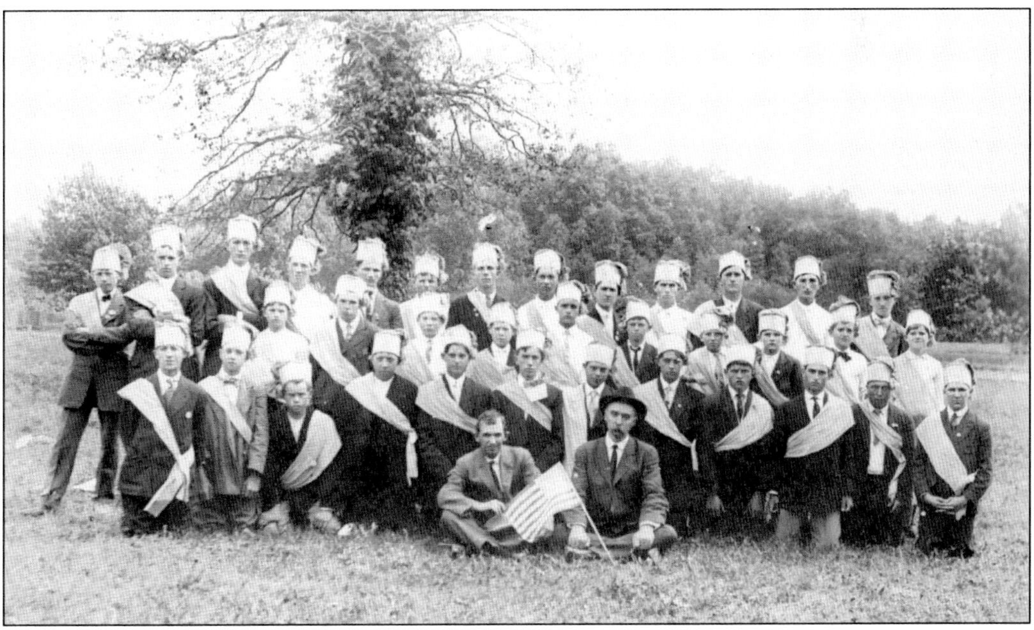

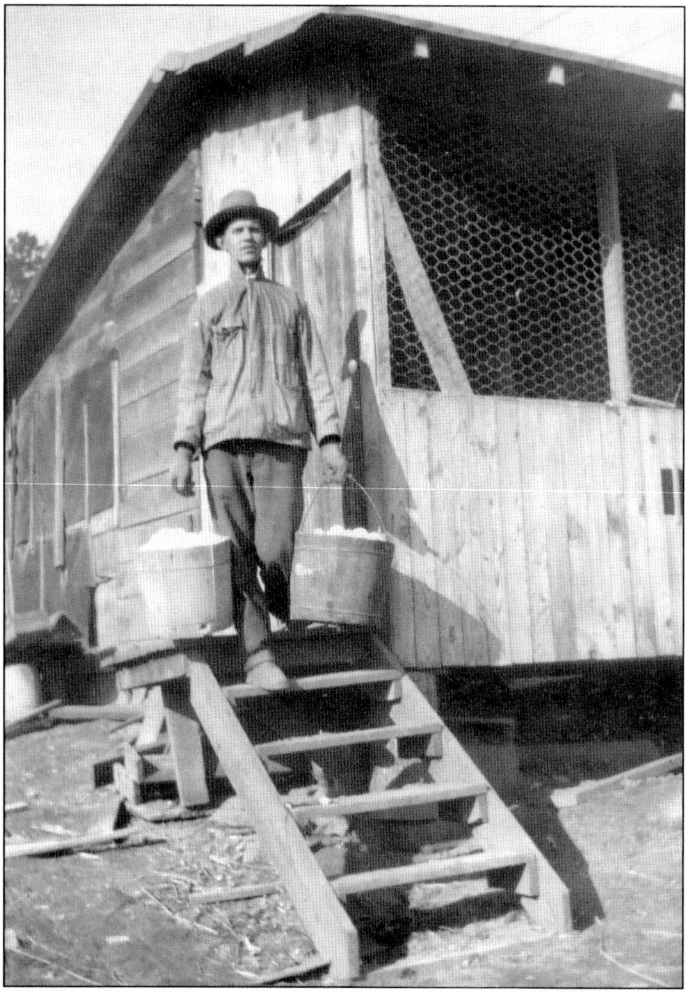

CHAMPION POULTRY FARM. T. O. Minton, owner and proprietor of Champion Poultry Farm, built his first chicken house in the Mount Pleasant community in 1923 to accommodate 150 pullets (young hens). He began with White Leghorns ordered directly from England and built an empire that was the largest commercial breeding farm in the South (and the third largest in the United States) during the 1930s and 1940s. His 500-acre farm could accommodate 35,000 layers and 30,000 pullets. He also owned incubator facilities for 164,000 hatching eggs, and his milling company produced feed for his own farm and for commercial selling as well. Pictured at left is Minton gathering eggs from one of his chicken houses; pictured below are free-range chickens on the Champion Poultry Farm. (Both courtesy of Eloise Church.)

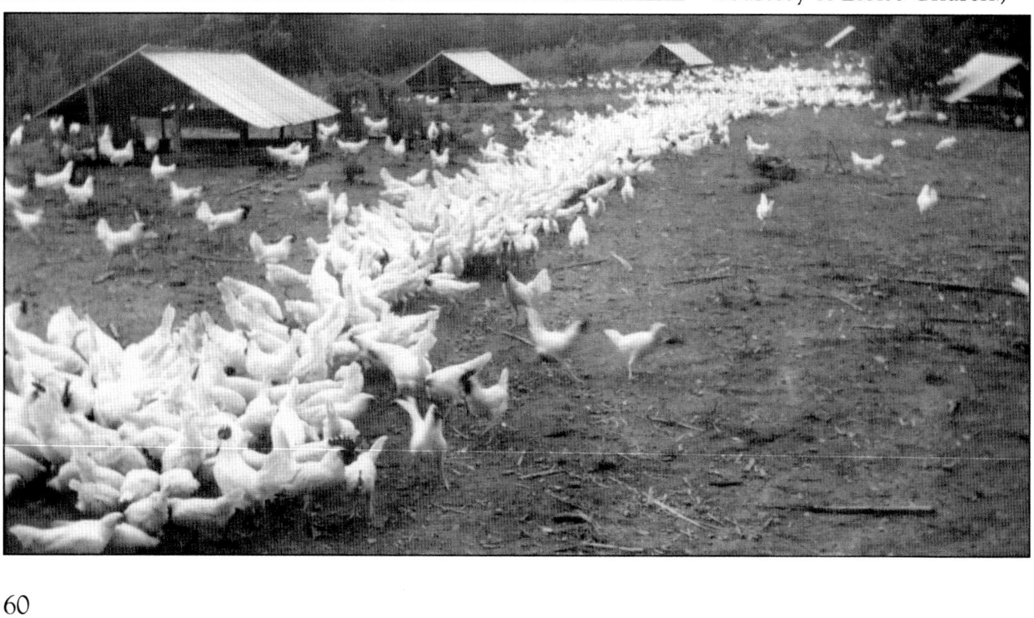

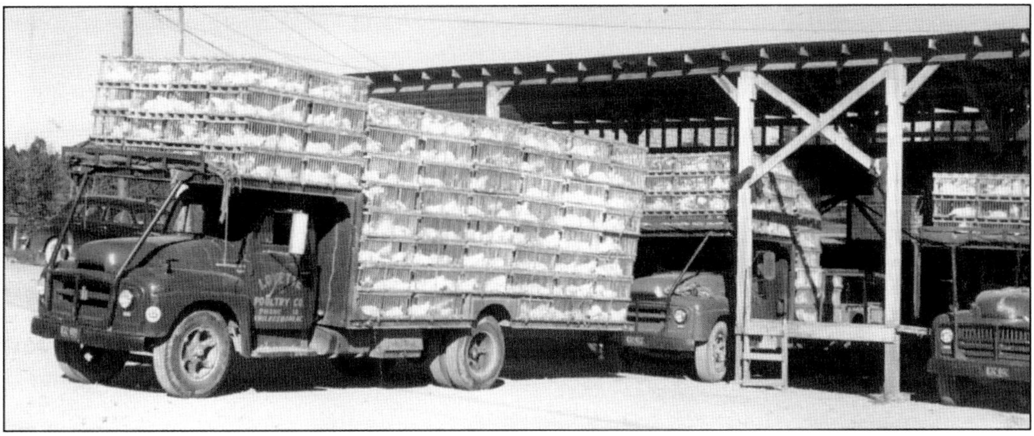

HOLLY FARMS. In 1942, Fred Lovette entered the chicken business with $3,000, a truck, and one employee. By the end of the 1950s, his interests could process 400,000 birds per week. In 1961, 16 firms engaged in various aspects of poultry production merged into Holly Farms Poultry Industries, Inc. This allowed Holly Farms to control every step of the production cycle. By 1976, production had risen to five million birds processed per week, and the company employed 7,000 people. In 1989, Holly Farms was acquired by Tyson Foods, Inc. Tyson, the largest industrial employer in Wilkes County, currently supports around 3,500 people. Shown above is a Lovette Poultry truck; shown below are chickens being processed in the Holly Farms plant. (Both courtesy of Wilkes Heritage Museum.)

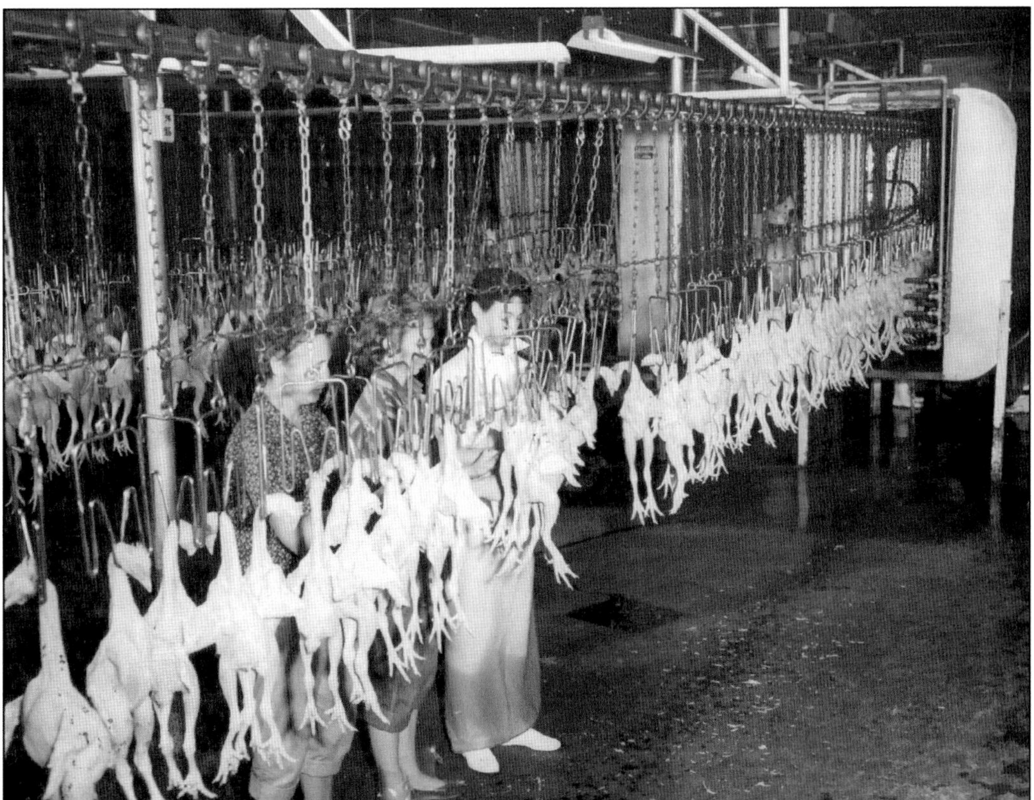

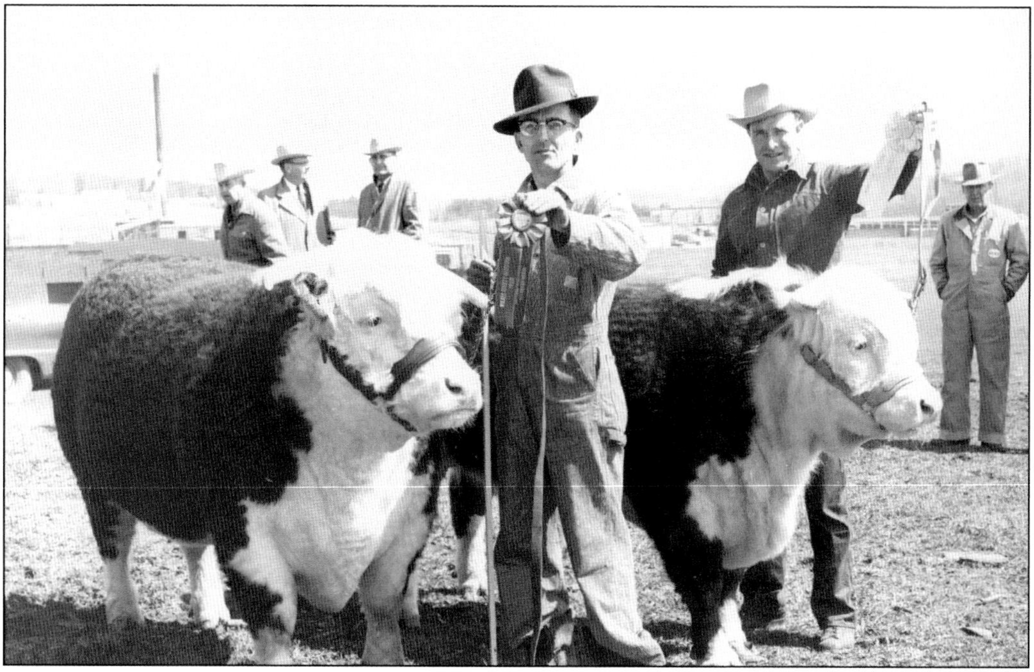

CHAMPION BULLS, 1956. Pictured on the left is the grand champion bull Homebuilder 11th, owned by Fred Vannoy, and on the right, the reserve champion owned by Robert Fender of Scenic Valley Farm. This photograph was taken at the Wilkes Hereford show and sale in March 1956. On this day, 55 purebred Herefords were sold for an average price of $130. (Courtesy of the *Wilkes Journal-Patriot.*)

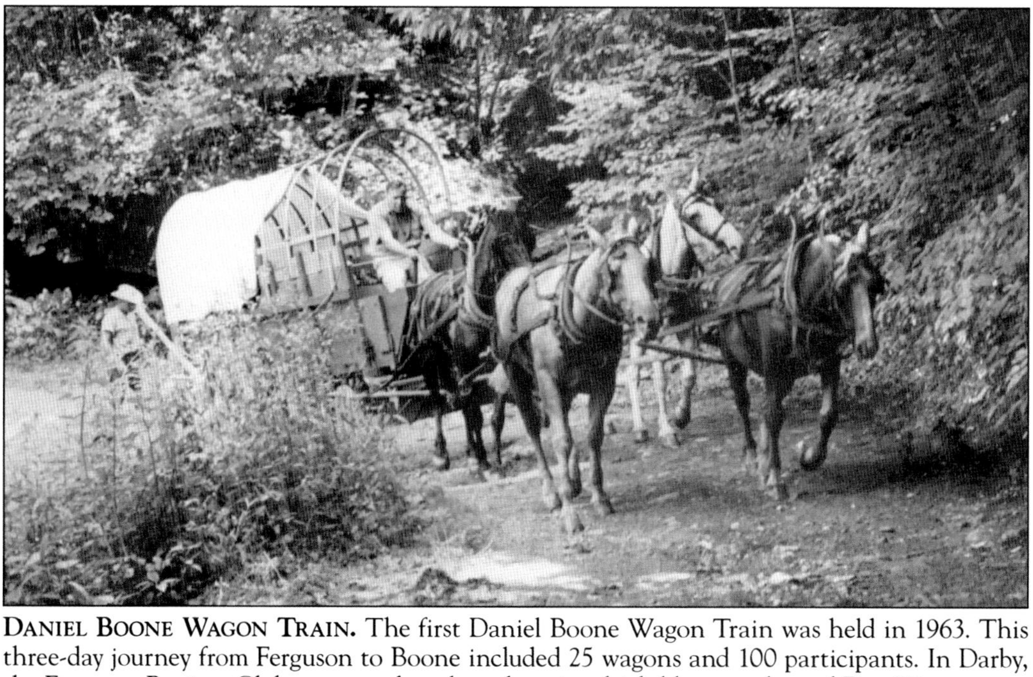

DANIEL BOONE WAGON TRAIN. The first Daniel Boone Wagon Train was held in 1963. This three-day journey from Ferguson to Boone included 25 wagons and 100 participants. In Darby, the Ferguson Ruritan Club sponsored a talent show in which bluegrass legend Doc Watson won second prize. (Courtesy of Wilkes Community College Library.)

DEER HUNTING. Deer hunting was once a necessity—venison meat was eaten and hides were used for moccasins, blankets, and pouches. In the early 1900s, deer became scarce, but now there are an estimated 30-45 deer per square mile in Wilkes County (even more in mountainous areas). Contemporary deer hunters in Wilkes hunt for both sport and taste. (Courtesy of Wilkes Community College Library.)

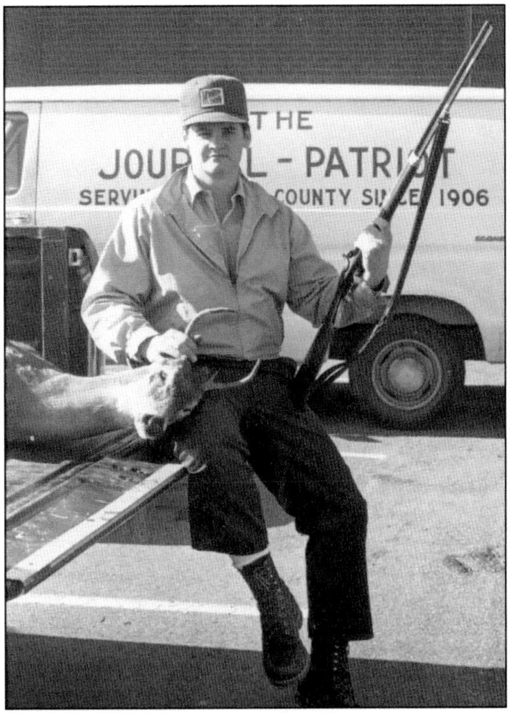

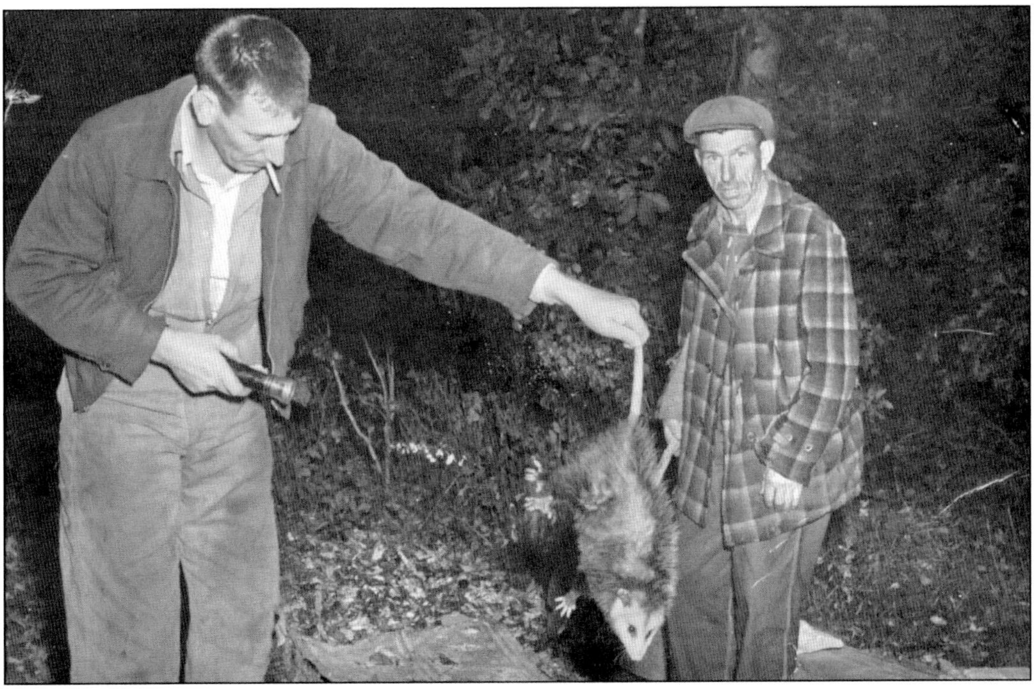

HUNTING OPOSSUM. Opossum pelts were once valuable to hunters and trappers. Opossum meat was also used to supplement rural diets, though many found the meat less palatable than other small game. Opossum hunting was often done late at night with dogs trained to tree the animals so hunters could shoot them. Pictured are Muncie Jordan (left) and Robert Swaim. (Courtesy of Georgia Cothren.)

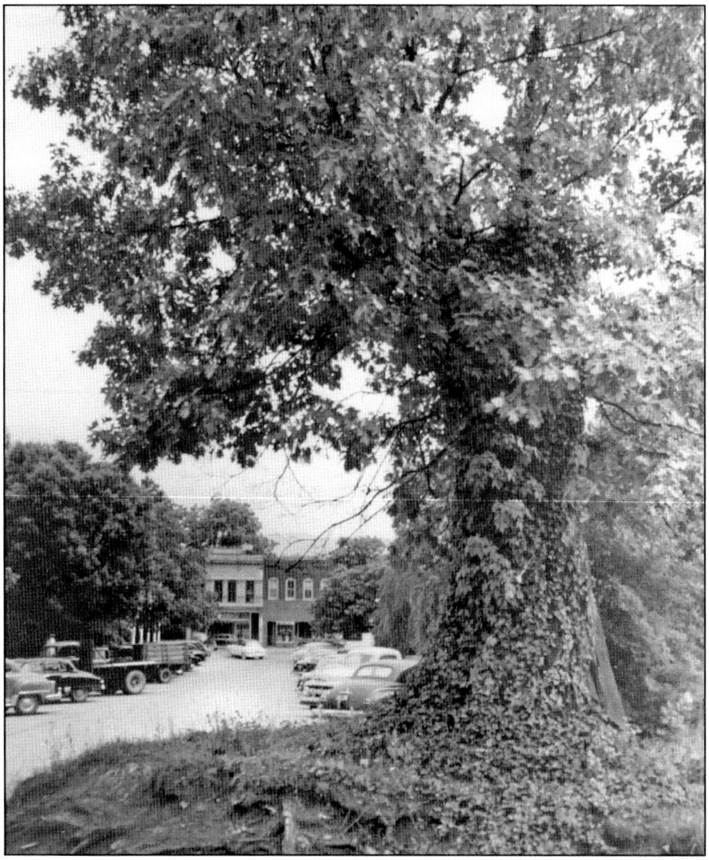

The Tory Oak. The Tory Oak stood on the courthouse square for more than three centuries. Legend holds that the Tory Oak was used by Col. Benjamin Cleveland to hang Tories during the Revolutionary War before large crowds that gathered on the courthouse square to witness the spectacle. In the 20th century, the tree began to decay and was destroyed by a storm in 1992. In 1997, a young oak sapling was planted at the site of the Tory Oak. The photograph at left shows the Tory Oak as it stood *c.* 1950; the photograph below shows a Confederate Veteran reunion held on the courthouse lawn *c.* 1910. (Both courtesy of Wilkes Community College Library.)

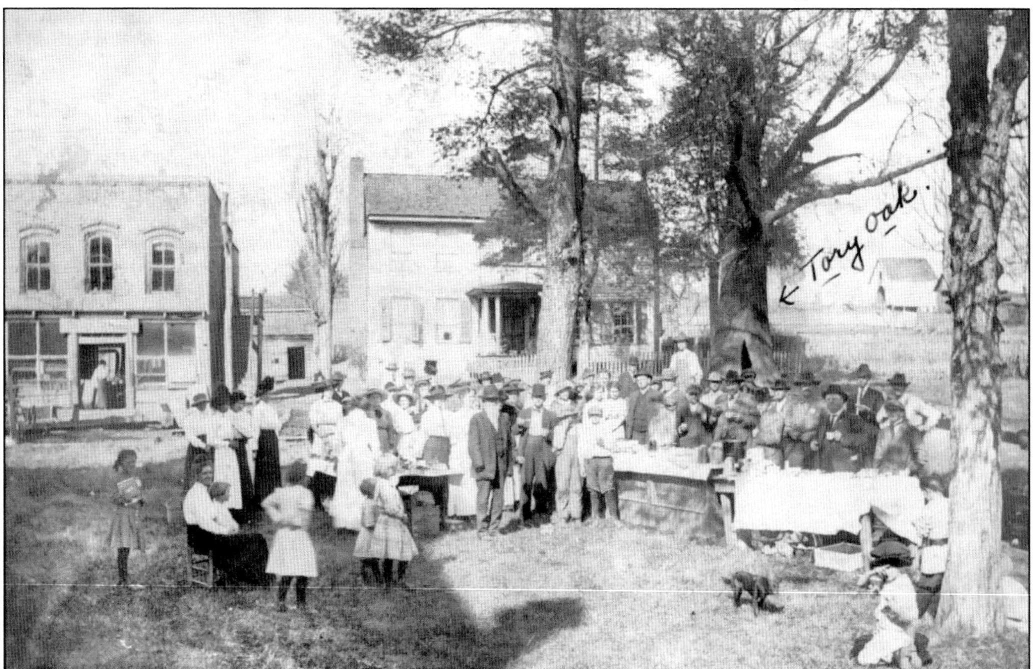

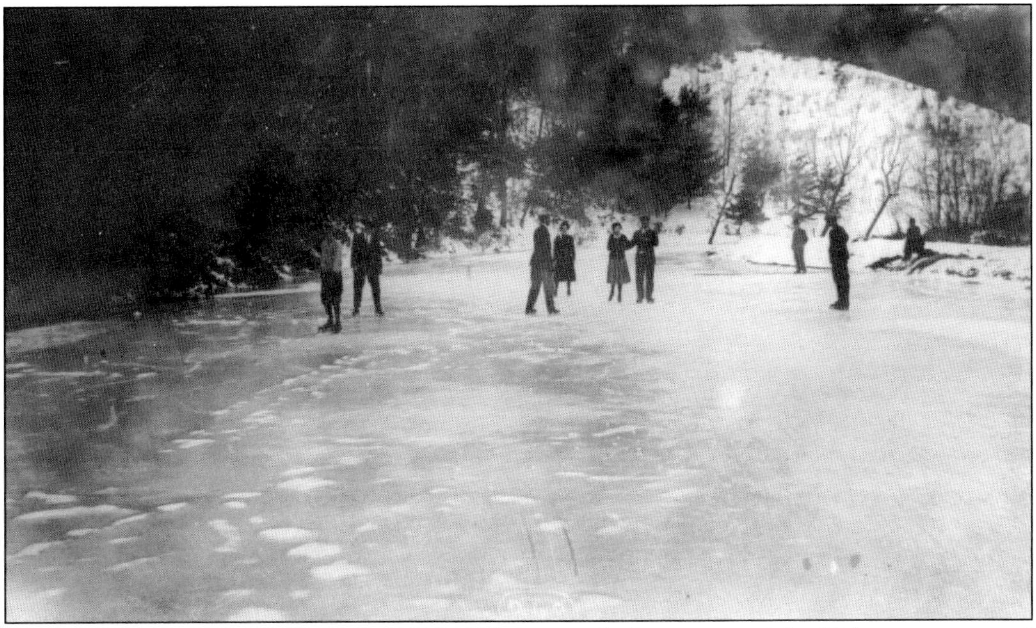

ICE SKATING ON REDDIES RIVER, C. 1900. Winters at the beginning of the 20th century proved remarkably cold. Residents recall wagons loaded with lumber were driven by oxen crossing the frozen Yadkin River. Folks sawed ice off rivers and ponds that they stored in sawdust in icehouses so they could use it at a later date. (Courtesy of Wilkes Community College Library.)

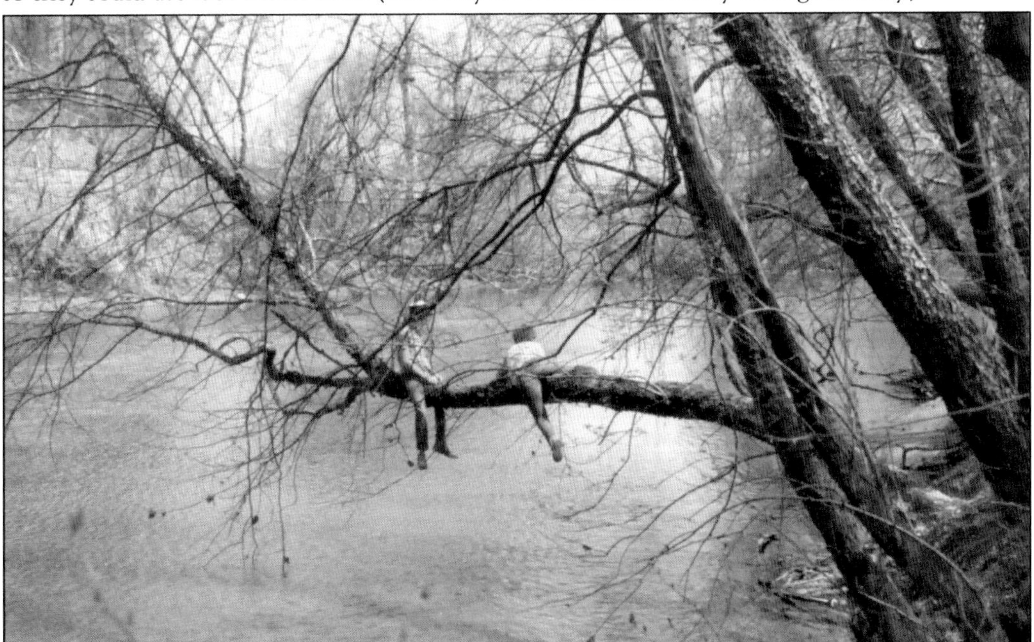

THE YADKIN RIVER. In 1820, the Yadkin Navigation Company sold stock with the intent of creating a navigable river from Wilkesboro to the east. Ultimately the river proved unsuitable for this venture. Today the Yadkin River provides water and opportunities for recreation to the citizens of Wilkes County. Pictured are Bill and Delores Horton enjoying an afternoon over the river. (Courtesy of Vergie Foster.)

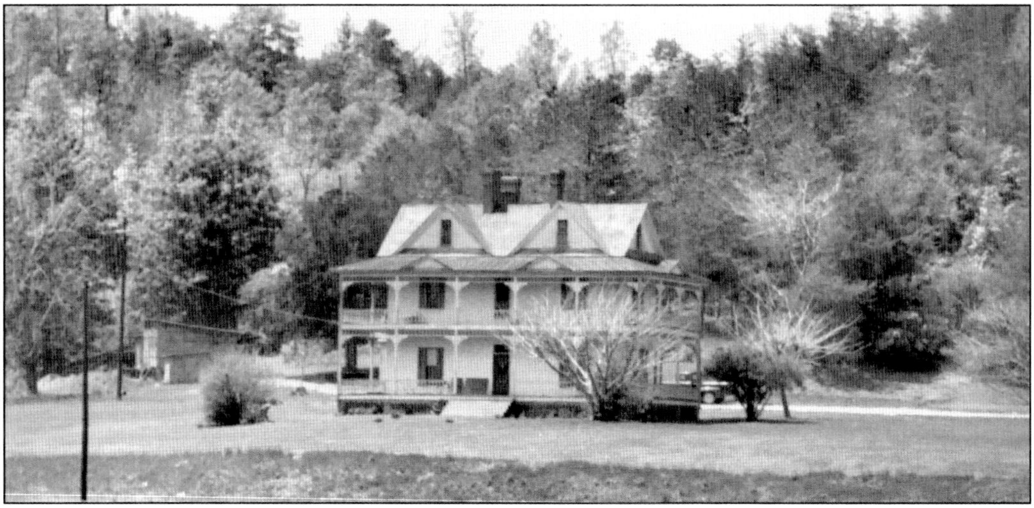

W. KERR SCOTT DAM. Devastating floods struck Wilkes County in 1899, 1916, and 1940. As a result, there was a concerted effort to dam the Yadkin River to prevent further flood damage. After much public debate, construction began *c.* 1960. W. Kerr Scott used his political influence to help bring the dam to fruition. The lake covers 1,500 acres and has a capacity of 153,000 acre-feet of water. There are about 55 miles of shoreline, and the area is home to numerous species of fish, waterfowl, flora, and other plants and animals. The purposes of the dam and reservoir are flood control, natural resource management, water supply, and recreation. Pictured above is the Higgins home, which stood in the bottomland now covered by the reservoir; pictured below is an aerial photograph during the construction phase. (Both courtesy of James Adams.)

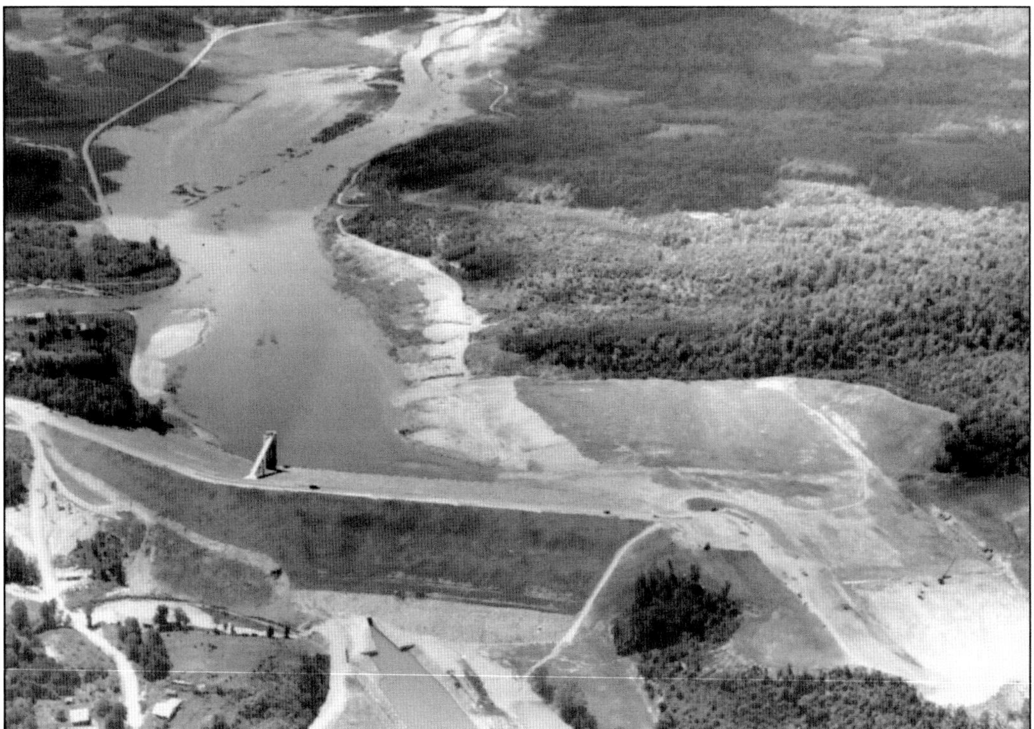

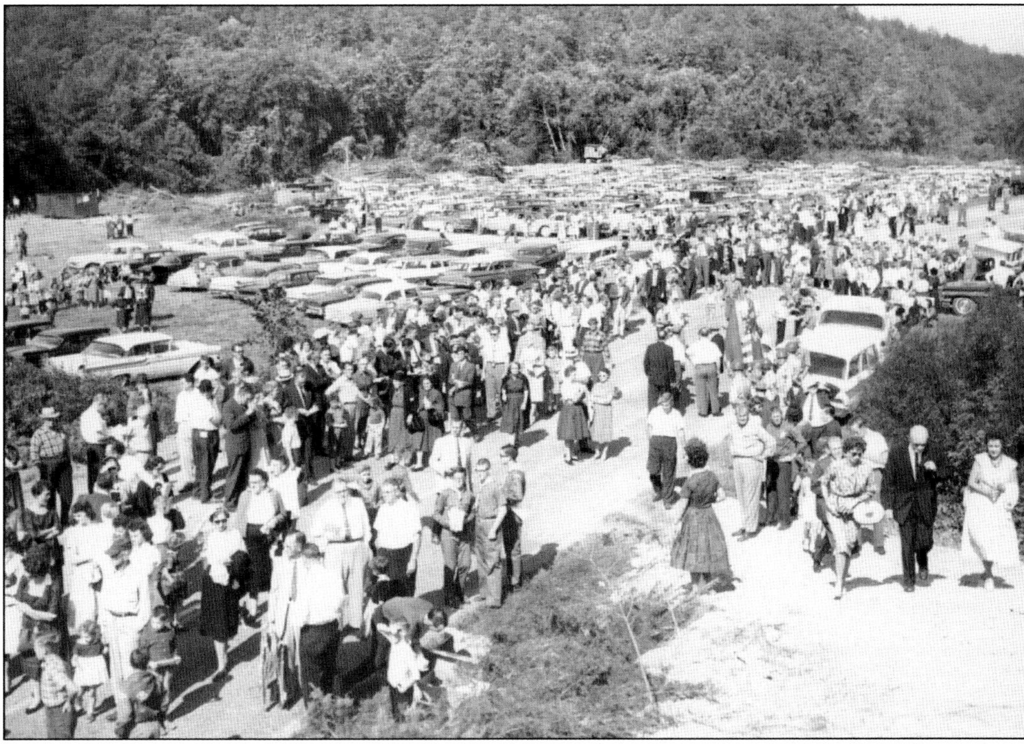

W. Kerr Scott Dam. The W. Kerr Scott Dam and Reservoir opened in 1963. For fishing enthusiasts, the lake has been stocked with alewife, blue catfish, blueback herring, channel catfish, largemouth bass, rainbow trout, smallmouth bass, threadfin shad, hybrid striped bass, tiger muskellunge, spotted bass, walleye, and white bass. For boaters, there are public-access boat ramps on the lake, as well as a marina. The Corps of Engineers maintains day-use facilities, including designated swimming areas, picnic shelters, campsites, and playgrounds. There is an outdoor amphitheater on the lake, the Forest Edge Community Amphitheater at Historic Fort Hamby, where *Tom Dooley: A Wilkes County Legend* is staged each summer. Pictured above is the groundbreaking ceremony; pictured below are boaters in the early 1960s. (Both courtesy of Wilkes Community College Library.)

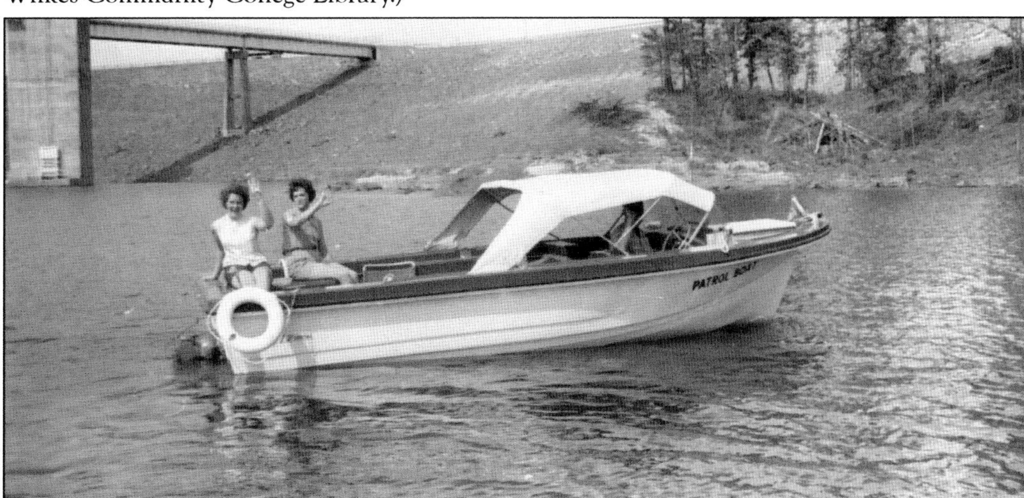

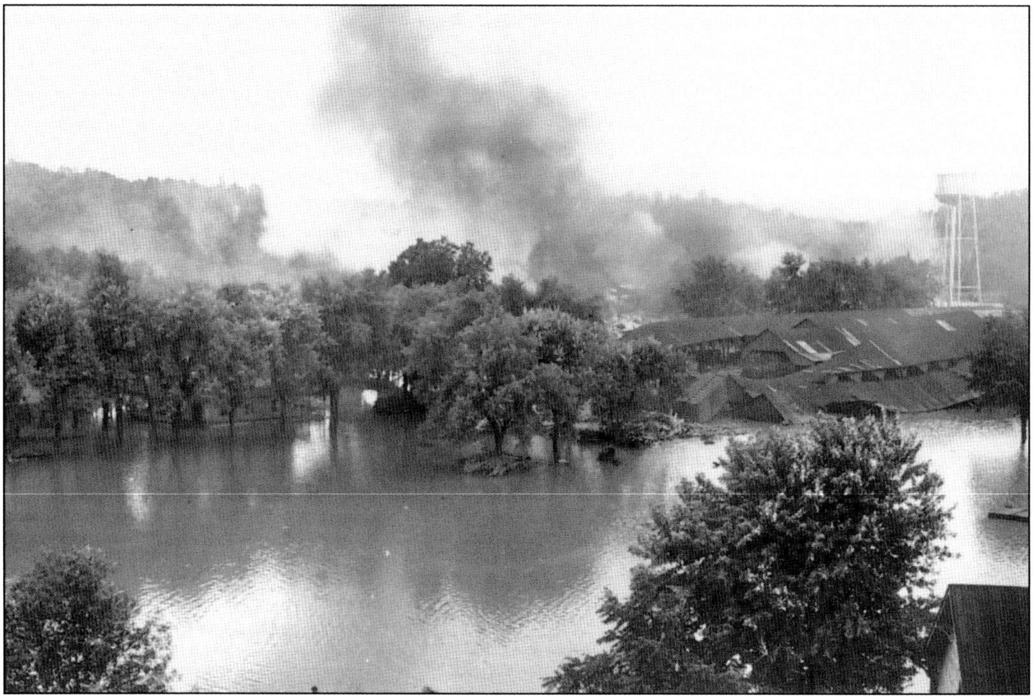

FLOOD OF 1940. During the summer of 1940, sudden cloudbursts erupted along the Blue Ridge Mountains, and water descended into the hollows and valleys between the Wilkesboros. The result was a flood that claimed eight lives, destroyed more than 150 homes, and caused $5 million in property damage. In places, waters of the Yadkin River rose more than 30 feet. The buildings on the fairgrounds in North Wilkesboro were washed away, including the grandstand and the National Guard armory. Train service was interrupted, and fires accompanied the water damage. Pictured above are floodwaters in the foreground and smoke from the fire that destroyed the International Shoe Tannery in the background. Pictured below are floodwaters near Forester's Nu-Way. (Both courtesy of Wilkes Heritage Museum.)

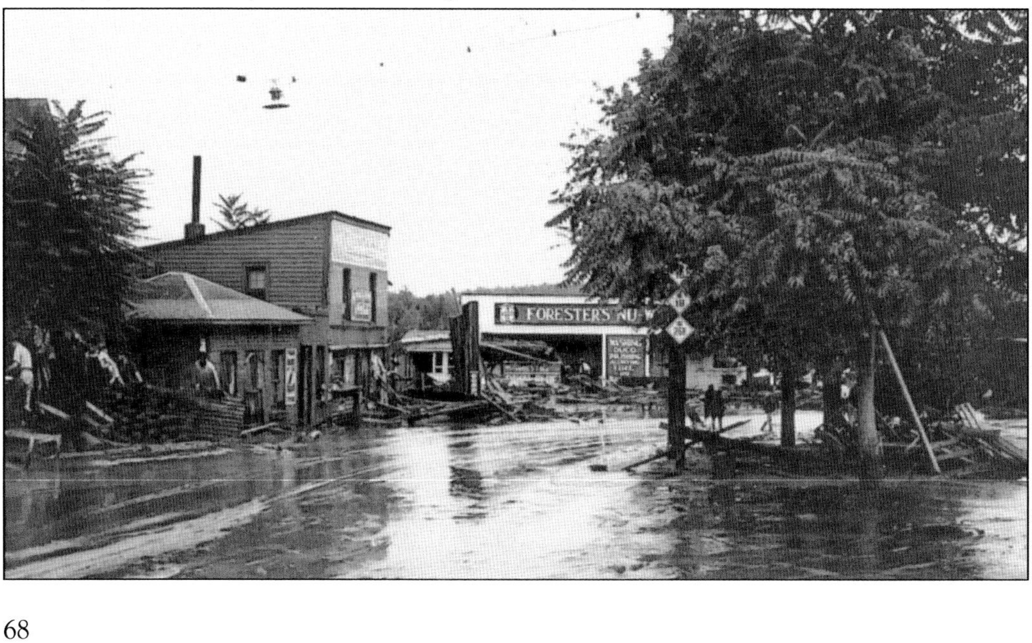

Five

Taking Care of Our Own

As Wilkes County developed and became more of a community and less a series of isolated farms, the need for public services like roads, post offices, and hospitals became apparent. Adequate transportation was one of the first requirements of the county. Far-flung communities separated by rivers and mountains coupled with wagon roads maintained by local road crews meant that travel could be treacherous, especially during rough weather. The 1920s brought state involvement and improved roads, including paved highways. Construction of a railroad to North Wilkesboro in 1891 facilitated the transportation of passengers and freight to markets. By 1948, North Wilkesboro had a private airstrip built by a group of local pilots.

Medical practice in Wilkes County also evolved to meet the changing community. Early physicians served patients without the benefit of modern medicine. They administered patent medicines and home remedies, operated on kitchen tables and under shade trees, and depended on patients' families rather than trained nurses for medical assistance. They traveled by horseback or in wagons to treat patients in their homes. Conditions improved under the leadership of Dr. Fred Hubbard, who constructed hospitals in North Wilkesboro in 1923 and 1952. In 1915, the County Home opened to house indigents, individuals with psychiatric disorders, and tuberculosis patients. During the 1950s, medical care was enhanced by the organization of the Wilkes Rescue Squad and introduction of volunteer fire departments in several communities. Rural post offices were consolidated into larger, more modern facilities. Groups like the American Legion and the Veterans of Foreign Wars were organized to support veterans.

Over the years, much has changed in Wilkes County. Gravel roads have been paved, modern airports have been constructed, and state-of-the-art hospitals and medical facilities have been opened. Great distances still separate some communities from larger towns, but those distances have been shortened by improved transportation and communication. Despite myriad changes, some things remain the same: local markets still provide small communities with groceries, gasoline, and gossip; the public library bookmobile still winds its way along crooked roads to eager readers; and the people of Wilkes County remain determined to improve themselves and their communities.

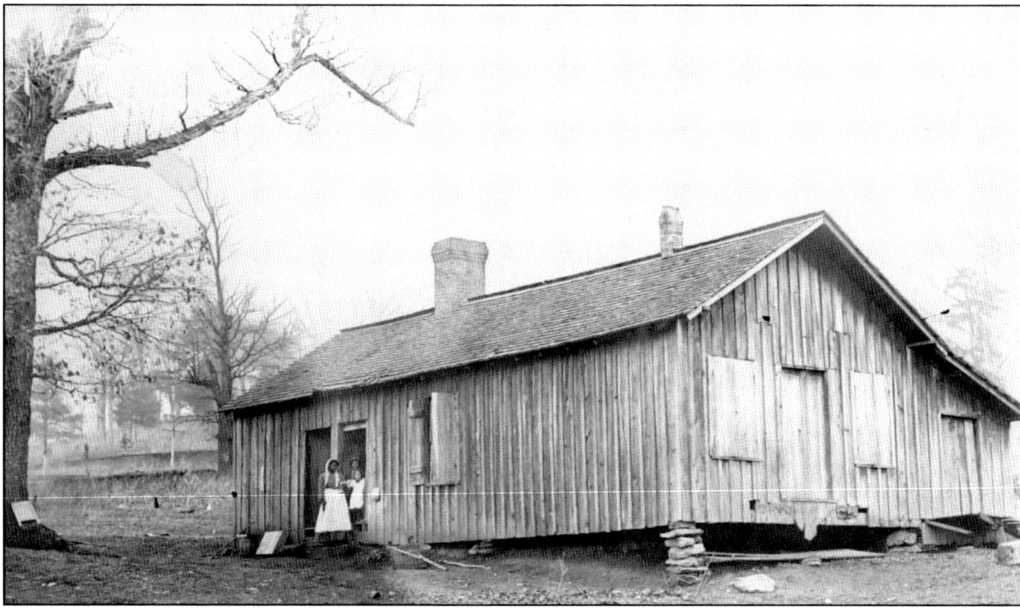

GORDON POST OFFICE. When the Northwest North Carolina Railroad Company built a line to Wilkes County, J. R. Finley set up shop in the town of Gordon, later chartered as North Wilkesboro. This storehouse was built in 1890, and Finley was appointed as Gordon's postmaster. This building was later demolished, and Forest Furniture Company was built on the site. (Courtesy of Wilkes Community College Library.)

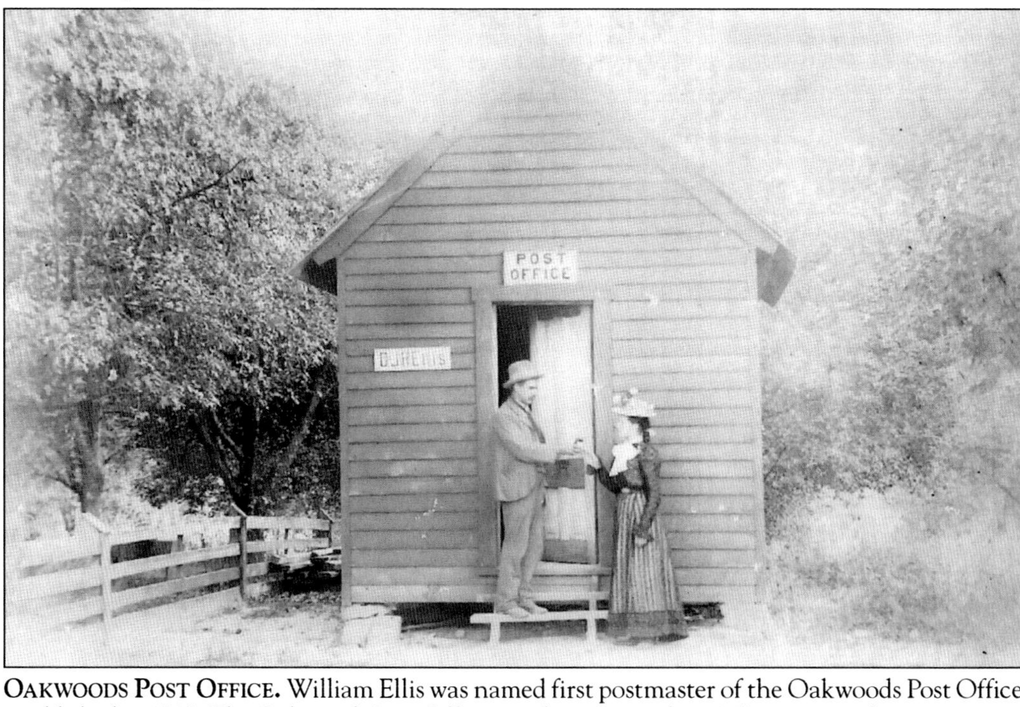

OAKWOODS POST OFFICE. William Ellis was named first postmaster of the Oakwoods Post Office, established in 1893. The Oakwoods Post Office was discontinued in 1953 as a part of a controversial federal effort to save money. Dr. J. H. Ellis, pictured here with an unidentified woman, met with patients at the Oakwoods Post Office. (Courtesy of Wilkes Heritage Museum.)

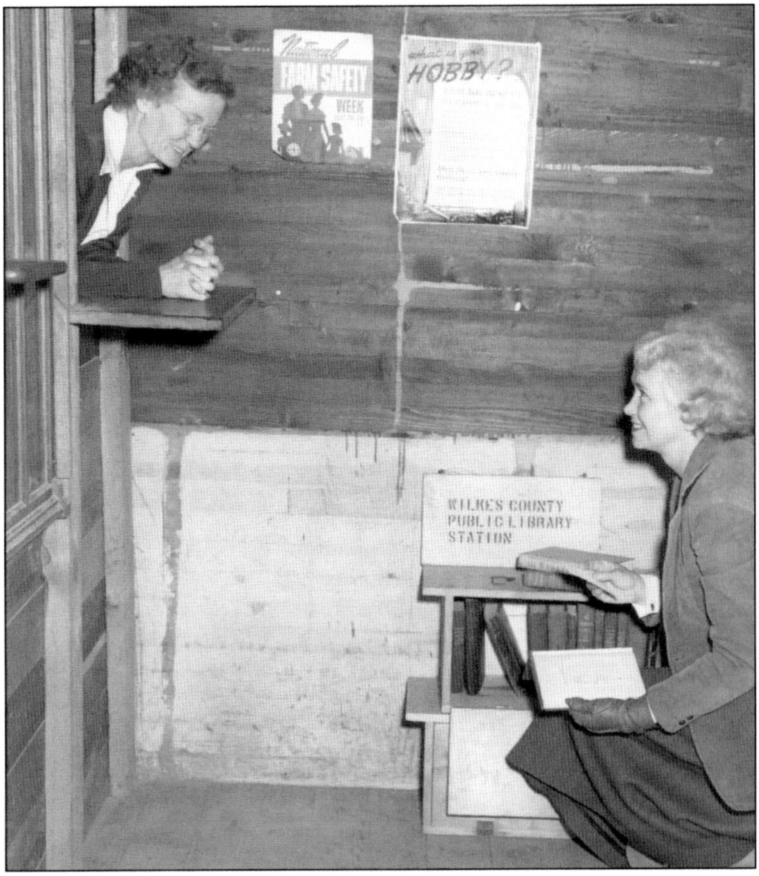

WILKES COUNTY PUBLIC LIBRARY. In 1918, Edward Finley requested that the North Carolina State Library send books to North Wilkesboro to be housed in Dean's Jewelry. In 1966, the library relocated to the North Wilkesboro Post Office building on C Street, where it remained for 33 years. The new library on Tenth Street opened in 1999. Book exchanges, such as the one pictured at right, were deposited at Millers Creek High School and other spots in the late 1930s. The *c.* 1930 photograph shows one of the bookmobiles. (Both courtesy of Wilkes County Public Library.)

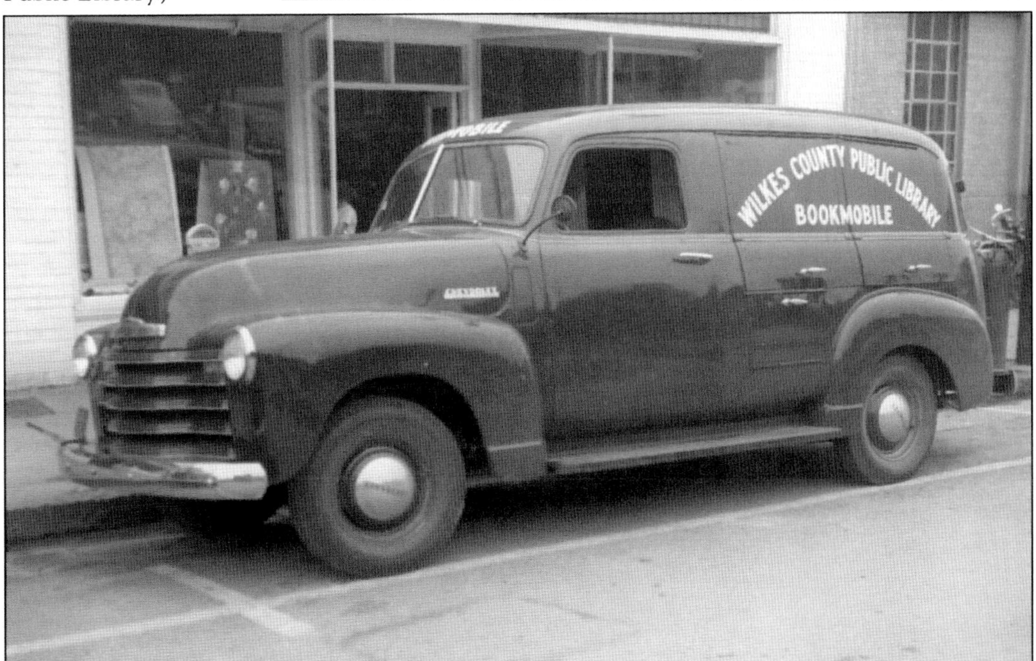

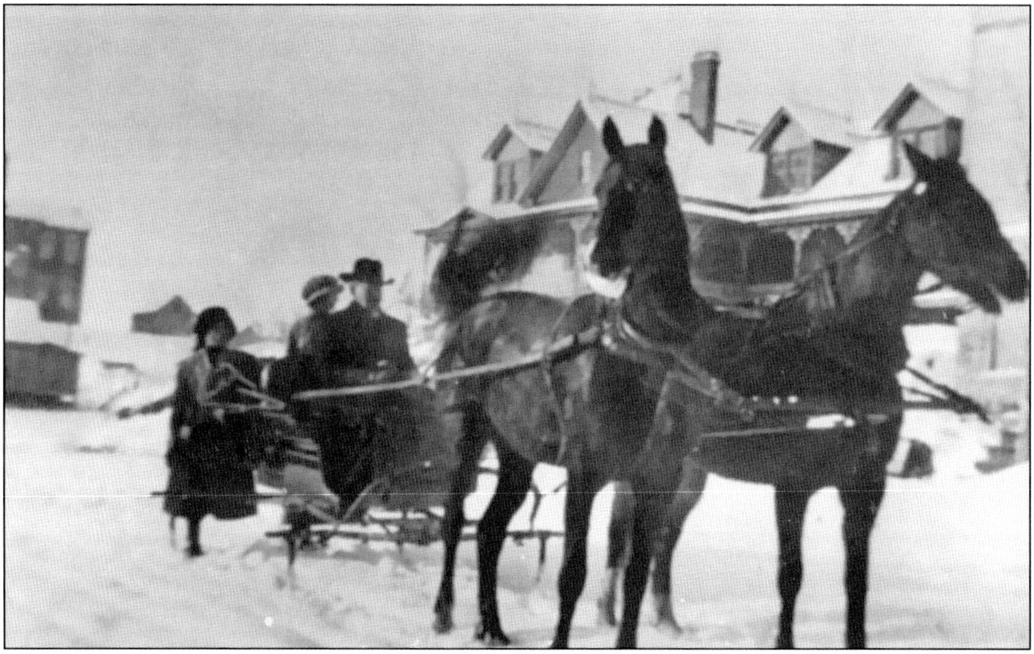

EARLY TRANSPORTATION. Prior to the introduction of the railroad and the automobile, horses provided the primary means of transportation in Wilkes County. Individuals rode astride their horses, while groups of people and cargo were transported with carriages and wagons. Because travel was slower, people outside of Wilkesboro and North Wilkesboro would often camp overnight. There were campsites along the old Boone Trail for travelers taking their wares to Ashe and Watauga Counties. In the photograph above, a horse-drawn sleigh carries a fashionable family through North Wilkesboro. In the photograph below, a woman is pictured fording the Reddies River. (Both courtesy of Wilkes Community College Library.)

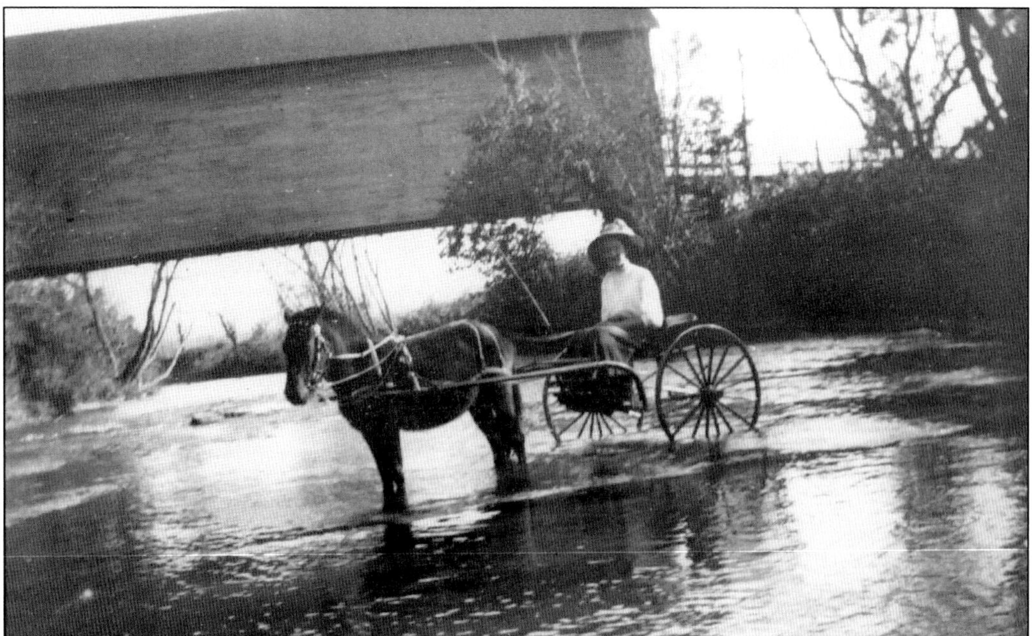

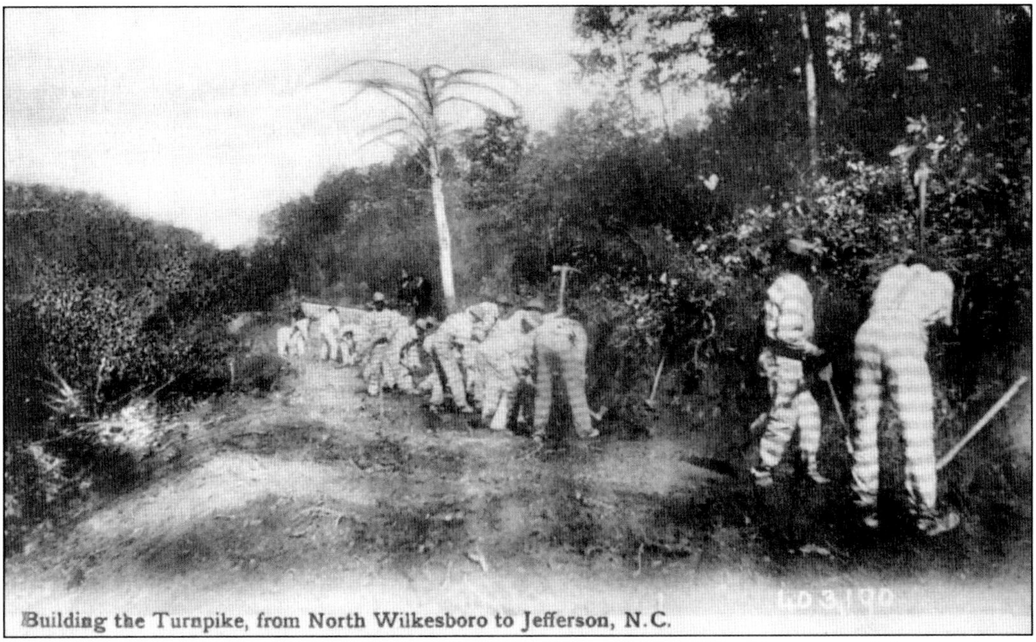

BUILDING THE TURNPIKE. The Jefferson Turnpike followed the Reddies River parallel to the Giant Lumber Company flume. It was created with convict labor arranged and paid for by the State of North Carolina. Ashe and Wilkes Counties agreed to provide guards, food, and shelter for the laborers. A flood in 1916 destroyed the turnpike. (Courtesy of Wilkes County Public Library.)

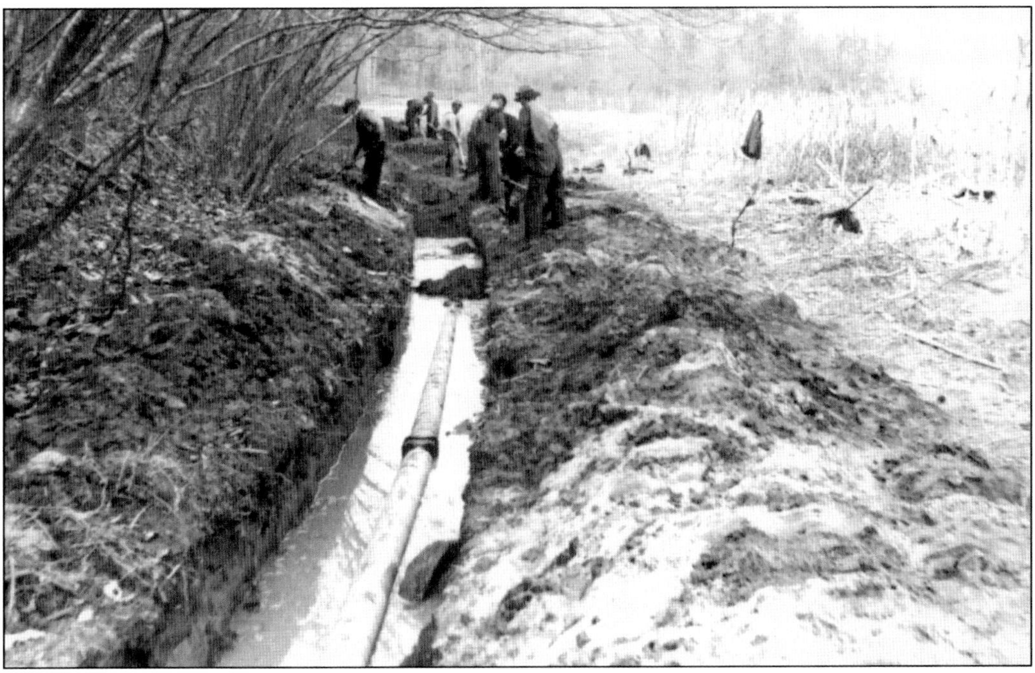

NEW WATER LINES IN WILKESBORO. One of the many activities completed by the Works Progress Administration in an effort to improve public health during the 1930s was the introduction of new water lines for improved service to the town of Wilkesboro. (Courtesy of North Carolina State Archives.)

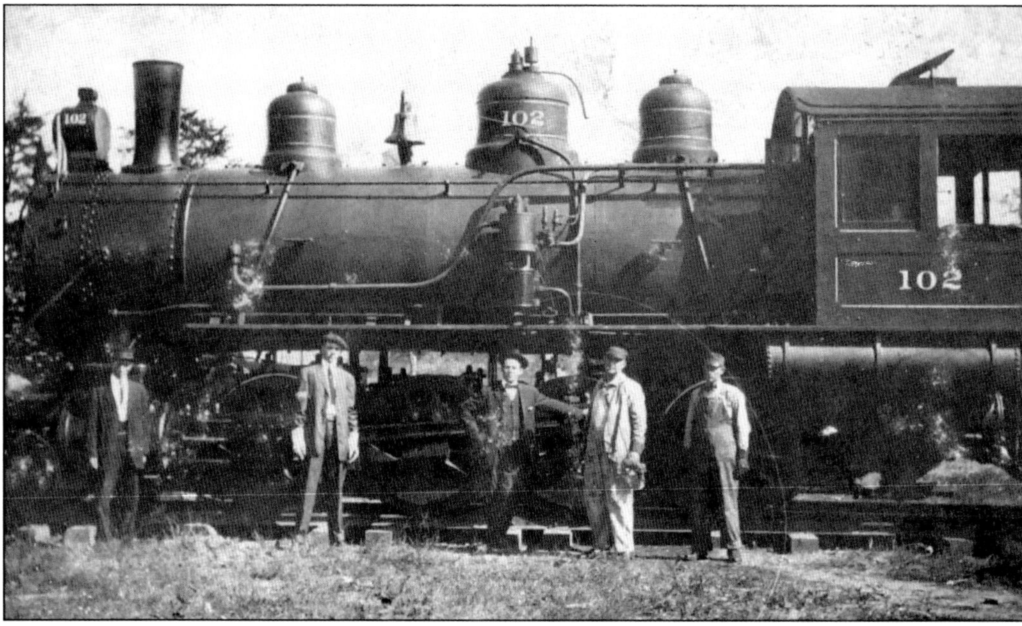

EARLY TRAINS. The town of North Wilkesboro was established to meet the train that connected Winston-Salem to Wilkes County. Originally, the line was meant to run to Wilkesboro, though this plan was not realized because the railroad company elected not to build across a flood-prone portion of the Yadkin River. The coming of the railroad changed the tone of the county, connected people to markets, and opened lines of travel and commerce as never before. Pictured above is a train car that served the town of Grandin in the western part of the county. Pictured below are individuals posing in front of a freight train during the early 1900s. (Above, courtesy of Wilkes Community College Library; below, courtesy of Mac Atwood.)

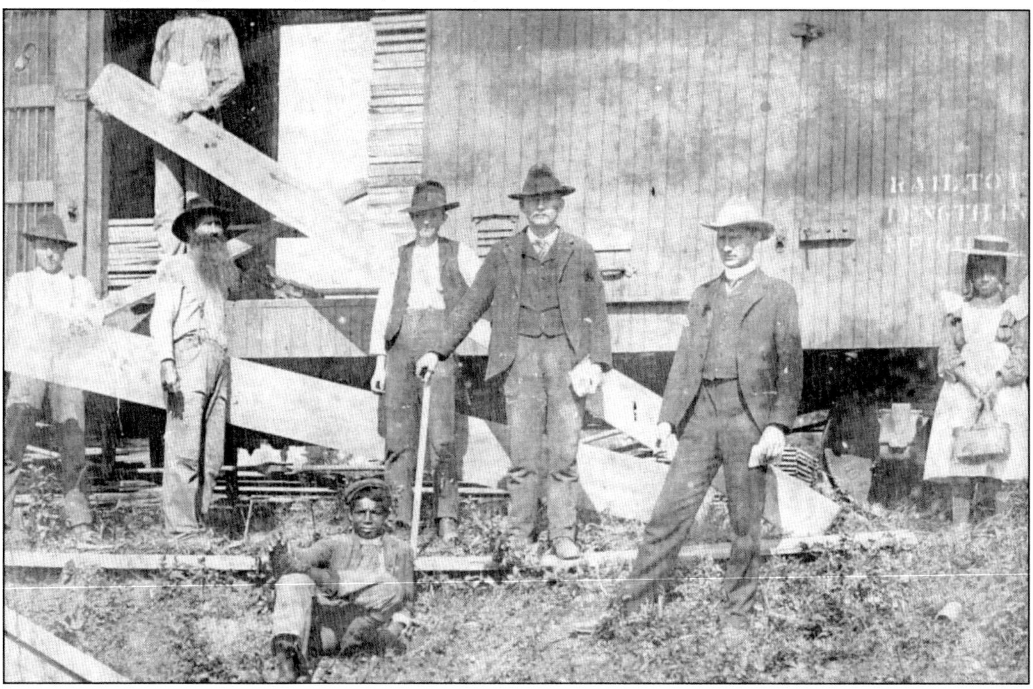

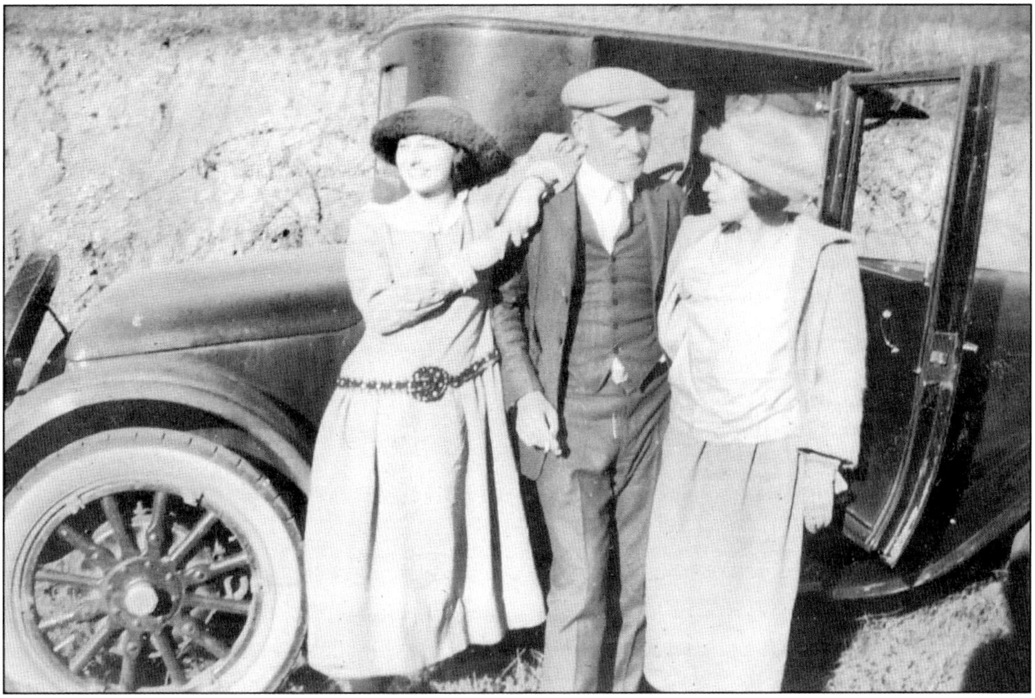

EARLY CARS. Early Ford Model Ts were shipped unassembled to North Wilkesboro via railroad cars. Assembled locally, the cars sold for $350 to $750 in 1915. In 1909, state law required motor vehicle operators to slow down to eight miles per hour when approaching a horse or draft animal in the road. As they rose in popularity, vehicles afforded a new level of freedom for those who could afford them. Pictured above are, from left to right, Roxie ?, Russell ?, and Loy Evans standing in front of an early automobile. Shown below is Wrenn Minton of the Mount Pleasant community, posing in front of his father's Model T, the first in that section of the county. (Above, courtesy of Wilkes Heritage Museum; below, courtesy of Eloise Church.)

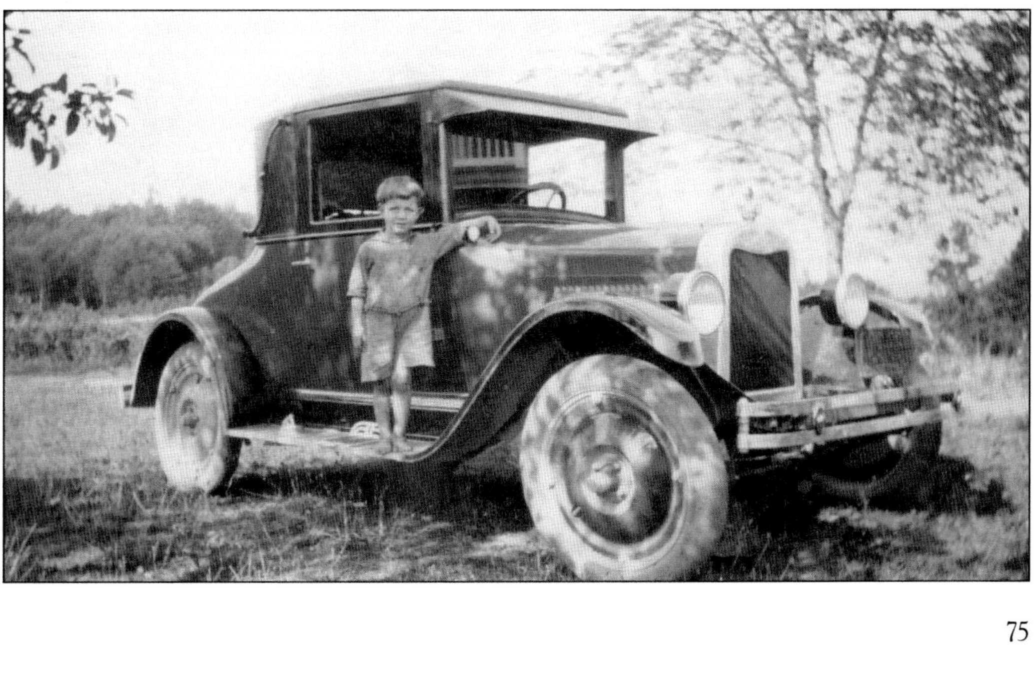

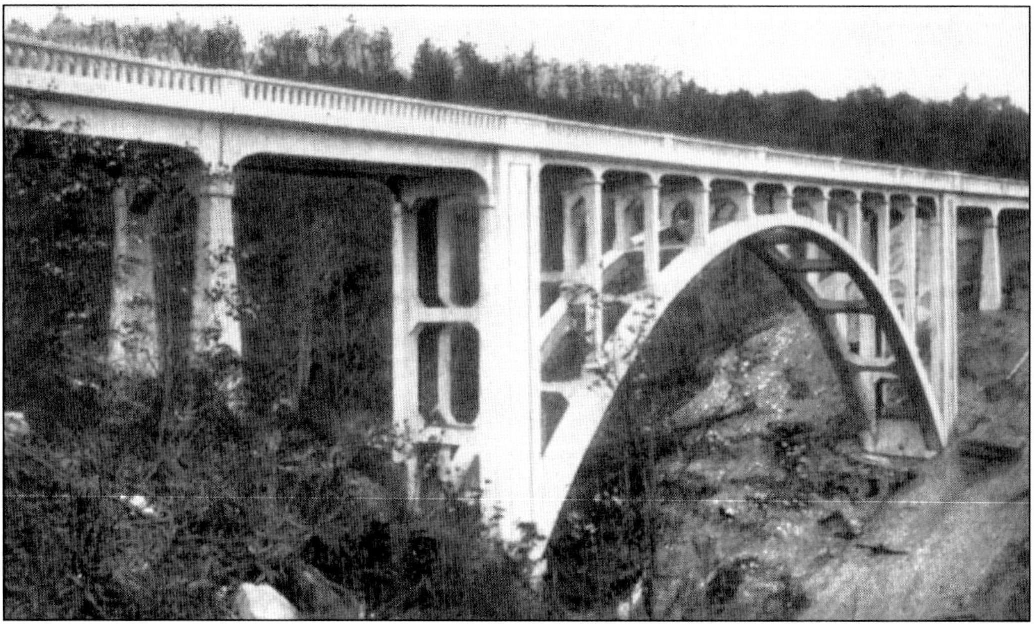

WADE HARRIS BRIDGE. Construction of the Wade Harris Bridge was completed in 1930. It was reportedly the tallest bridge in the state with a span of 110 feet above the Lewis Fork Creek gorge. It was named for Wade Harris, a railroad executive and editor of the *Charlotte Observer* from 1892 to 1935. (Courtesy of North Carolina Collection, University of North Carolina Library at Chapel Hill.)

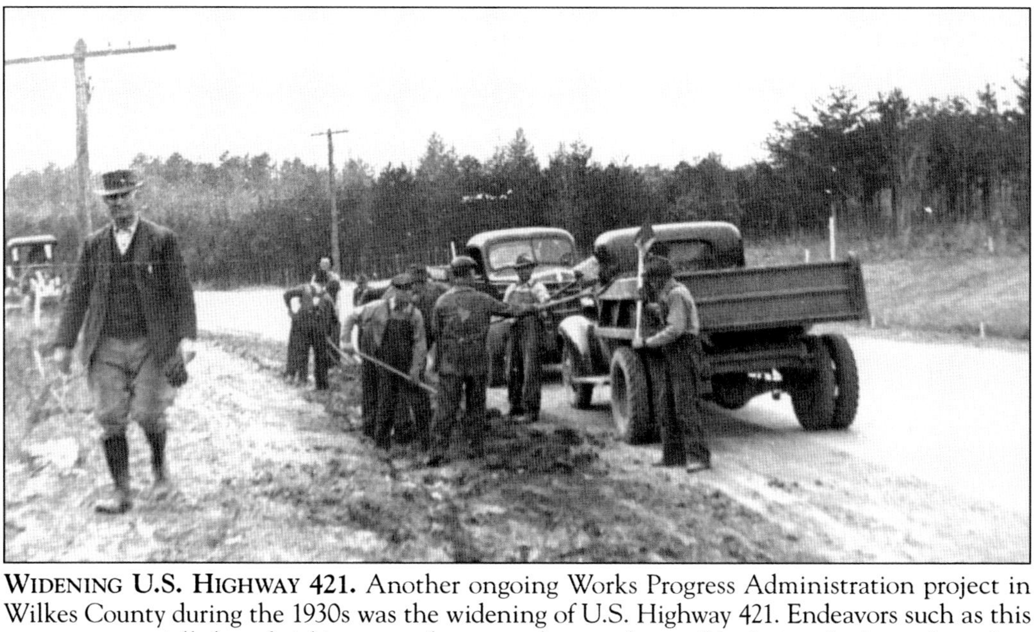

WIDENING U.S. HIGHWAY 421. Another ongoing Works Progress Administration project in Wilkes County during the 1930s was the widening of U.S. Highway 421. Endeavors such as this one were especially beneficial in areas where travel was only possible during the best of weather. (Courtesy of the North Carolina State Archives.)

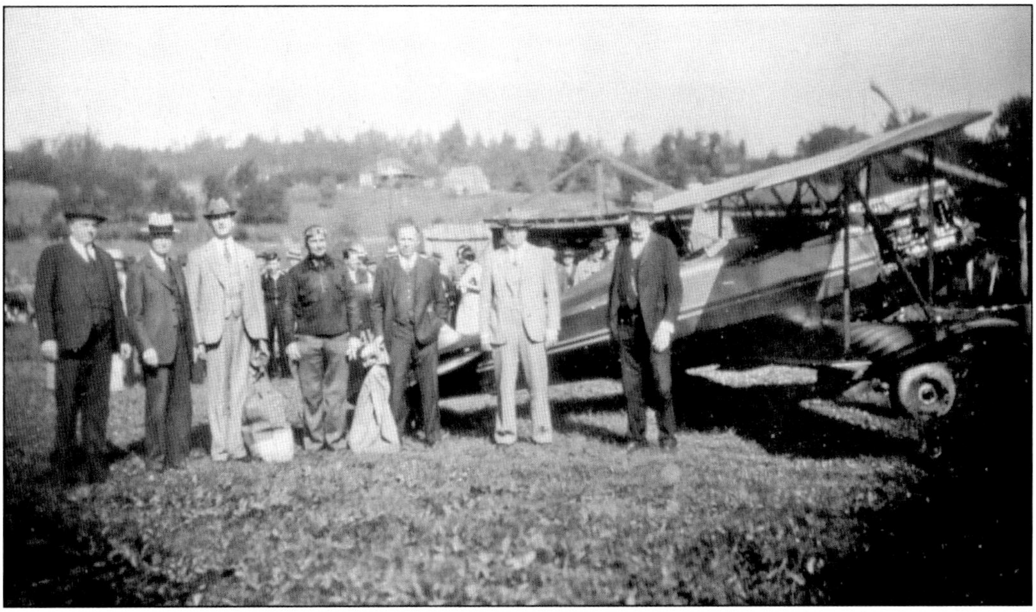

EARLY AVIATION. Early grass airstrips in Wilkes County facilitated trips aboard private aircraft for leisure and recreation. Light for evening landings was provided by flares and automobile headlights. As commercial air traffic increased with the acquisition of planes by local companies, including Lowe's and Holly Farms, the need for an airport became apparent, and the facility on Highway 268 west of Wilkesboro was built. Pictured above c. 1920 are, from left to right, J. B. Williams, J. R. Finley, J. C. Reins, Johnny Crowell, F. W. Graham, R. T. McNeill, and A. A. Finley commemorating airmail week. Wood Wallace, pictured below, earned $1 per person for Sunday afternoon flights in an OX-5. He was also a flight instructor who was credited with having taught 300 students, some of whom became bomber pilots in World War II. (Both courtesy of Wilkes Heritage Museum.)

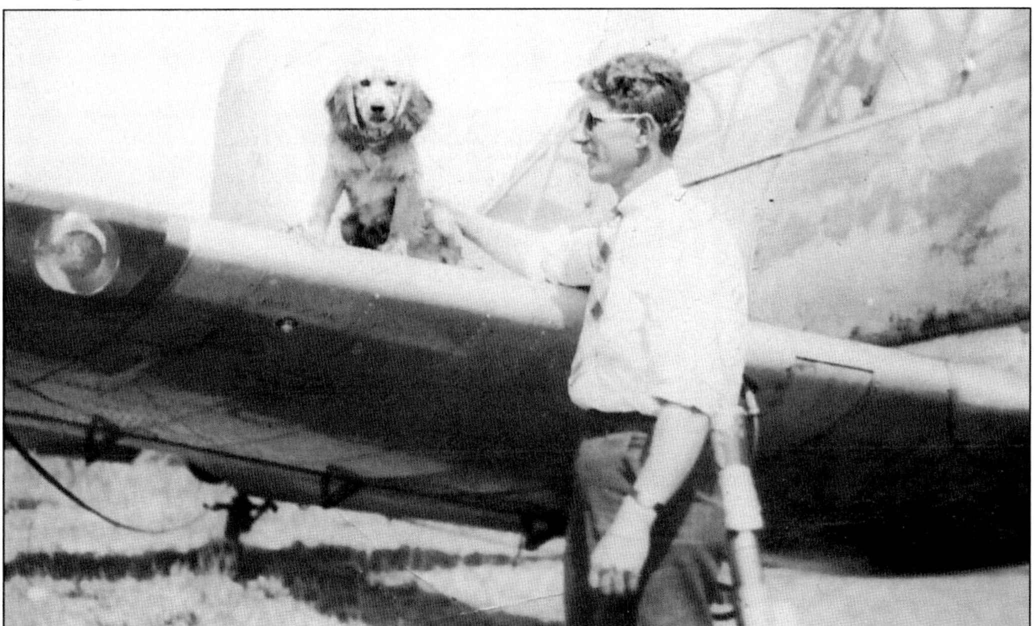

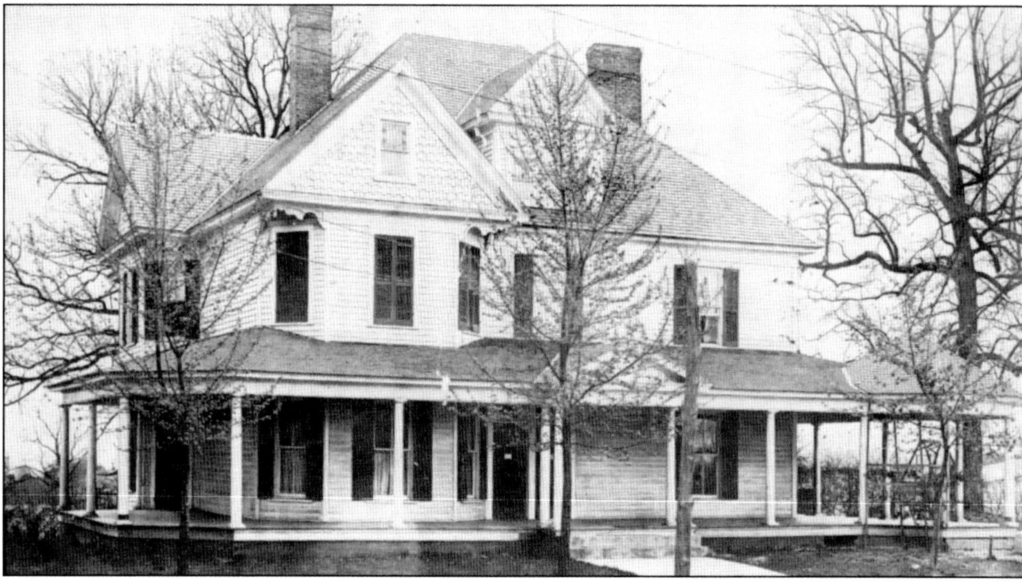

Early Hospitals. The first hospital in Wilkes County was started in 1923 by Dr. Fred C. Hubbard on Eighth Street in North Wilkesboro. Prior to this, Hubbard assisted Dr. J. W. White as White performed surgeries on patients on their kitchen tables and under the shade trees in their yards. In 1952, Wilkes General Hospital was built on land Hubbard contributed. Hubbard served in the U.S. Army Medical Corps during World War II, practiced medicine as a surgeon for nearly 70 years, wrote a history of medicine in Wilkes County, and served as surgeon emeritus at Wilkes General Hospital until his death in 1986. Wilkes Regional Hospital opened at its present location in 1952. (Both courtesy of Wilkes Heritage Museum.)

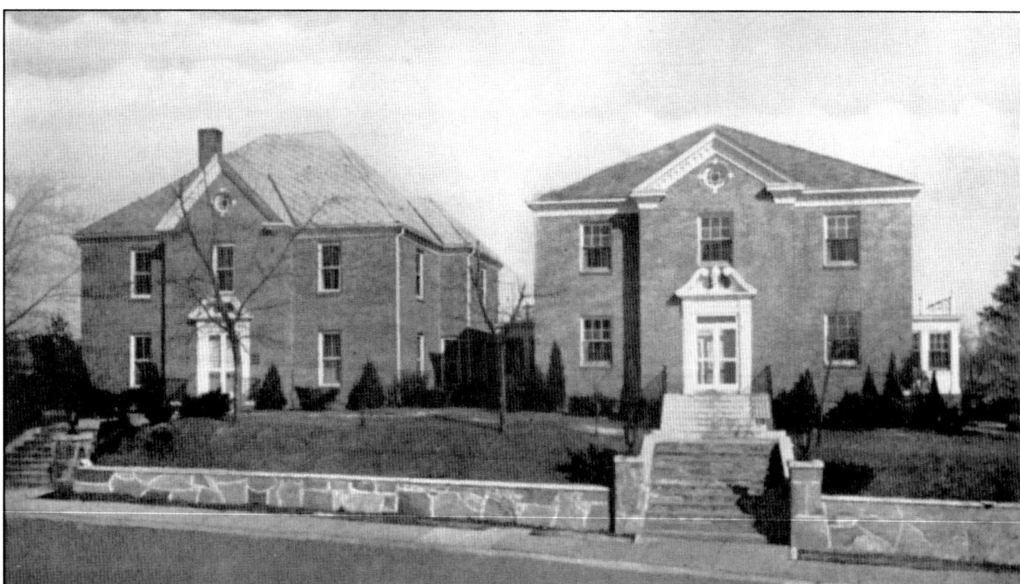

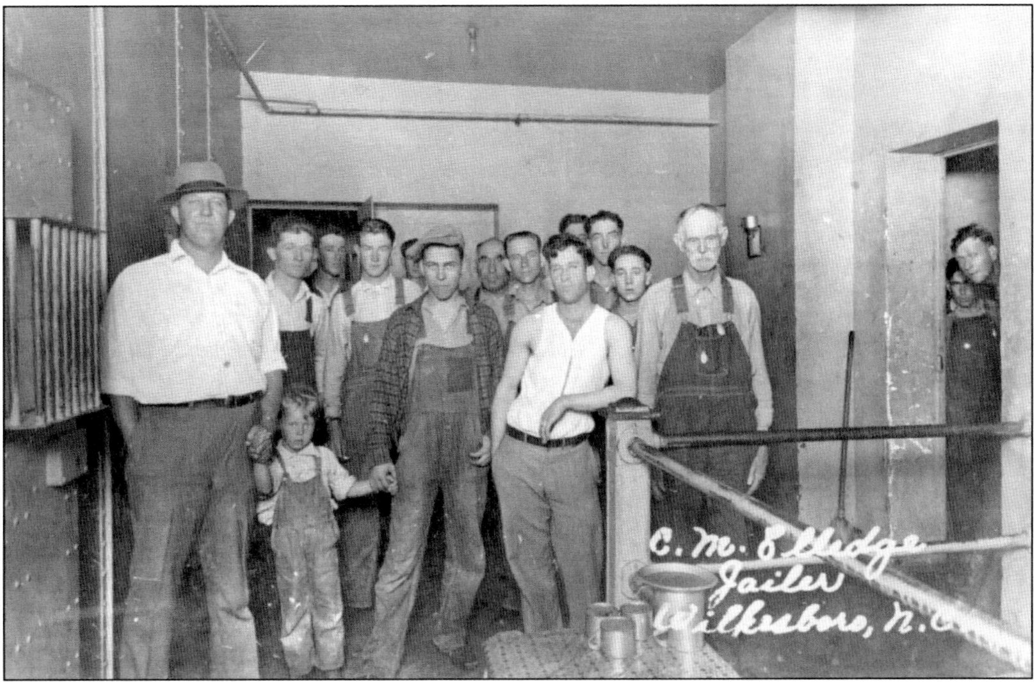

WILKES COUNTY JAIL. The men in this *c.* 1930 photograph are being detained for making moonshine. Josh Pruitt stands on the back row, just right of the man in front wearing the hat. Burley Bauguess stands second from the left, behind the little boy. The jailer at the time was C. M. Elledge. (Courtesy of Jason Duncan.)

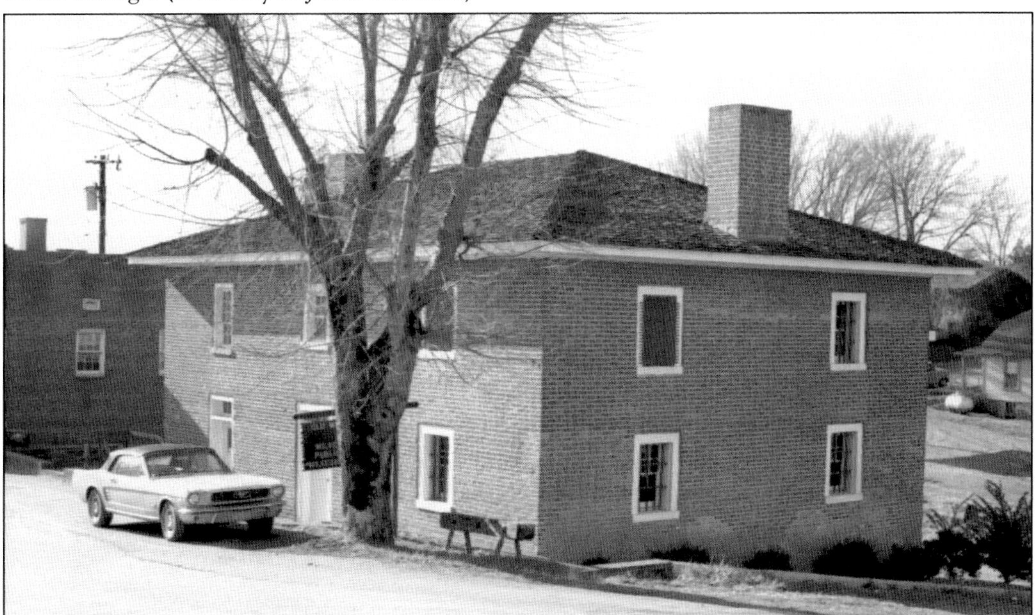

OLD WILKES COUNTY JAIL. Completed in 1860, this jail housed Confederate provisions along with Union prisoners. Tom Dula was incarcerated here before standing trial for murder, as was outlaw Otto Wood. The building served as a jail until 1915, when a new jail was built. The old jail is now operated as a museum by Old Wilkes, Inc. (Courtesy of North Carolina State Archives.)

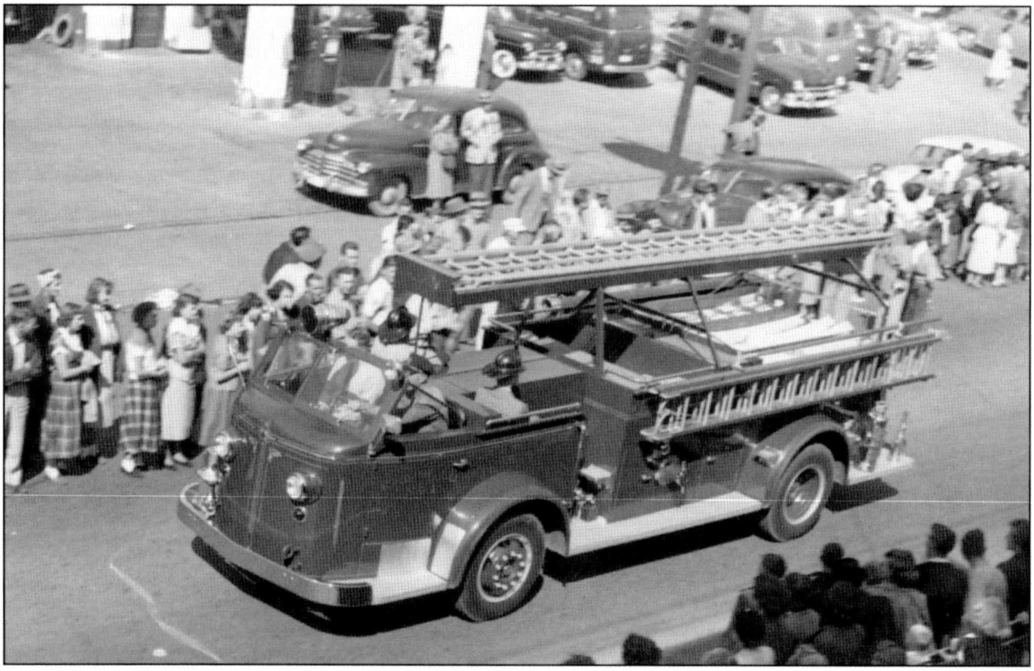

NORTH WILKESBORO FIRE DEPARTMENT. The fire department was established in 1910 with 20 charter members. The first equipment consisted of a reel mounted on two wagon wheels with a 500-foot hose. It was pulled manually to the scene of the fire. This truck, a 1951 American La France, was sold in the spring of 2005 for $3,500. (Courtesy of Wilkes Community College Library.)

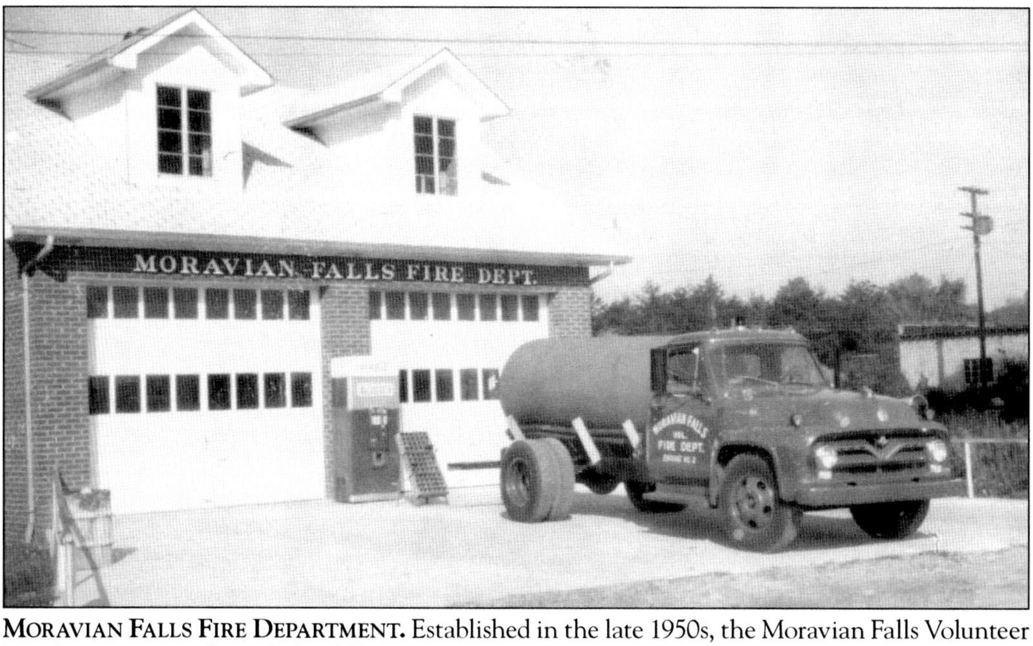

MORAVIAN FALLS FIRE DEPARTMENT. Established in the late 1950s, the Moravian Falls Volunteer Fire Department elected the following officers: L. G. Critcher, president; Joel Bentley, vice president; Lacy Ferguson, treasurer; Ruth Hubbard, secretary; and Hal Hawkins, chairman of the finance committee. They purchased a GMC truck with American La France firefighting equipment. (Courtesy of Wilkes Community College Library.)

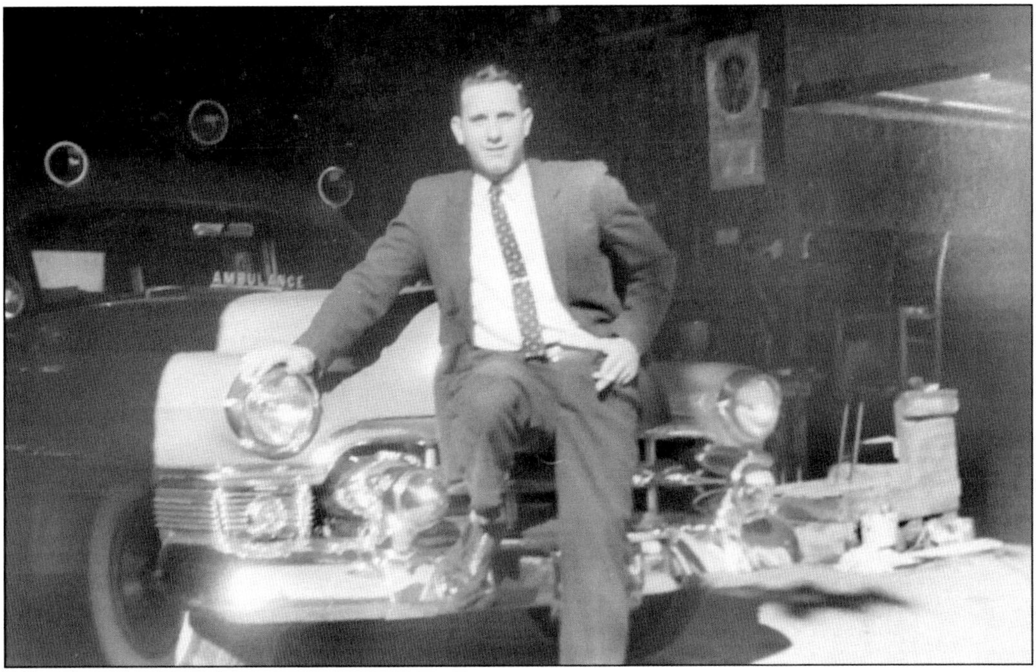

1953 AMBULANCE. Prior to the creation of organized emergency medical service (EMS) teams, funeral homes operated ambulance services. Many of the vehicles owned by Reins-Sturdivant (established in 1933) served as both ambulance and hearse. This 1953 Cadillac ambulance that served Wilkes County was equipped with three 2-barrel carburetors on a V8 engine. James Richardson, the driver, stands in front of the vehicle. (Courtesy of James Richardson.)

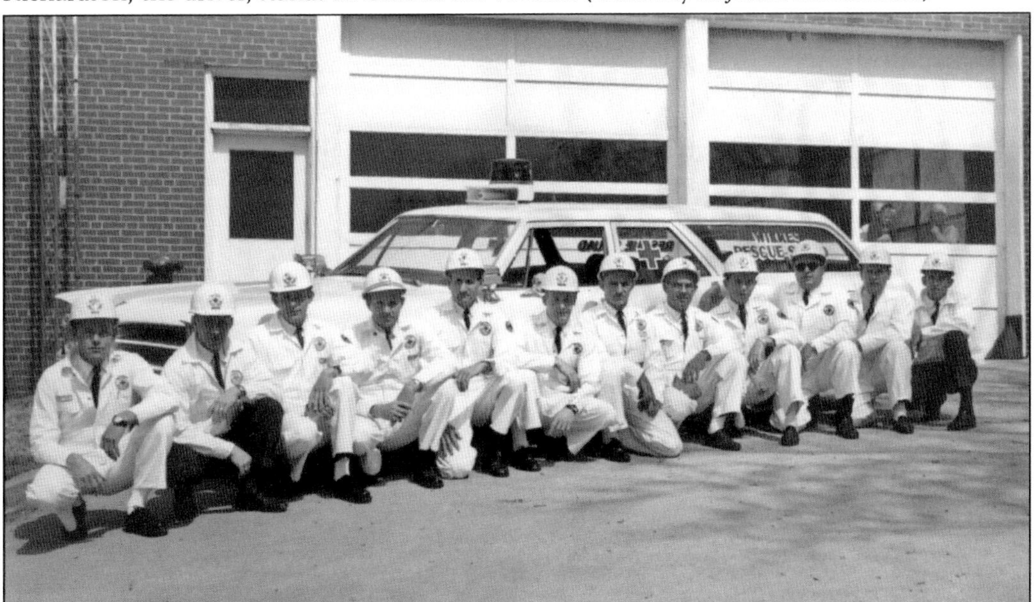

WILKES COUNTY RESCUE SQUAD. The Wilkes County Rescue Squad was organized in 1955 to provide EMS, extrications, and mountain searches. Wilkes County EMS was established in 1971. Both organizations provide advanced life support to the citizens of Wilkes County. (Courtesy of Wilkes Community College Library.)

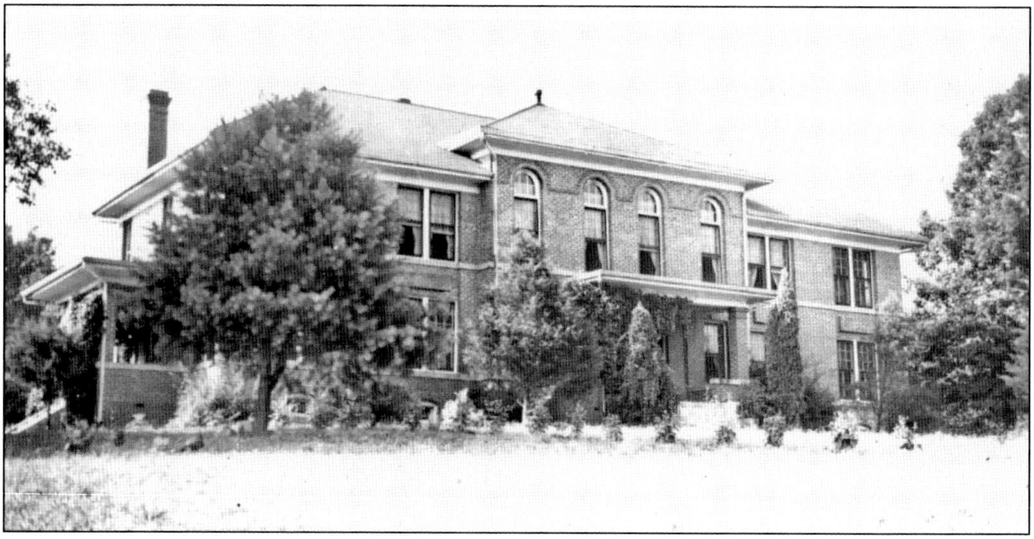

COUNTY HOME. Constructed in 1915, the County Home compound consisted of several other buildings, including a colored ward and a tuberculosis hut. The county sold 250 acres of farmland in parcels to industries including Coca-Cola Bottling and Carolina Mirror following the 1940 flood. The home closed in 1952. (Courtesy of Wilkes Community College Library.)

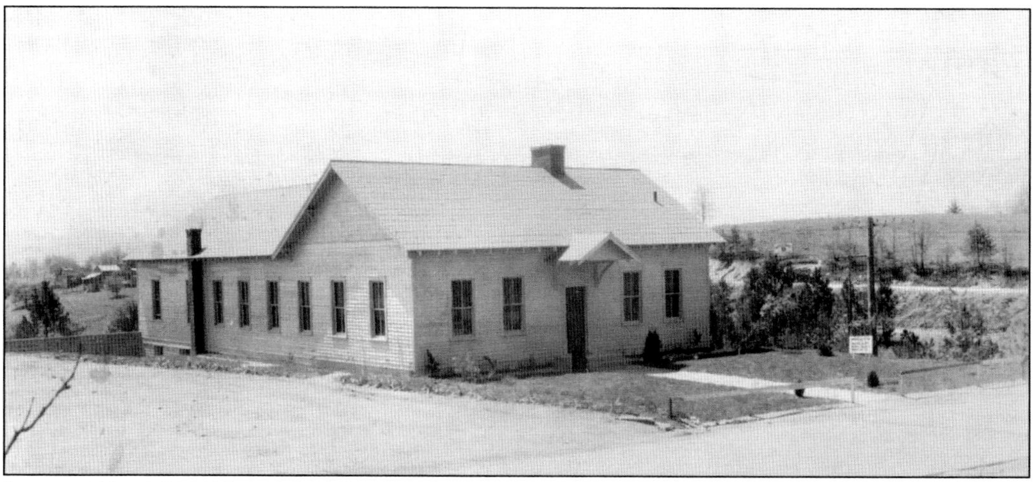

LEGION HUT. Post No. 125 of the American Legion was organized in the fall of 1921 with 19 charter members. It was located on Finley Avenue. North Wilkesboro High School dances were often held at the Legion Hut, as were bingo games, square dances, and other social events. (Courtesy of Wilkes Heritage Museum.)

Six

Bartering and Trading

Wilkes County's amenities combined to make the county a center of business and industry for northwest North Carolina. The first industries developed to take advantage of the lush forests that covered the county. Manufacturers produced portable sawmills to outfit lumber companies, tanneries sprung up in Stanton and North Wilkesboro, and furniture manufacturing became a major industry. The forests also provided furs and herbs to dealers. All these industries benefited from the coming of the railroad, and other industries followed. Wilkes County has boasted mirror manufacturing plants, a coffin factory, a pottery, ham and poultry processing plants, machine shops, cotton mills, hosiery mills, and glove manufacturers.

Merchants have also thrived in Wilkes County, from one-room general stores to nationwide home-improvement empires. By 1850, Wilkes County merchants Waugh and Finley had established a chain of general merchandise stores, and by 1953, N. B. Smithey oversaw 17 regional stores. Brame Drug not only provided medicines and milk shakes to locals but also produced its own patent medicines that were distributed nationwide. Outside the Wilkesboros, most communities had their own small mercantile, many of which served as store, post office, and public library.

As business and industry flourished in Wilkes County, so did banking and commerce. The first bank was established in 1891, with others following in 1903 and 1923. Banking has remained an important industry in the county. The first bank continued operations through several consolidations with larger institutions. Lowe's Companies and Tyson Foods, two Fortune 500 companies, maintain operations here. Wilkes County remains a center of business and industry for northwest North Carolina. The people still provide an abundant workforce, the county's location still links the mountains to the piedmont, and the county is still a beautiful place to work.

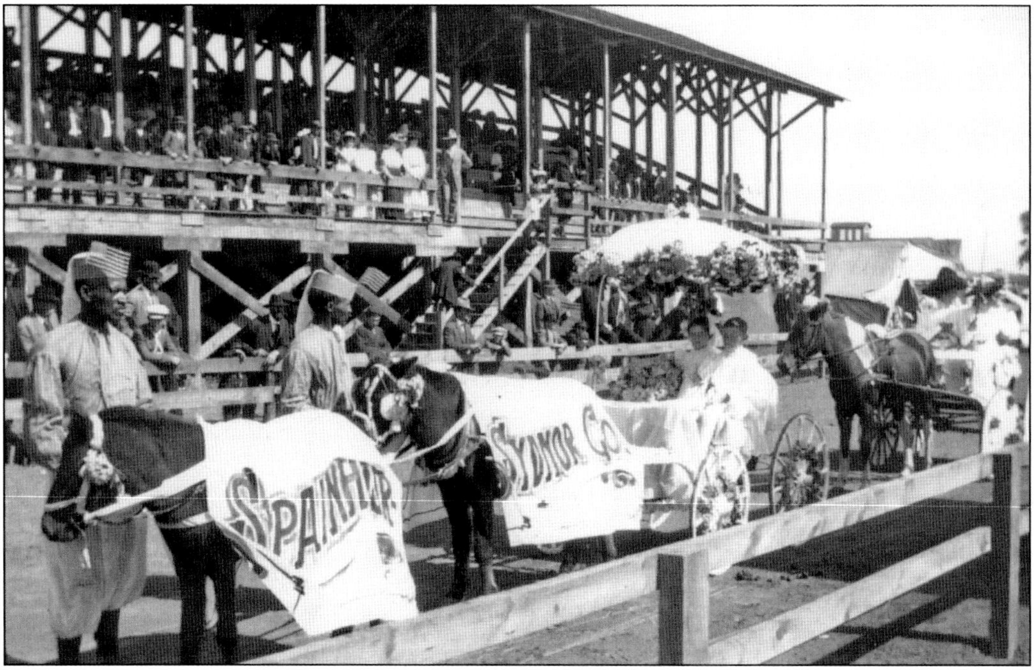

SPAINHOUR-SYDNOR COMPANY. The Spainhour-Sydnor Dry Goods Company was chartered in 1906 by R. A. Spainhour, F. G. Holman, J. E. Spainhour, and W. A. Sydnor. The company operated stores in Wilkes, Lenoir, Elkin, Hickory, Statesville, and Winston-Salem. In the early 1920s, they carried textbooks used at North Wilkesboro Elementary School. (Courtesy of Wilkes Community College Library.)

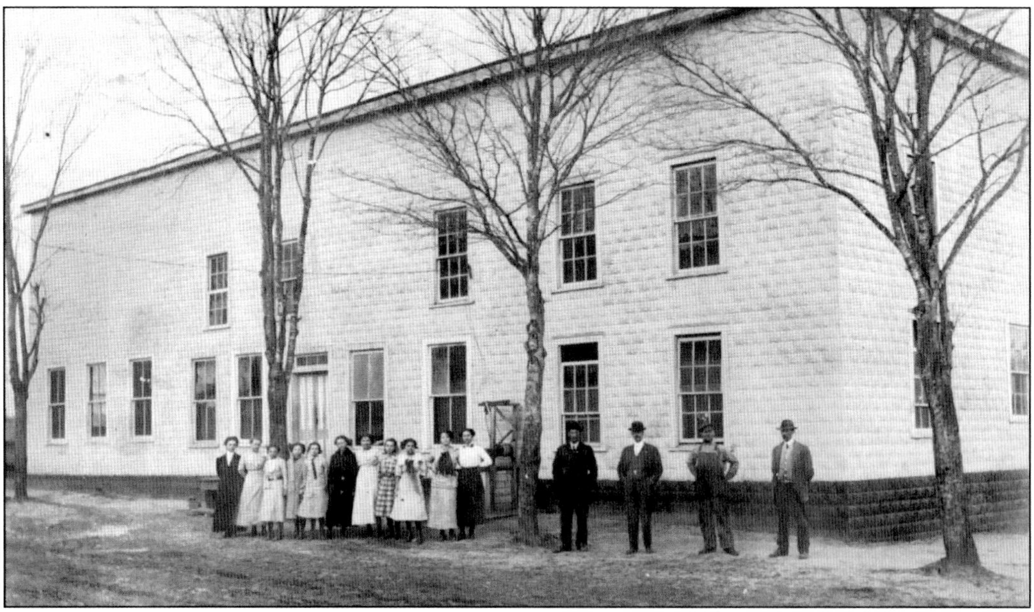

THE YELLOW JACKET. Founded by R. Don Laws in 1895, *The Yellow Jacket* aimed to "swat all liars and leeches, hypocrites and humbugs, demagogs and dastards." Sharp barbs, pointed humor, and political jabs captivated 250,000 subscribers until fire destroyed the factory in 1943. (Courtesy of Wilkes Community College Library.)

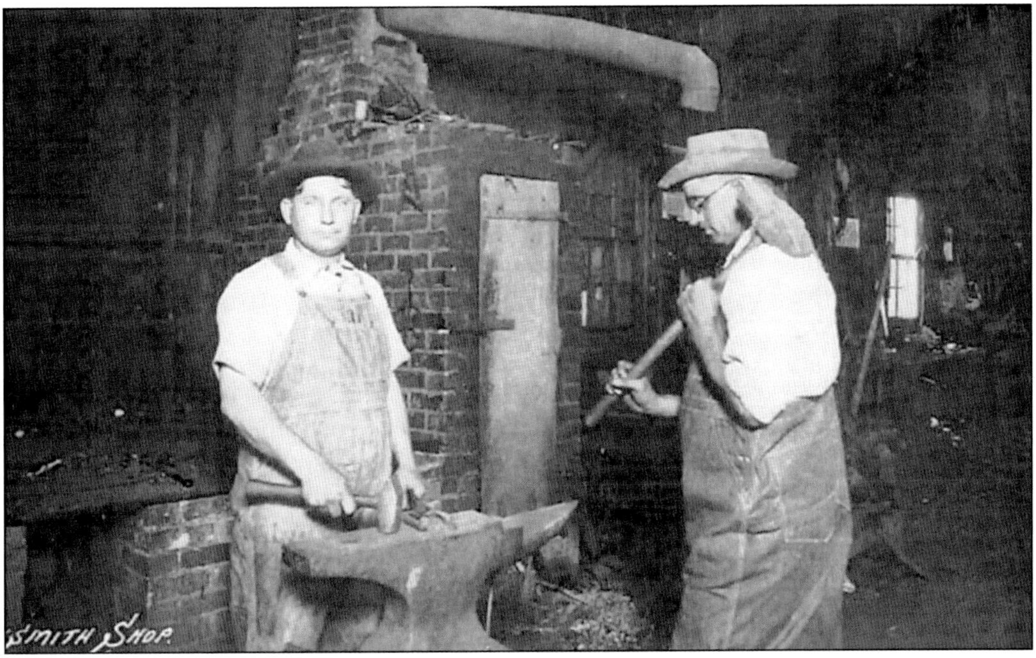

Early Blacksmiths. Blacksmiths forged horse and mule shoes and made almost all the iron hardware needed for new buildings, including hinges, handles, and nails. They also made andirons, pothooks, and locks and sharpened tools. By 1820, there were at least three blacksmiths practicing their trade in Wilkes County. (Courtesy of Wilkes Heritage Museum.)

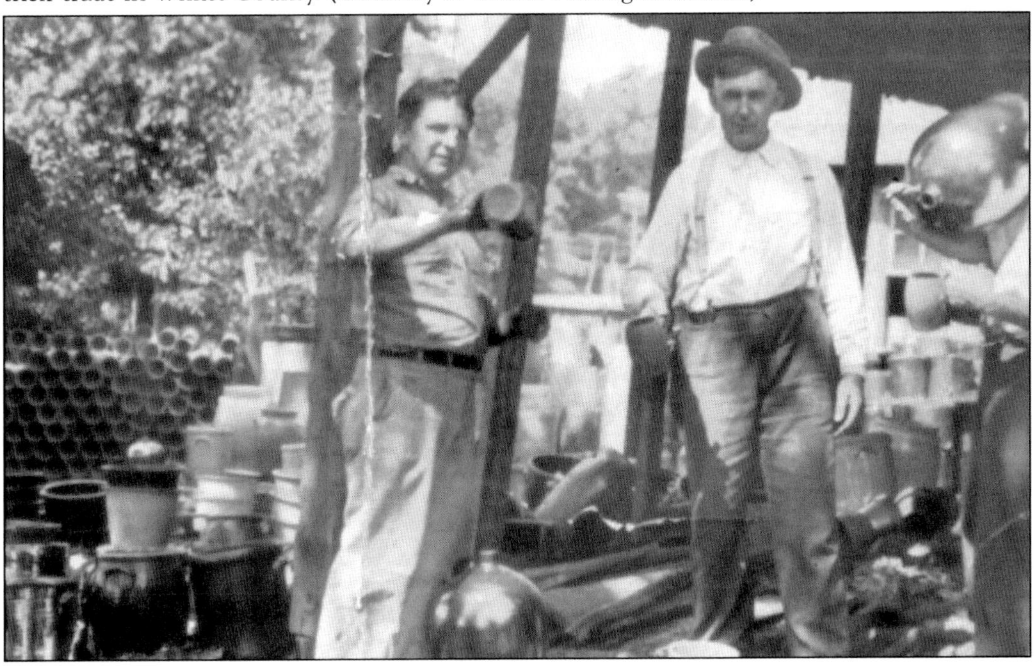

Kennedy Pottery. B. J. and Dave Kennedy started Kennedy Pottery in 1896 in Wilkesboro, in part because of the abundance of clay in Wilkes County. They made stoneware, pitchers, jugs, and flowerpots. The pottery closed in 1968. Tyson Foods now stands on the former site of Kennedy Pottery. (Courtesy of Wilkes Heritage Museum.)

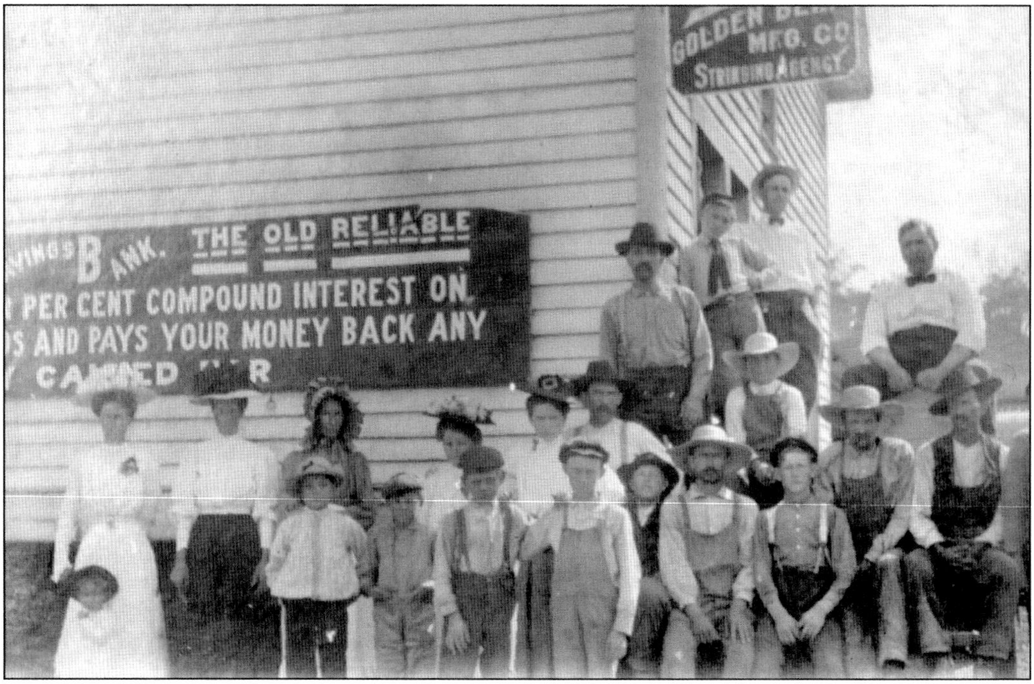

TOBACCO STRINGING, C. 1930. Tobacco stringing (sewing drawstrings into cotton tobacco bags) was a common way of earning money in North Carolina and Virginia in the late 19th and early 20th centuries. Golden Belt Manufacturing Company was based in Durham, but more than 75 households in Wilkes County received income from them through a local bag agent. For many families this was their only source of income. Mrs. Samuel Stayley of the Reddies River community, pictured below (left), was 83 years old when this picture was taken and had five children living at home. The family earned about $5 a month stringing tobacco bags. (Both courtesy of North Carolina Collection, University of North Carolina Library at Chapel Hill.)

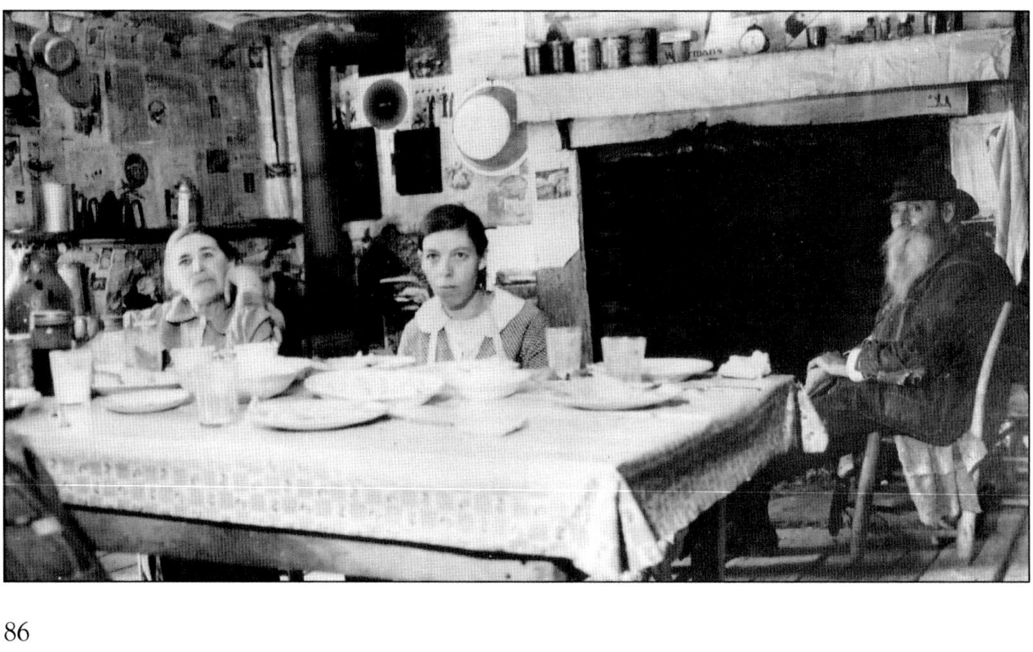

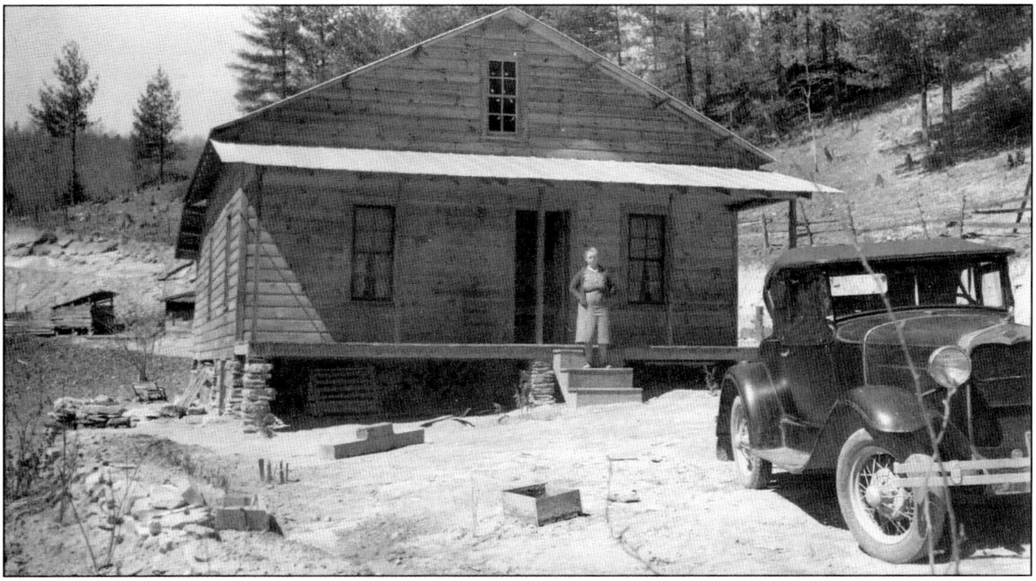

TOBACCO STRINGERS, 1939. Pictured above is Mrs. Dillard Taylor of the Reddies River community. When this photograph was taken, she lived with her husband and three of her five children. Her husband worked for a furniture factory for $11 a week while she earned $20 a month stringing bags. The car in the photograph belonged to her son. Pictured below is Mrs. Fidell Shepherd, also of the Reddies River community, and her three children. Her husband worked for the Public Works Administration earning $24 a month. She could string 500 tobacco bags a day. Both families owned their own homes and kept cows, pigs, and chickens. (Both courtesy of North Carolina Collection, University of North Carolina Library at Chapel Hill.)

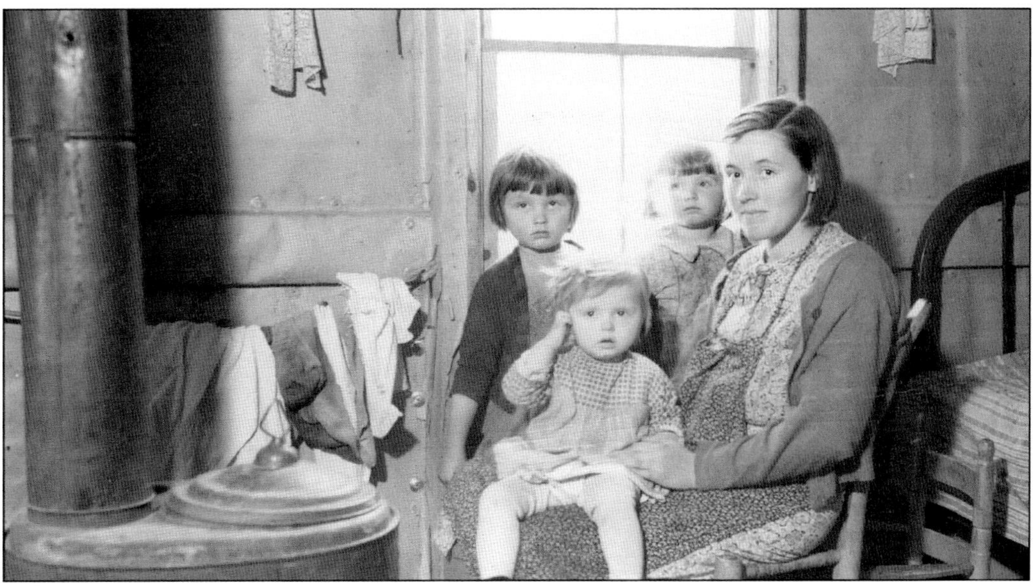

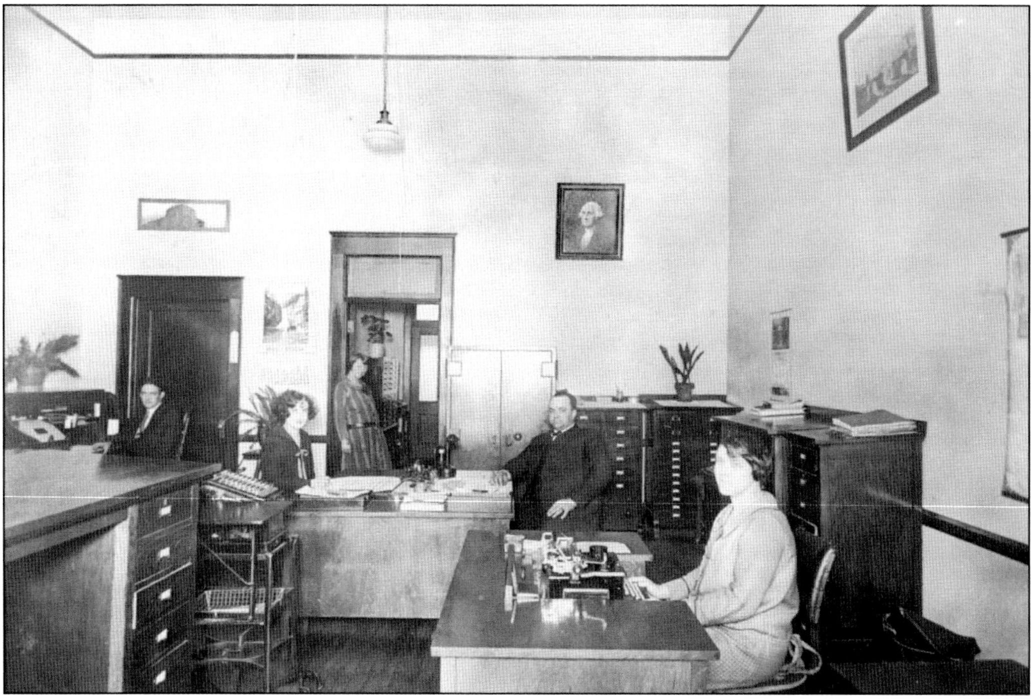

NORTH WILKESBORO BUILDING AND LOAN. The North Wilkesboro Building and Loan Association opened its doors in April 1903. For many years, it was the most active financial institution in home building in Wilkes County. The first officers were J. C. Smoot, president; Frank Hackett, attorney; and A. V. Foote, secretary/treasurer. Among those pictured are J. B. Williams (second from right) and Elizabeth Barber (second from left). (Courtesy of Wilkes Community College Library.)

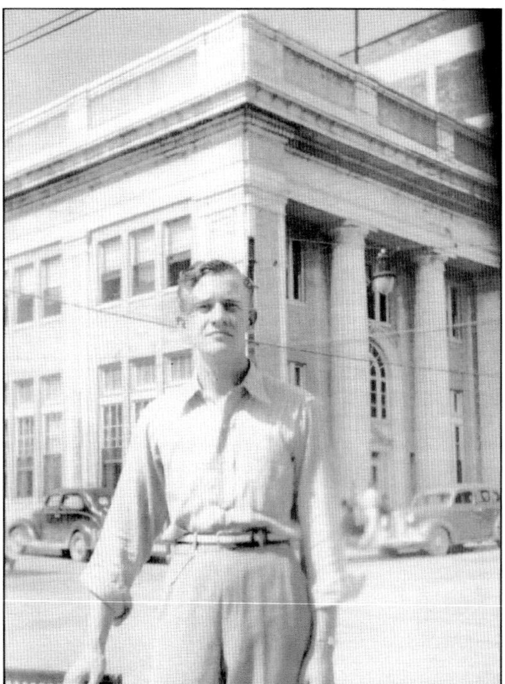

BANK OF NORTH WILKESBORO. This neoclassical revival brick-and-stone building was constructed in 1923. This was the second location for the bank; the first location stood on the opposite corner. The building has housed the offices of the Town of North Wilkesboro since 1999. Jay Brewer stands in front of the building. (Courtesy of North Wilkesboro High School Alumni Association.)

DEPOSIT AND SAVINGS BANK. The Deposit and Savings Bank was organized in 1903. This stone building was constructed on Main Street in North Wilkesboro in 1906. The first officers were W. F. Trogdon, president; W. W. Barber, vice president; H. O. Absher, cashier; and Ella Campbell, teller. The building later became the headquarters of the Northwestern Bank. (Courtesy of Wilkes Heritage Museum.)

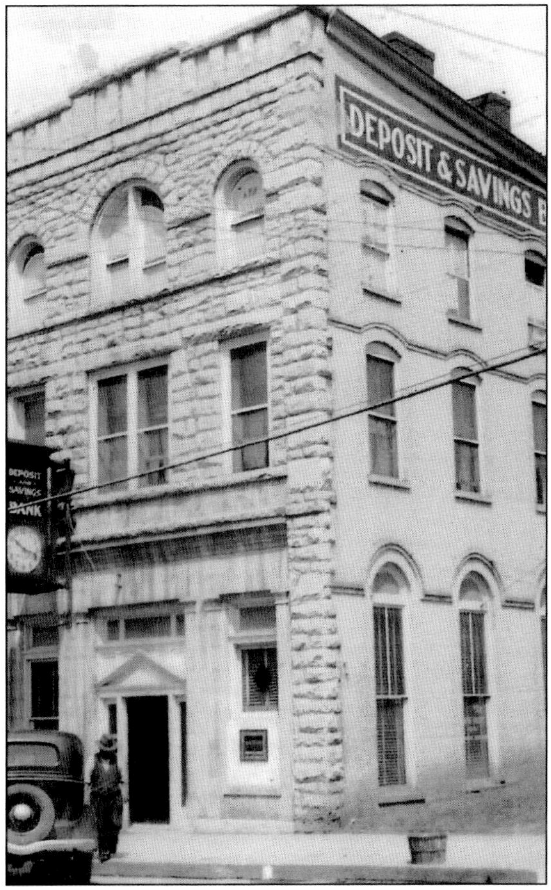

HOTEL WILKES. This five-story building was constructed in 1926 to replace the Hotel Gordon, which had served North Wilkesboro since 1904. The fireproof building cost $165,000 and contained 63 guest rooms. The hotel was sold in 1981 to Wilkes Towers and currently serves as a residential complex for senior citizens. (Courtesy of Wilkes County Public Library.)

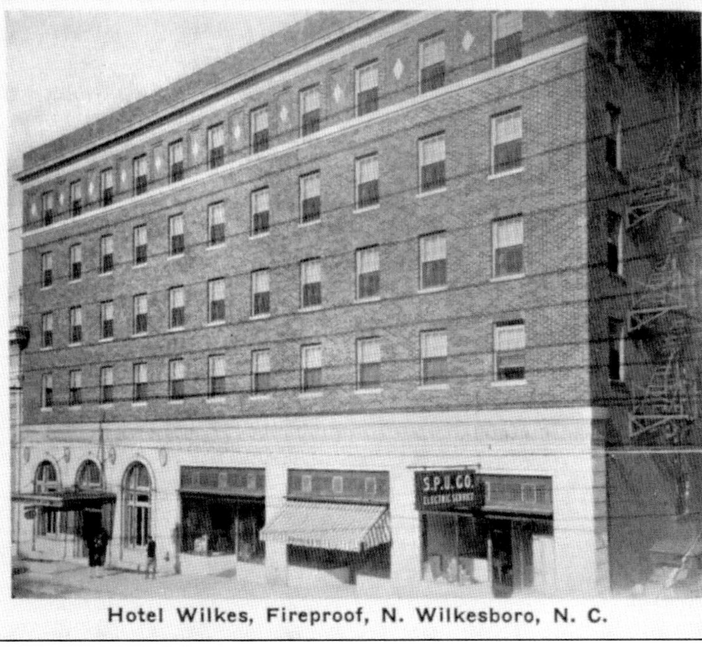

Hotel Wilkes, Fireproof, N. Wilkesboro, N. C.

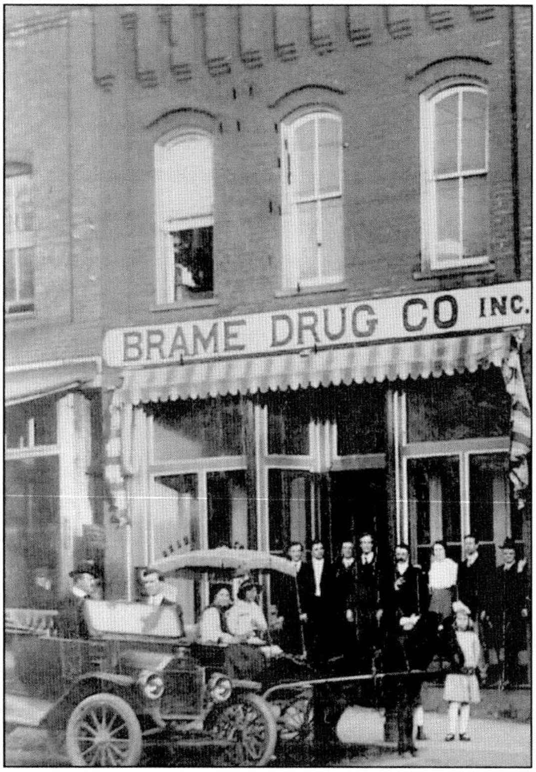

Brame Drug. Brame Drug was the first brick building in downtown North Wilkesboro, and it had a gas tank prior to 1918, believed to be the first of its kind in North Wilkesboro. The Brames made many popular remedies, including Brame's Pain Knocker, Dental Fluid, and Croup and Pneumonia Salve. (Courtesy of Wilkes Community College Library.)

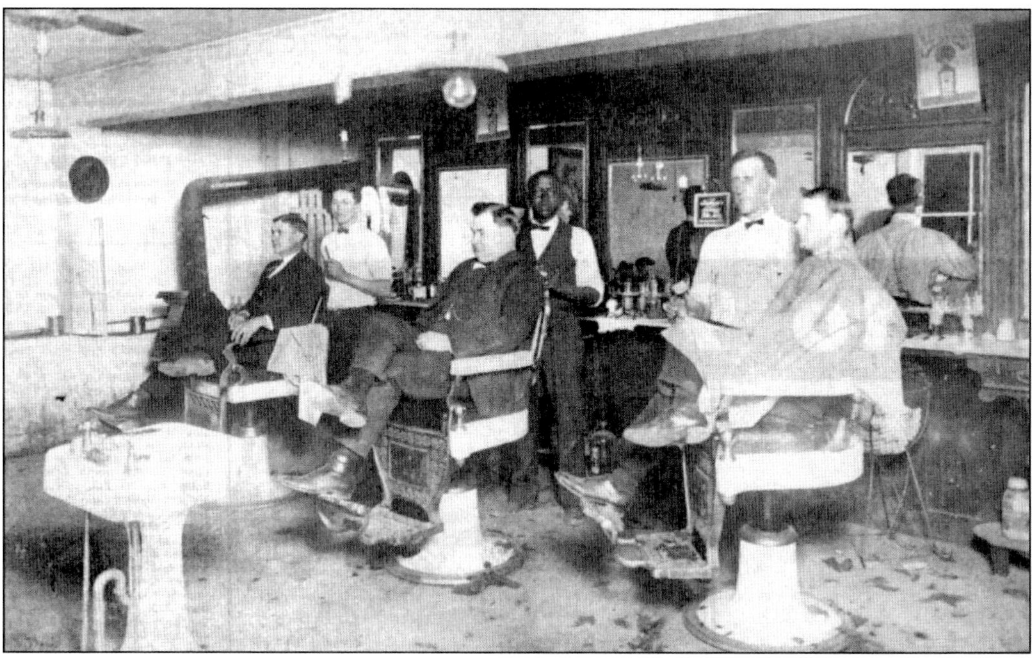

Huey Reid's Barbershop. The barbershop has always been a place for men to exchange news and talk politics. Pictured here in Huey Reid's barbershop on Tenth Street in North Wilkesboro are, from left to right, (seated) Richard Canter, Roscoe Vannoy, and Grady Canter; (standing) Huey Reid, Will Canter, and Tom Forester. (Courtesy of the *Wilkes Journal-Patriot.*)

CHURCH'S HARDWARE. The local hardware store has always been a central meeting place in small towns. A trip to the local hardware store was as much about men gathered around a woodstove discussing local politics as it was about buying screws by the piece and nails weighed out by the pound. Pictured in front of Church's Hardware are, from left to right, Carl Miller, Ernest Miller, and proprietor Edward Church. (Courtesy of Eloise Church.)

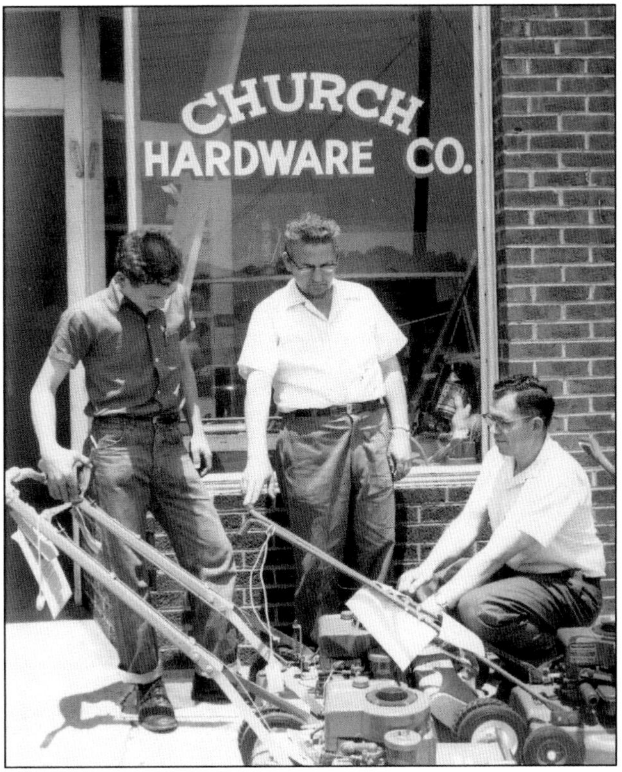

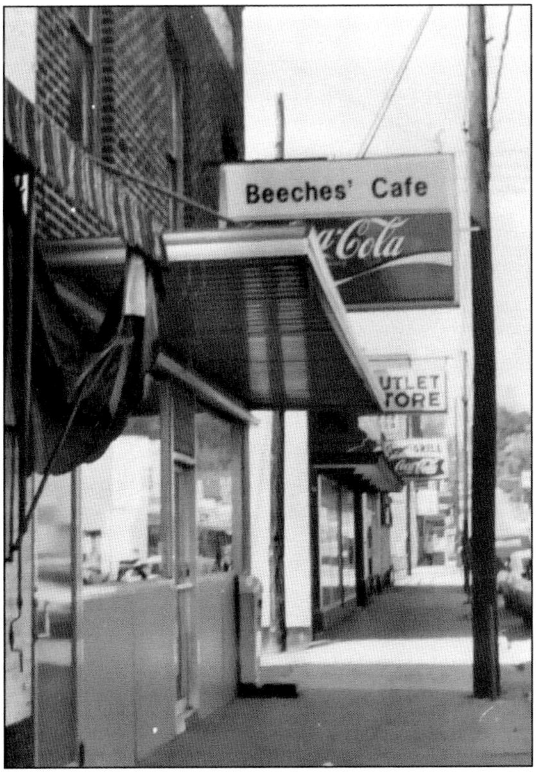

BEECHES', C. 1960. Beech Blankenship opened Beeches' Café in 1928. Turtle soup was one of the house specialties. Beech's son, Harold, carried on the family tradition, first in the original Beeches' location and later at Harold's restaurant on Highway 115. Dale's and Mary's later occupied the building on Tenth Street; in 2007, the Key City Grille opened in the former Beeches' location. (Courtesy of Gail Haynes.)

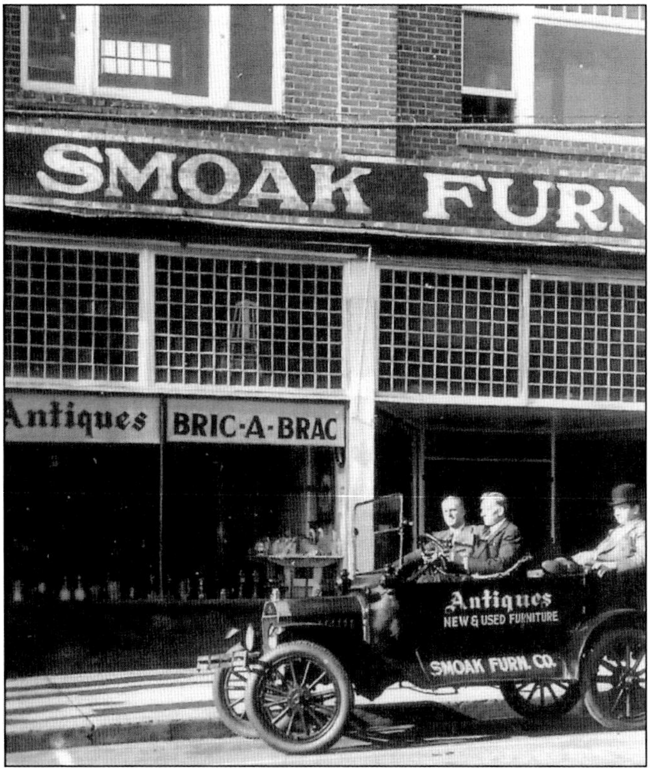

SMOAK BROTHERS. The Smoak brothers began selling furniture, appliances, and carpets, as well as buggies, in North Wilkesboro in 1903. One of their most popular items was called the "Range Eternal" and was billed as "the most economical and perfect range ever presented in the United States." (Courtesy of Wilkes Heritage Museum.)

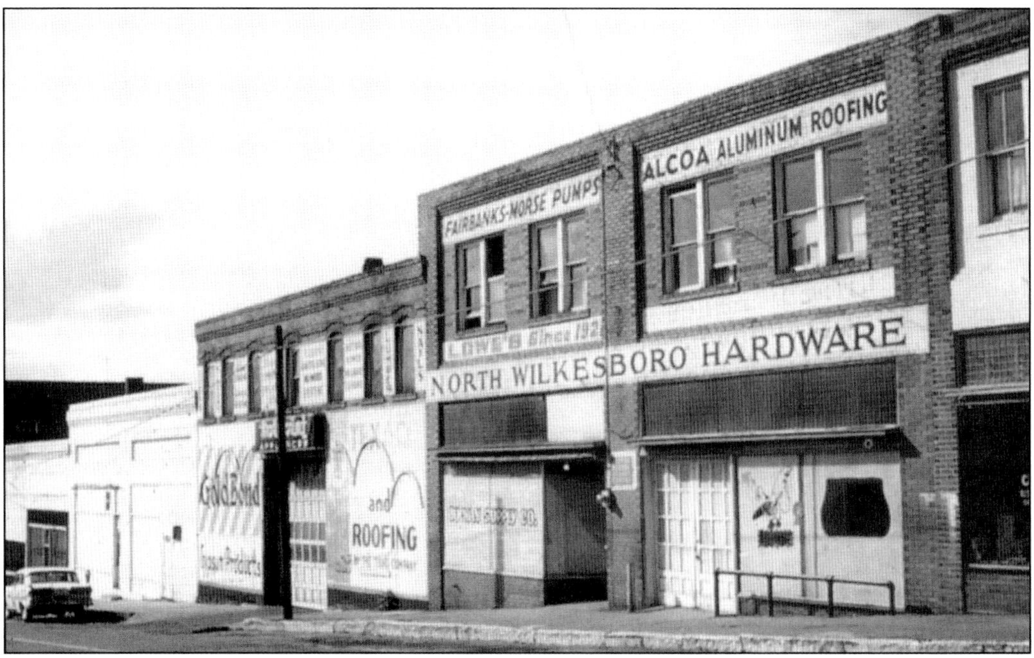

LOWE'S HARDWARE. The original Lowe's North Wilkesboro Hardware was opened on C Street in North Wilkesboro by L. S. Lowe in 1921. He sold it to his son, Jim, in 1940 for $4,200. Lowe's opened a second store in Sparta in 1949 and has continued to expand, currently operating more than 1,400 stores across the United States. (Courtesy of Lowe's Photo Archive.)

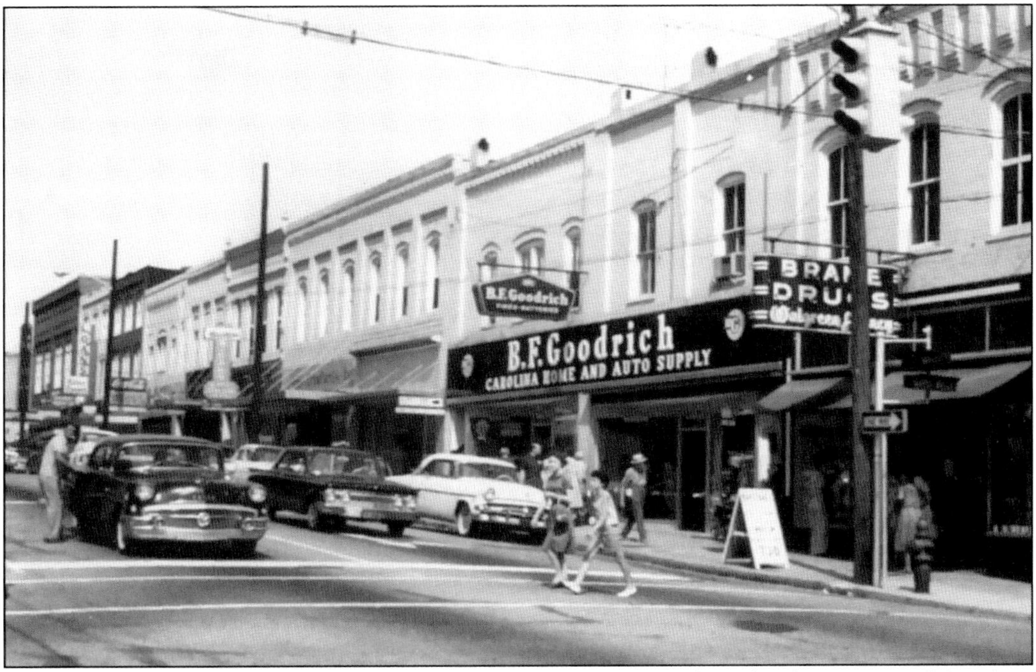

CAROLINA HOME AND AUTO SUPPLY, C. 1960. James Flake Cook and Bob Kite started Carolina Home and Auto Supply in North Wilkesboro in 1946. Cook bought out Kite's interests in the mid-1960s. When Cook's son, James, entered the business in 1964, sporting goods and supplies became a major part of Cook's merchandise. Cook's moved to its current location in West Park in 1974. (Courtesy of Gail Haynes.)

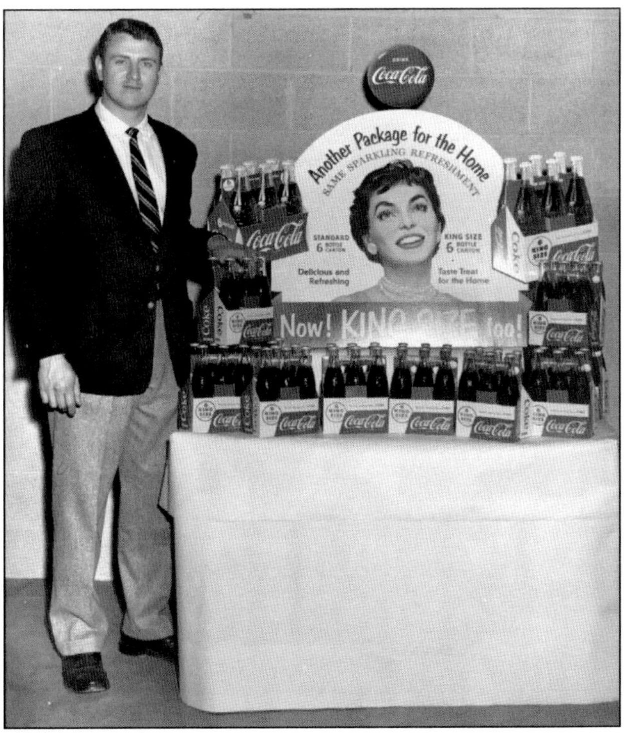

COCA-COLA BOTTLING. Red Top Bottling Company on Tenth Street began operations in 1909. The company, operated by the McNeil family, was reincorporated in 1919 as the North Wilkesboro Coca-Cola Bottling Company. In 1954, a new location was constructed on Highway 268. The plant closed in 1985 after the Western Carolina Coca-Cola Bottling Company acquired the business. (Courtesy of Wilkes Community College Library.)

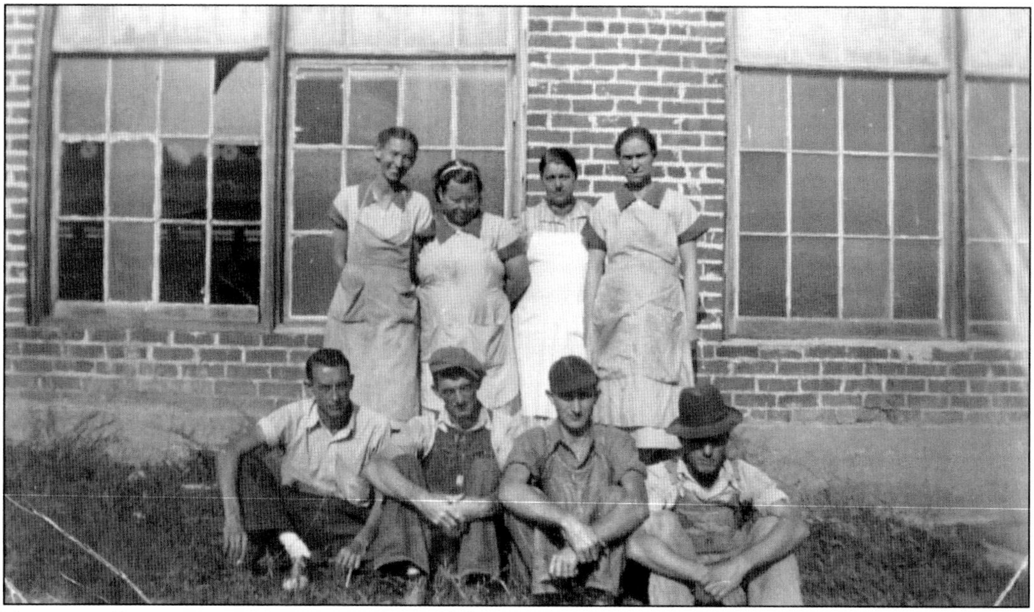

ROARING RIVER COTTON MILL. The mill, built in 1911, was later purchased by Bill Palmer. The Grier Cotton Mill used the facility to spin cotton, and the building was later used for machine storage until it burned. In this *c.* 1930 photograph are, from left to right, (first row) unidentified, Paul Alexander, Rex Baldwin, and Fred Alexander; (second row) Grace Shumate, Annie Lee Roope, Grace Bell Swaim, and Verti Shumate. (Courtesy of Georgia Cothren.)

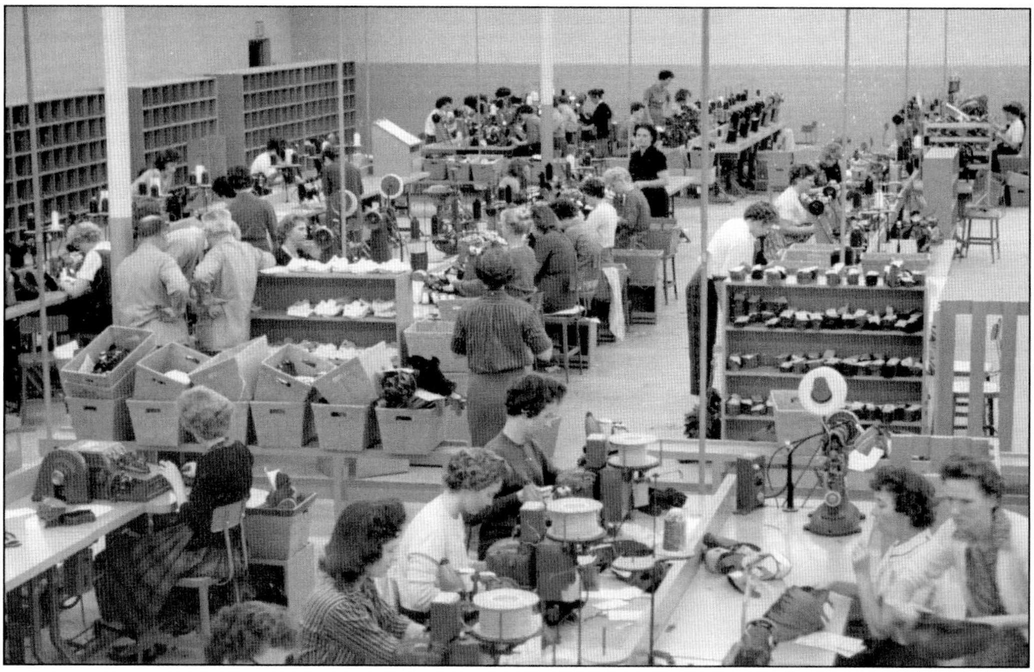

BLUE RIDGE SHOE COMPANY. Grading on the Blue Ridge Shoe Company building began in 1960. The primary product manufactured at Blue Ridge Shoe's 61,000-square-foot facility was children's shoes. The building later housed operations for Golden Needles before their operations were moved offshore. (Courtesy of Wilkes Community College Library.)

Seven

Watering Holes and Hangouts

Wilkes County has always had its share of gathering places. These are places remembered most vividly, places where serendipitous things happen, places of which legends are born. City streets, courthouse squares, public parks, coffee shops, theaters, ice cream parlors, racetracks, clubhouses, and churches are all gathering places. The beauty lies in the fact that in gathering places the community comes to life. These spots hum with multi-generational activity: talking, playing, people-watching, flirting, and catching up. In gathering places, communities are bound together in fellowship and mutual interest.

Downtown North Wilkesboro was a prime gathering place, especially on Saturdays when the streets were filled with people. Wags remember the corner of D and Sixth Streets where women would gather and exchange gossip. A passersby would note that the "Sixth Street Sentinel was going to press." Public spaces along Main and Tenth Streets offered men and women an opportunity to talk politics. Men gathered in barbershops, city hall, the Opera House, and the Amuzu, Orpheum, and Allen theaters to make important decisions and to hold events.

For rural residents, country stores, post offices, and gas stations were popular gathering places. From Calvin Cowles' store in Elkville, to the Gerald McGee store in Ferguson, to H. C. Greene's store in Clingman, to the old Traphill Country Store, these places drew men around potbellied stoves to exchange ideas and enjoy each other's company. The stock sale, the community market on the parking deck, and the farmer's market at Smoot Park drew people together in a similar fashion. Restaurants were also popular hangouts. Jack's, Super Service, City Café, Ideal Grill, Hester's, Harold's, the Ponderosa, Embers, Woodie's, and other local eateries drew regular crowds.

Gathering places make people feel interconnected. They provide an opportunity to exchange information, wisdom, and values. Be they charming, historic, celebratory, or spiritual in nature, gathering places provide that feeling of home that can only be found in communities like Wilkes County.

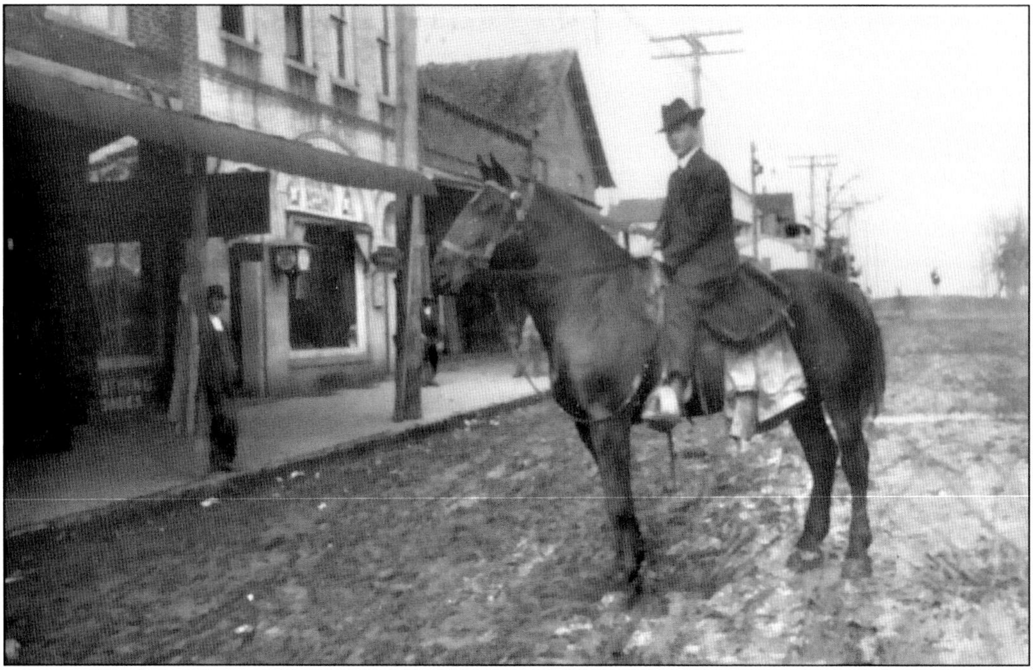

Dirt Streets in North Wilkesboro. Early on, the streets of North Wilkesboro were dirt, and sidewalks were constructed of boards. Later some streets were paved with cobblestones, which became slick when wet, rendering them virtually impassably by wagons. Sixth and Ninth Streets, with their steep hills, were particularly treacherous, even to early automobiles. (Courtesy of Wilkes Community College Library.)

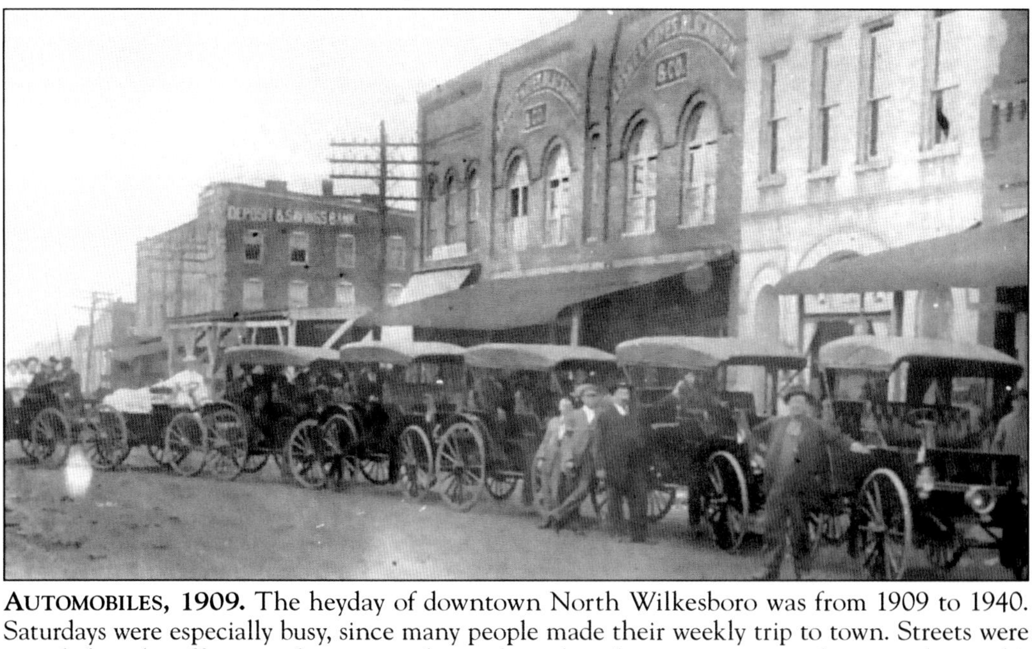

Automobiles, 1909. The heyday of downtown North Wilkesboro was from 1909 to 1940. Saturdays were especially busy, since many people made their weekly trip to town. Streets were crowded, and traffic was often jammed; people gathered in groups to catch up on the week's events. Pictured are automobiles gathered in downtown North Wilkesboro in 1909. (Courtesy of Wilkes Community College Library.)

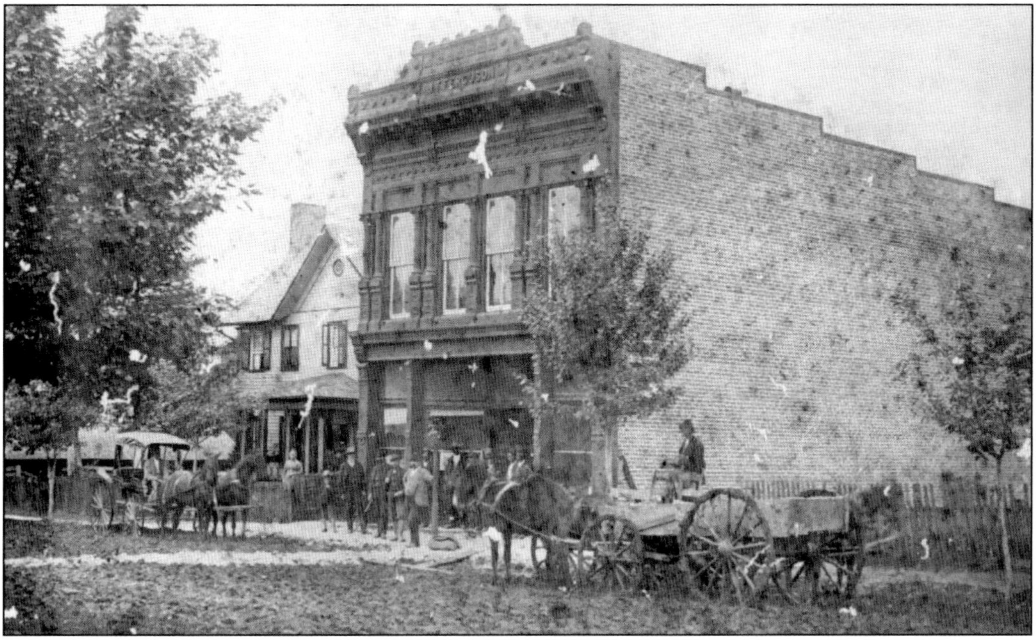

J. T. FERGUSON BUILDING. The pressed metal and cast-iron facade covering the brick foundation of the 1887 Jesse T. Ferguson store in Wilkesboro was produced by Mesker Brothers of St. Louis, Missouri. In addition to operating the general store, Jesse Ferguson was a Civil War veteran who became sheriff of Wilkes County and later mayor of Wilkesboro. (Courtesy of Wilkes Heritage Museum.)

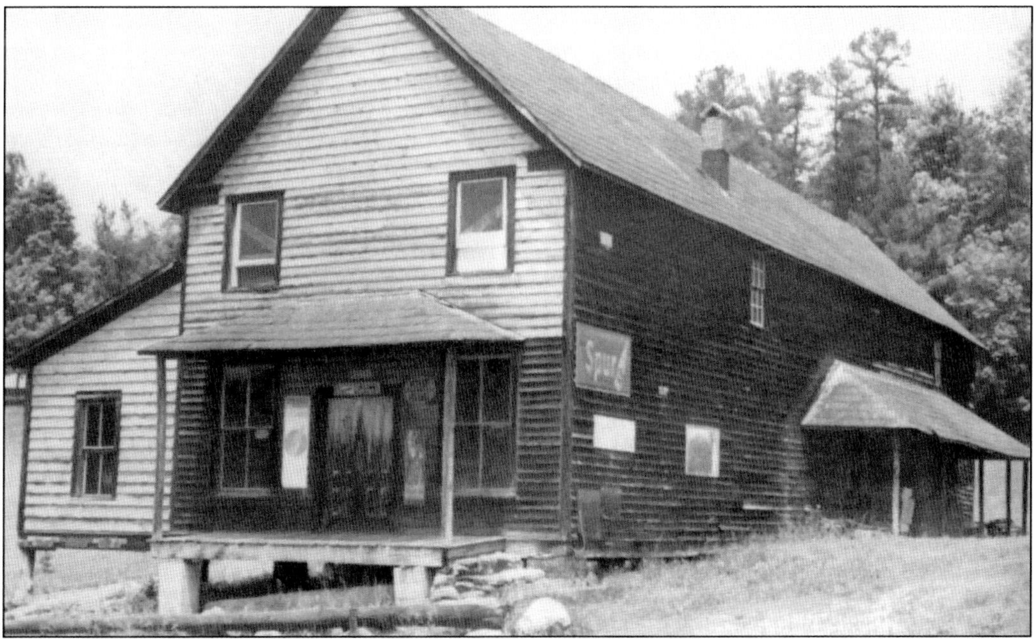

READY BRANCH STORE BUILDING. This store, originally known as the Church store building, is located in Ferguson. It was built c. 1878 and operated by L. L. Church until about 1920. From 1920 to 1945, it was operated by Zora Church Eller. In 1945, Gerald and Estelle Church McGee purchased the business and operated the store until 1958. (Courtesy of Wilkes Genealogical Society.)

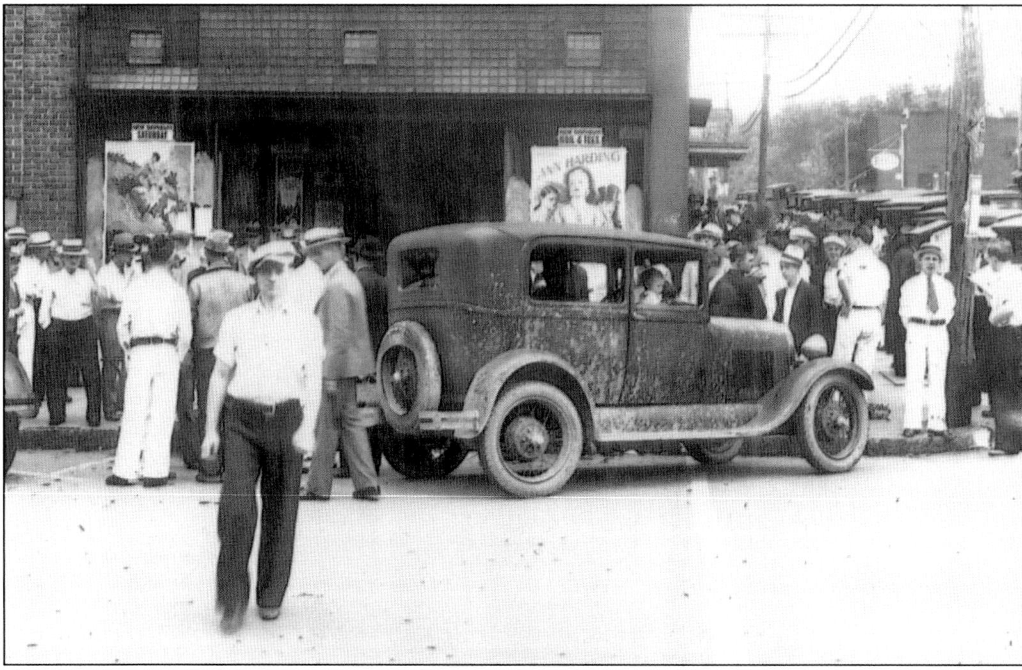

ORPHEUM THEATER. Before television became popular, children flocked to the theater on Saturdays to watch cowboy serials. Theaters in the 1940s often doubled as gathering places for town meetings and social events. This picture was taken in front of the Orpheum Theater in North Wilkesboro. (Courtesy of Wilkes Community College Library.)

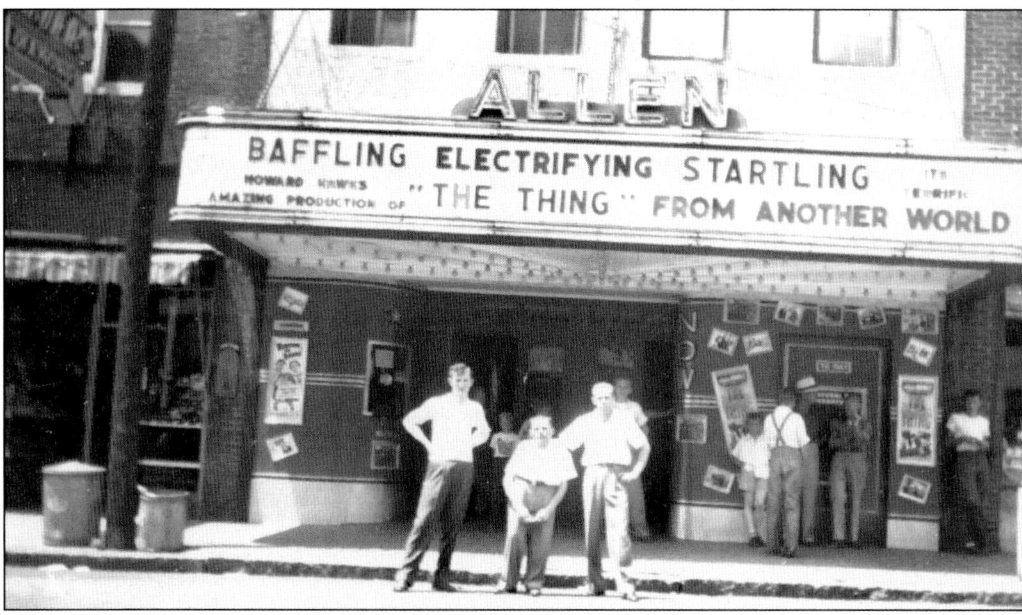

ALLEN THEATER, C. 1940. The Allen Theater, located in downtown North Wilkesboro, was owned by W. J. Allen. The Allen and the Liberty theaters were open seven days a week with shows held at 1:00 p.m., 3:00 p.m., 5:00 p.m., 7:00 p.m., 9:00 p.m., and 11:00 p.m. The Orpheum Theater was also owned by Allen. The Allen Theater burned in 1961. (Courtesy of Wilkes Heritage Museum.)

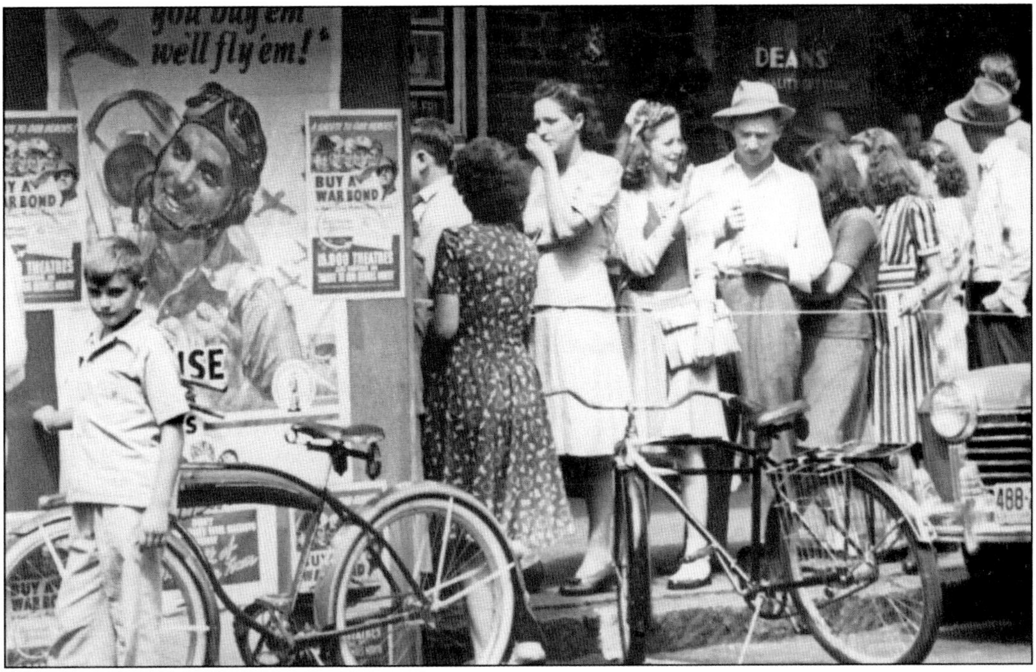

DOWNTOWN NORTH WILKESBORO, C. 1940. This photograph shows downtown North Wilkesboro in the 1940s. Notice the signs advertising war bonds. In 1943, the Wilkes County bond quota was $374,000. Firms and investors purchased bonds, generating more than $670,000 in revenue in a bond drive that year designed to help fund the U.S. war effort during World War II. (Courtesy of Wilkes Heritage Museum.)

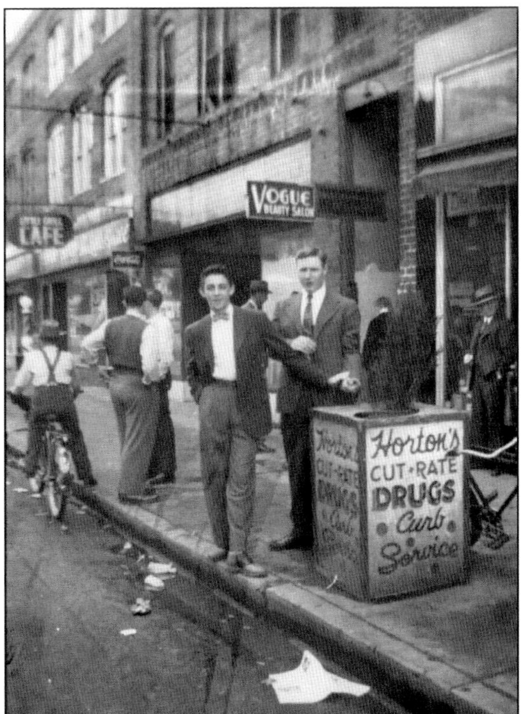

HORTON'S DRUG STORE, 1940S. Horton's Drug Store, built c. 1904, was established by W. P. Horton. Bea Jennings operated a photography shop above the drugstore in the 1930s. From 1910 to the 1920s, the building was used as the North Wilkesboro Post Office with part of the Hotel Blumont on the upper story. Horton's Drug Store closed in 1981. (Courtesy of Wilkes Heritage Museum.)

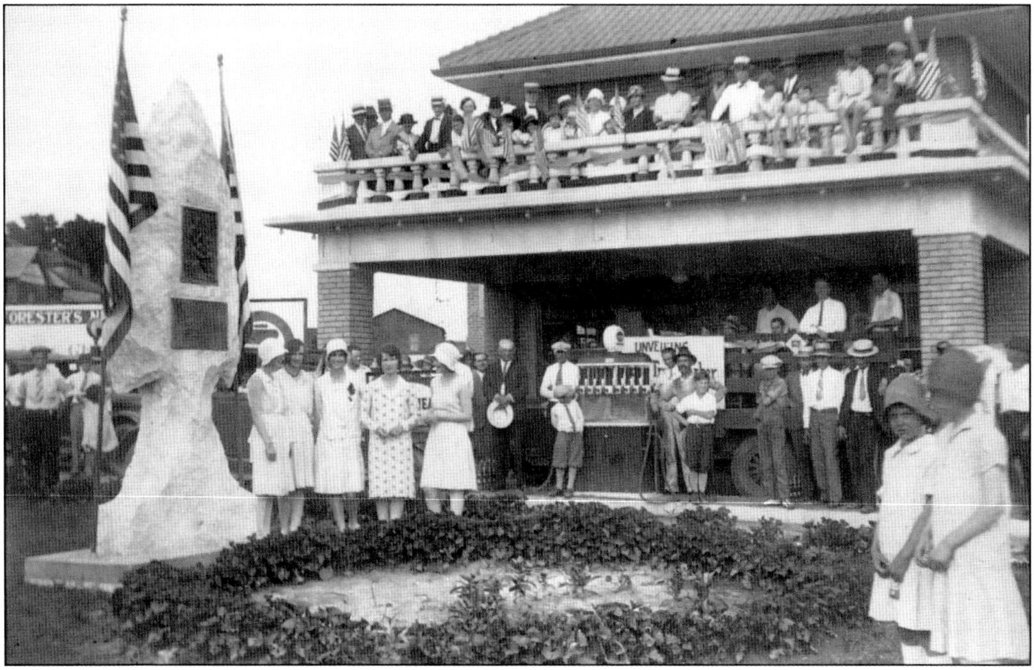

FORESTER'S NU-WAY. Forester's Nu-Way was founded in the late 1920s by Floyd C. (Tom) Forester. It was a meeting place for Democratic leaders and contained a small zoo with lions, bears, monkeys, and exotic birds. The 1940 flood washed away many of the animals, though the zoo operated until the early 1950s. Pictured is a celebration in the 1930s. (Courtesy of Wilkes Community College Library.)

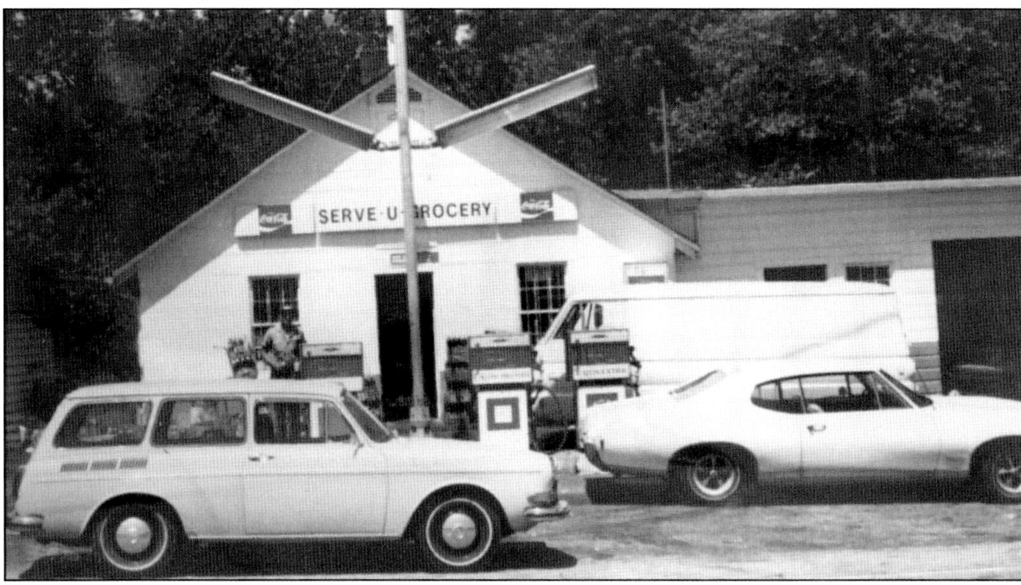

HAYES GROCERY. In 1945, Robert Hayes opened Serve-U-Grocery near Pads Road in Millers Creek. R. D. Hayes and Sons store at the intersection of N.C. 16 and old U.S. Highway 421 was operated by Rob's brother, Arlie. Serve-U-Grocery closed in 1983 when Arlie retired, and Rob returned to the original store, renamed Hayes Serve-U-Grocery, to operate it until it closed in 2000. (Courtesy of Wilkes Community College Library.)

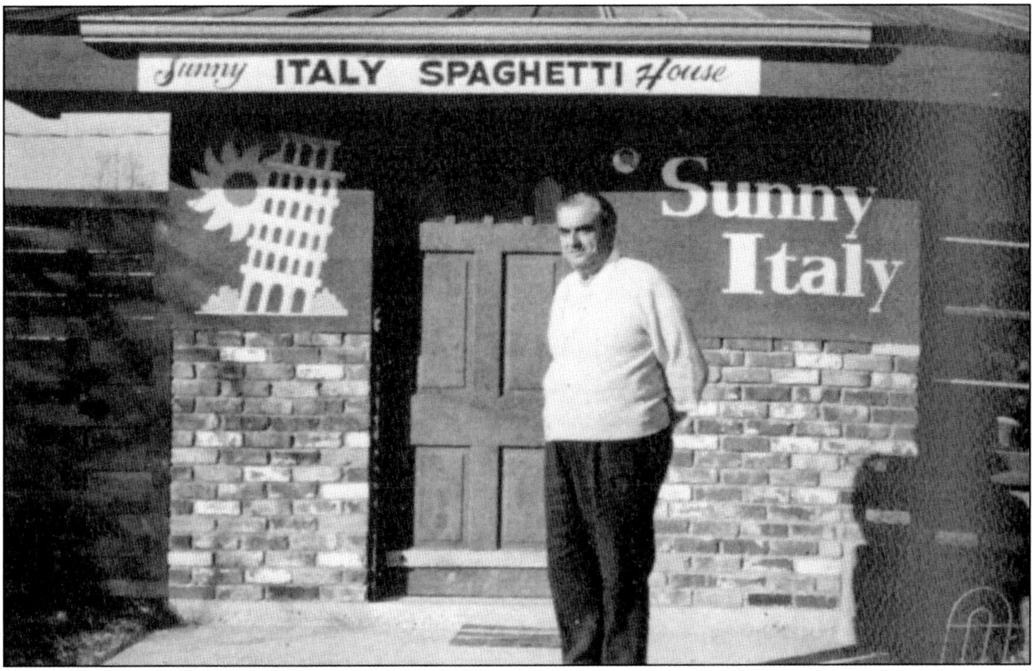

SUNNY ITALY, 1960S. Sunny Italy was opened in 1967 by John and Daisy Roselli. John (pictured here) had previously operated the Green Pig restaurant and Club Valencia. Wilkes County native Daisy made salads and desserts while husband John made sauces and pastas. Now son David helps Daisy operate this family eatery that specializes in traditional Italian cooking. (Courtesy of the *Hawkeye*.)

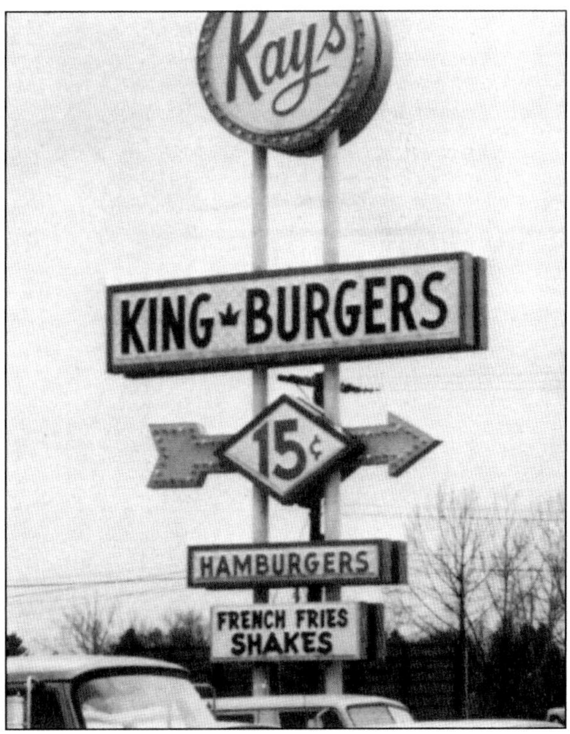

RAY'S KING BURGER. Ray's King Burger was among the first places in Wilkes County to serve hamburgers. After Ray's closed, Hadley's moved into the location from Wilkesboro Boulevard where it had operated as Southern Barbecue, Dixie Barbecue, Dixie Diner, and finally Hadley's to honor cook Hadley Phillips. (Courtesy of the *Hawkeye*.)

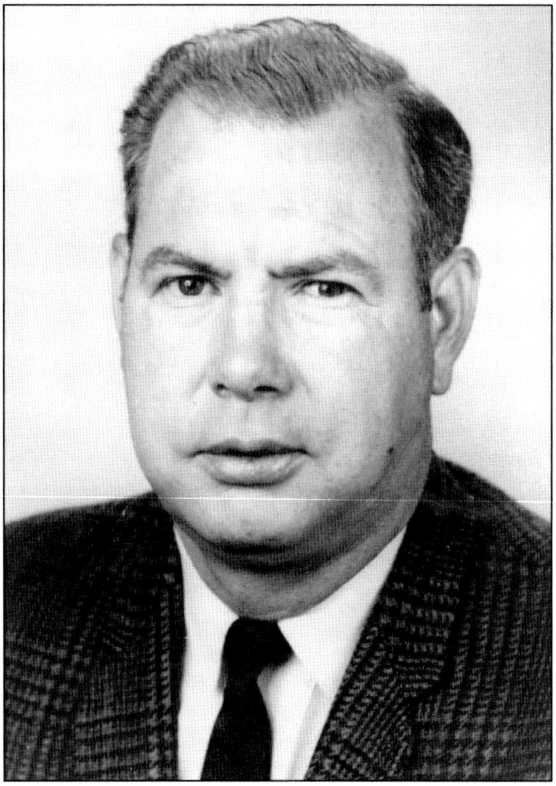

GLENN'S TASTEE FREEZ. Glenn Johnson's first Tastee Freez shop was located on Main Street in North Wilkesboro. In 1963, he moved to the corner of West Main and Curtis Bridge Road in Wilkesboro, where he continues his successful ice cream/restaurant business more than four decades later. In 2003, Johnson celebrated the 40th anniversary of the restaurant, selling some menu items at 1963 prices. Glenn's offers 50 flavors of milk shakes, banana splits, hamburgers, pizza, and onion rings. An active member of the community, Johnson (pictured left *c.* 1963) has also served as a commissioner for the town of Wilkesboro. Pictured below is Glenn's in September 1963. (Both, courtesy of Glenn Johnson.)

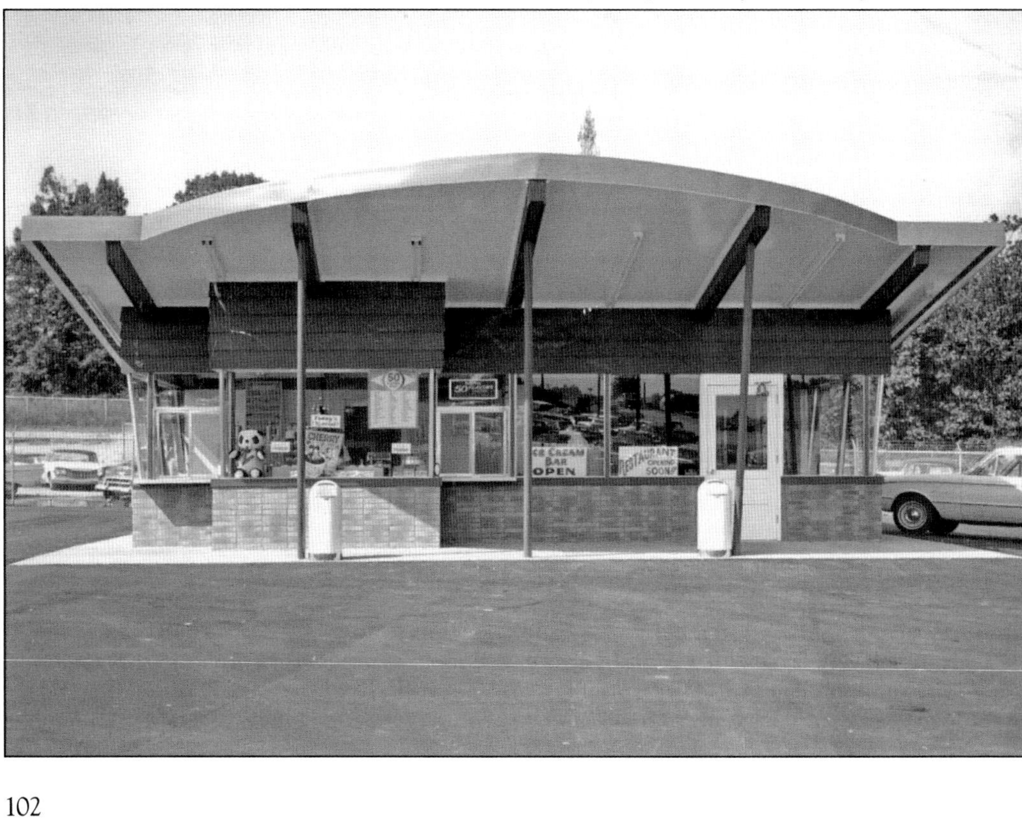

Eight

Down Home People

Many of the early settlers of Wilkes County were of Scottish and Irish descent. Rugged frontiersmen came to North Carolina via Pennsylvania and Maryland seeking land and independence. They were shaped by the harsh physical realities of life in the Carolina backcountry. Clearing forests, building homes, and toiling the land, they grew self-sufficient. At the same time, they turned to each other for support in times of need.

Since the Revolutionary War, the men of Wilkes County have served their country admirably in conflicts at home and abroad. The Battle of Kings Mountain, Gettysburg, the Battle of the Bulge, and the raising of the flag at Iwo Jima were all witnessed by brave Wilkes County fighting men. The women of Wilkes tended the homes, took care of the children, served in the military, fought for votes, gathered together, and made life more comfortable for all.

An entrepreneurial spirit grew, technology changed society, and Wilkes County began to take great pride in its small businesses. People gathered together in groups like the Women's Christian Temperance Union, the Knights of Pythias, the Odd Fellows, the Commercial Club, the Dokies, the Grange, and the Friday Afternoon Book Club. They brought their children together through Boy Scouts, Girl Scouts, and 4-H. Through it all, the county became a close-knit community where the roots of family run deep.

Wilkes County is an increasingly diverse area comprised of many nationalities and religions. Yet through it all, they have remained essentially the same. They work hard, they value their families, they help their neighbors, and they appreciate their heritage. They have been farmers and Freemasons, soldiers and statesmen, bootleggers and bankers. They built businesses. They raised families. They served their country. They fought for what they believed in. They lived and loved, laughed and cried, and made Wilkes County the place it is today.

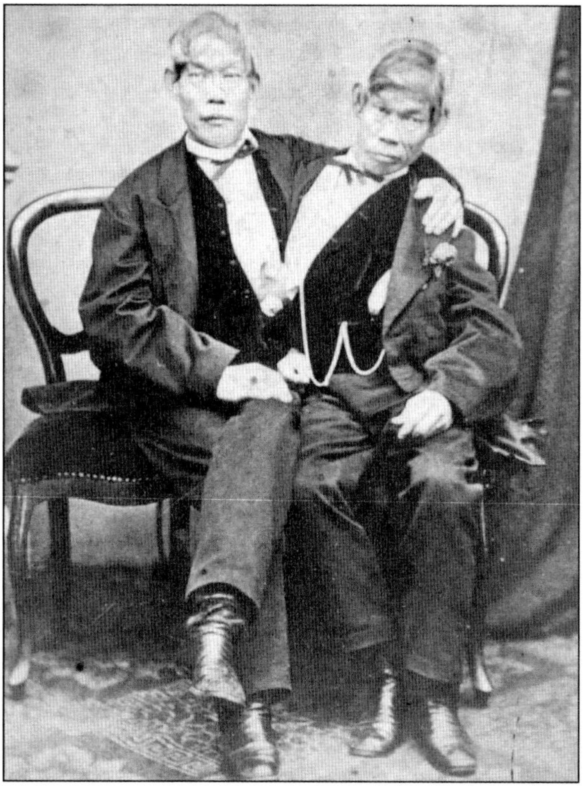

SIAMESE TWINS. Chang and Eng Bunker, born in Siam in 1811, traveled extensively as showmen before retiring in the 1830s. They built a home in Traphill *c.* 1842. Chang married Adelaide Yates, and Eng married her sister Sarah in 1843. Between them, they sired 21 children. The Bunkers died in 1874. (Courtesy of North Carolina Collection, University of North Carolina Library at Chapel Hill.)

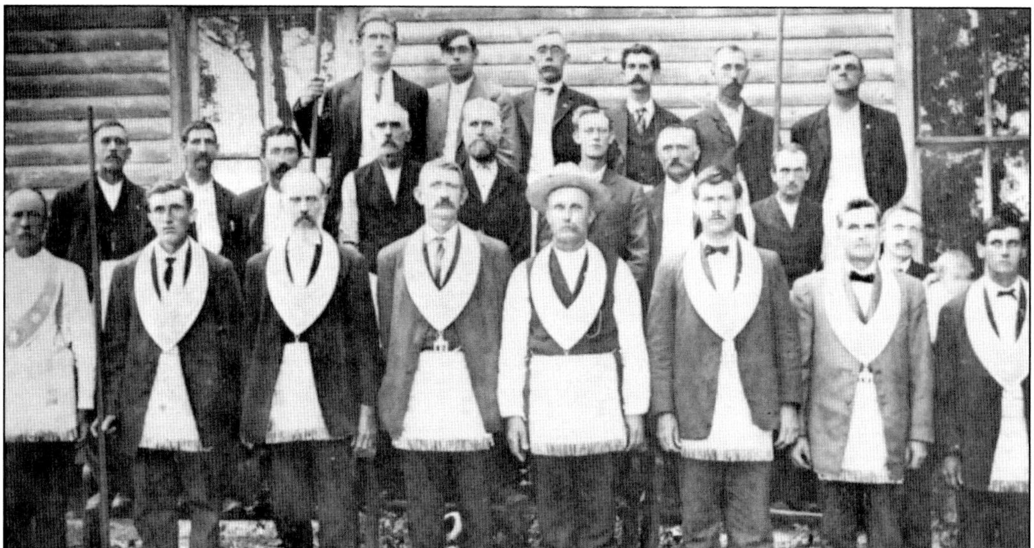

TRAPHILL MASONIC LODGE. The lodge was chartered in 1875. Pictured from left to right are (first row) John Wood, A. C. Yale, William Sparks, Thomas Bryan, James Sparks, Millard Caudill, James Kilby, and Gaither Pruitt; (second row) Dave Bryan, Bob Stiller, Joe Lyon, W. H. Lyon, Joseph Spicer, John Myers, Major Joines, C. W. Wood, and Avery Billings with son; (third row) Chy Pruitt, Rob Waddell, Thomas DeBorde, Clarence Holbrook, Gideon Lyon, and W. R. Shepherd. (Courtesy of Wilkes Genealogical Society.)

JAMES LARKIN PEARSON. Though he had little formal education, Pearson went on to become poet laureate of North Carolina, a post he held from 1953 until his death in 1981. After working with R. Don Laws of *The Yellow Jacket*, Pearson began his own paper, *The Fool-Killer*. (Courtesy of Wilkes Community College Library.)

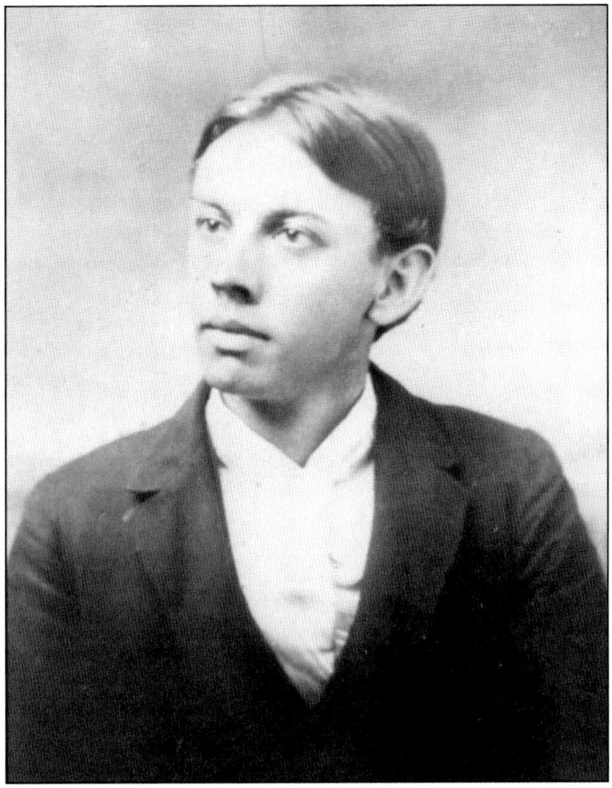

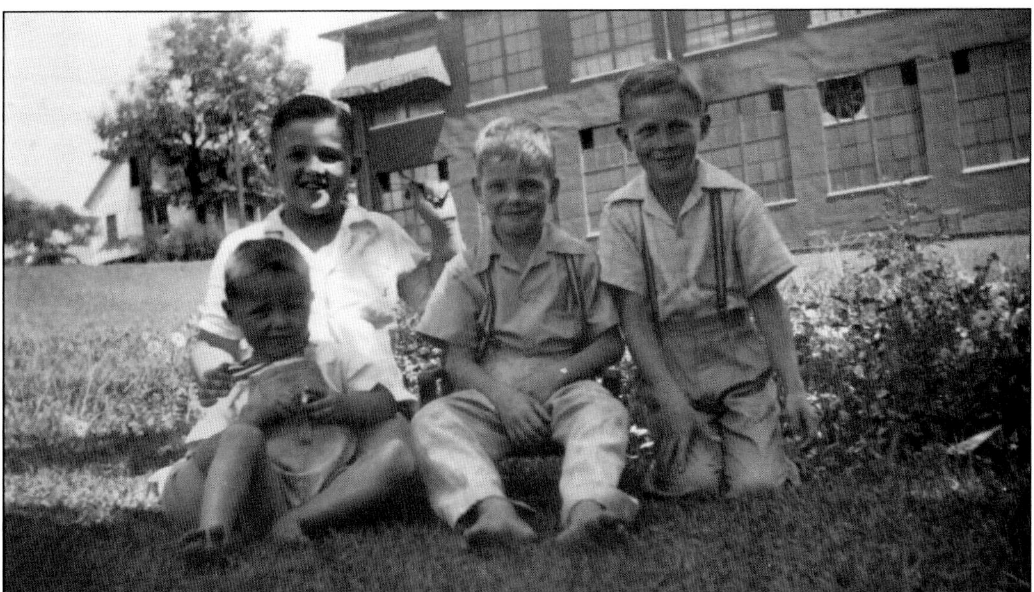

WILKES HOSIERY MILLS. The mill, established by P. W. Eshelman in 1918, was the first hosiery mill in Wilkes County to employ women. It was located in North Wilkesboro, first in the Opera House, then on A Street, and finally on F Street. Pictured in front of the mill are, from left to right, Jerry McNeil, Shang Reins, J. V. Reins and James Sidney Reins. (Courtesy of Nicole Brown de Bruijn.)

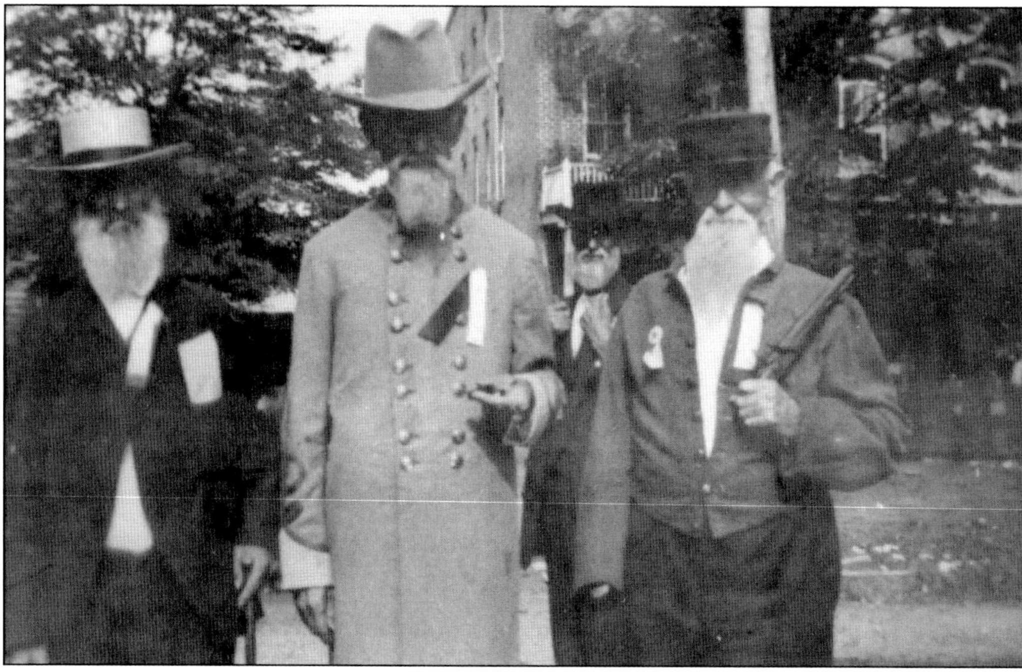

CONFEDERATE VETERANS, 1922. Though Wilkes County overwhelmingly opposed secession, more than 1,000 Wilkes County men fought in the Civil War, more than any other county in North Carolina except Mecklenburg. Casualties were heavy; one in four North Carolina soldiers fell in battle. Most owned no slaves but fought for their honor, their families, or simply because they had to. In August 1910, about 150 Confederate veterans of Wilkes County organized a group called the M. S. Stokes Camp of Confederate Veterans in memory of Col. Montford Stokes. Officers were E. S. Blair, commander; R. M. Staley, vice commander; J. S. Forester, secretary and treasurer; J. T. Ferguson, commissary; W. S. Meadows, chaplain; James Hickerson, sergeant; and Nellie White, mascot. The last Confederate reunion was held in 1926, pictured above and below. (Both courtesy of Wilkes Community College Library.)

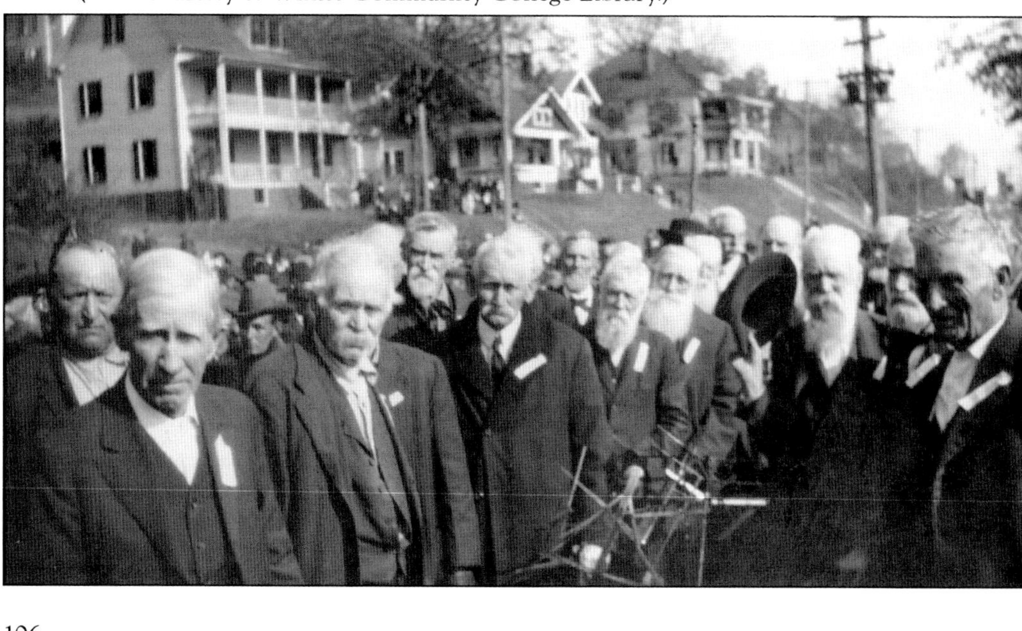

PAUL CROUCH. A Moravian Falls native, Crouch became active in the U.S. Communist Party in the 1920s while serving in the U.S. Army. He was imprisoned in Alcatraz for promoting his political views. Upon release, Crouch gained notoriety as a vocal proponent of the Communist movement. During the McCarthy era, he became an FBI informant and testified against the Communist party. (Courtesy of James Larkin Pearson Library, Wilkes Community College.)

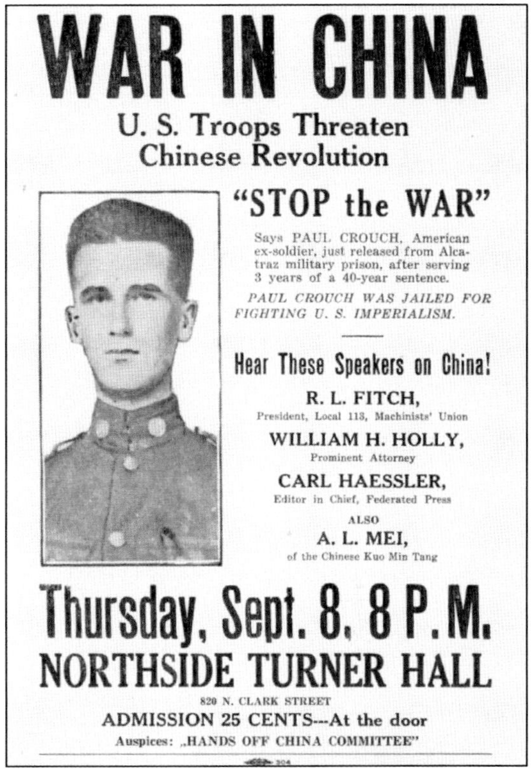

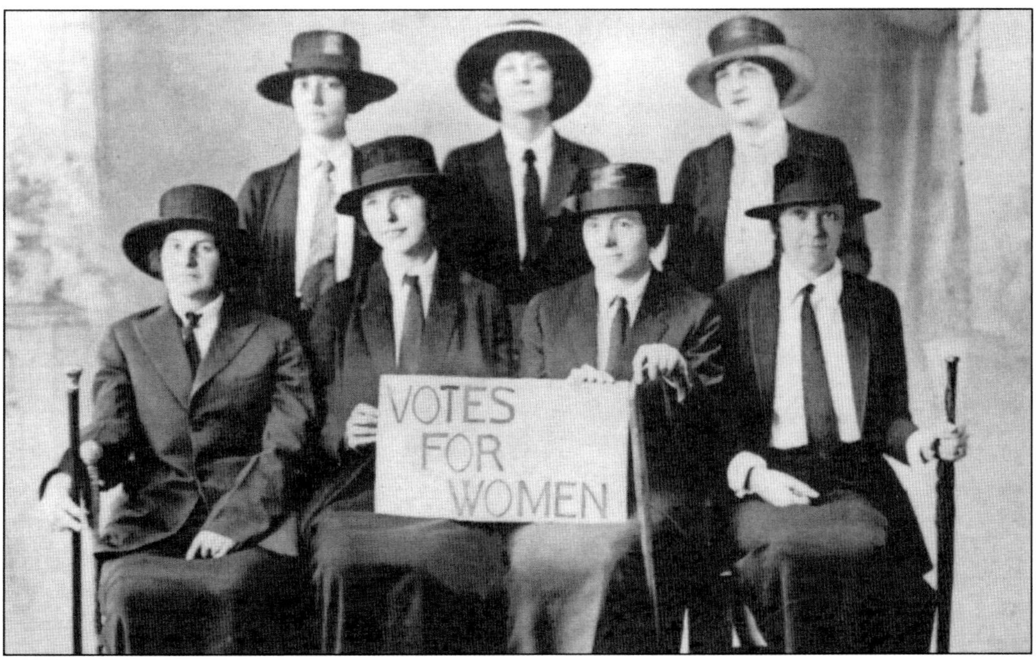

WILKES COUNTY SUFFRAGETTES. In this photograph, a group of Wilkes County suffragettes strike a pose for the right to vote prior to the passage of the 19th Amendment of 1920. Among those pictured are (front row, second from left) Lewis Carter and (front row, far right) Bernice Horton. (Courtesy of Wilkes Genealogical Society.)

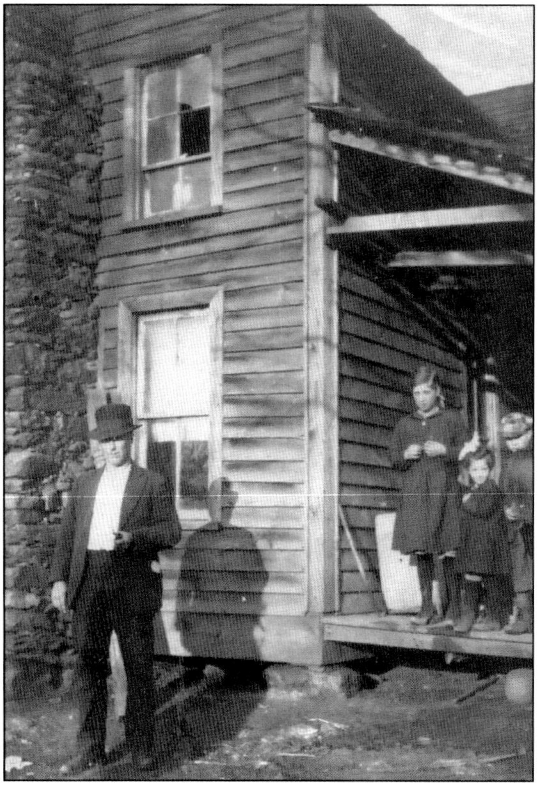

HOME IN BIG IVY. Shown here are Heg H. Beshears (left), his daughter Ivy Richardson, and two unidentified children. Beshears was engaged in lumbering and cattle raising. He was a leader in farming, served as a school committeeman in his community, and was an active Democrat nominated for office on several occasions. (Courtesy of James Richardson.)

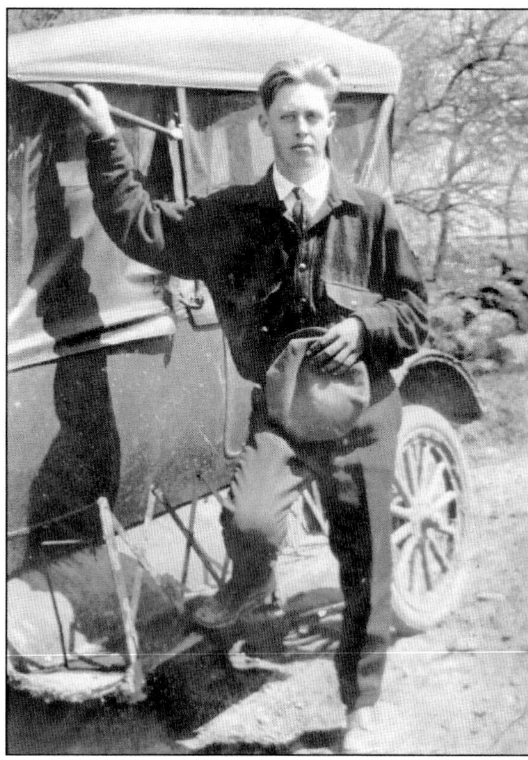

RONALD BARNETT. Barnett was among the many people who left Wilkes County to migrate westward. He migrated to Montana. Earlier Wilkes County residents migrated first to Ohio, Tennessee, and Kentucky, then further west to Montana and Wyoming. Many sought financial opportunities they believed surpassed those available along the East Coast. (Courtesy of Linda Triplett.)

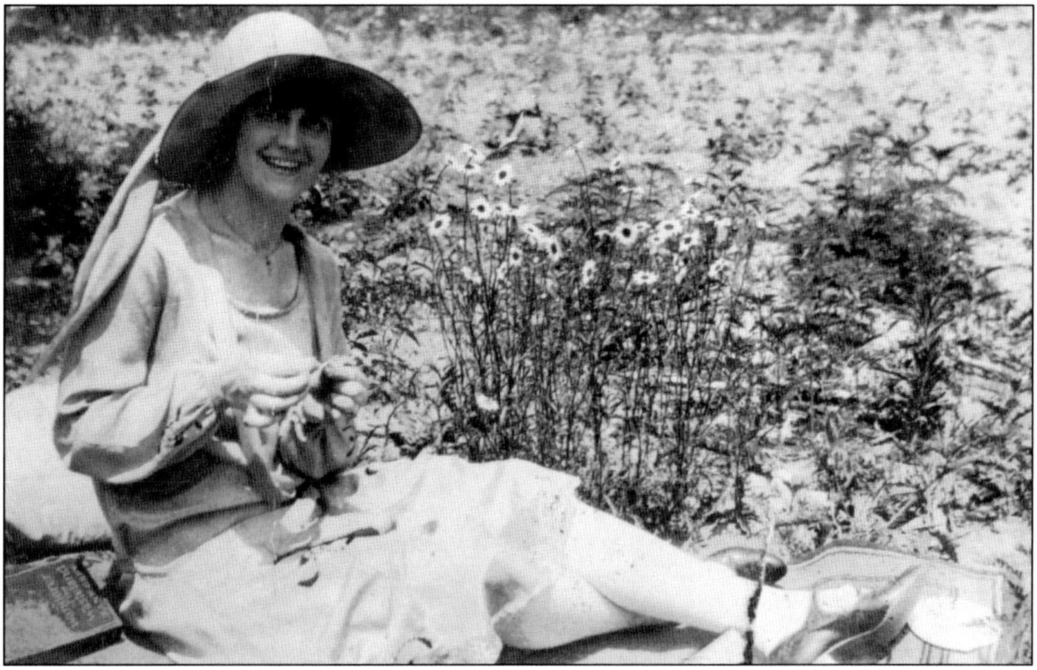

FLOSSIE TRIPLETT, 1920S. In the 1920s, ladies enjoyed picnic excursions to picturesque spots in the countryside to enjoy a meal, good conversation, and a good book. In this photograph, Flossie Triplett relaxes in a field near her home in the Mount Zion community. Beside her is the Zane Grey novel *Wanderer of the Wasteland.* (Courtesy of Linda Triplett.)

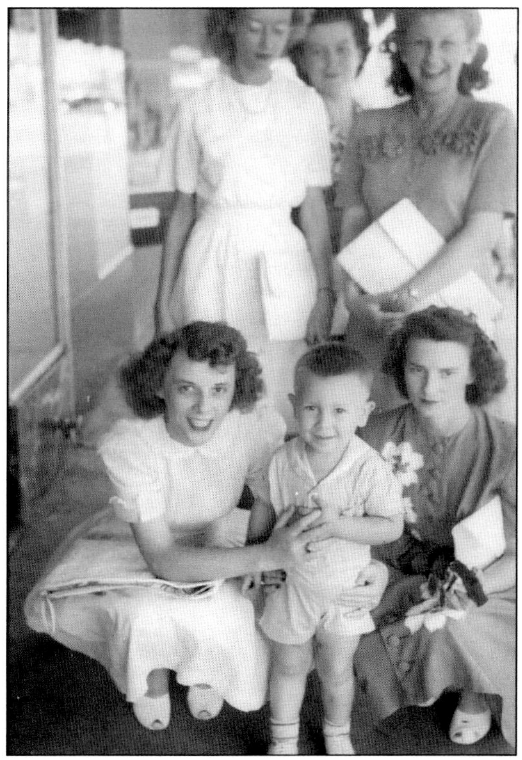

KILBY SISTERS. T. G. Kilby was a lumber buyer for Oak Furniture. Pictured are his four daughters and friends posing by a sandwich shop on Main Street in North Wilkesboro. Shown from left to right are (first row) Mabel, an unidentified boy, and Ruby; (second row) Fannie Ruth and Thelma with the mother of the unidentified boy behind them. (Courtesy of North Wilkesboro High School Alumni Association.)

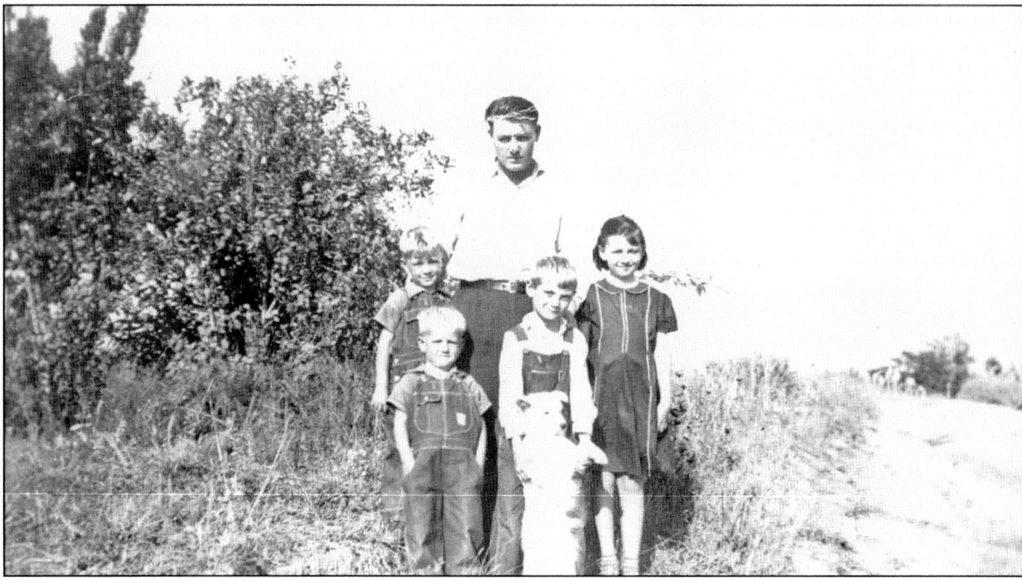

Swaim Family, 1940s. Families in Wilkes County have always been close-knit. Cousins are often as close as siblings, working side-by-side and playing together. In this 1940s photograph, Tom Bell (rear) poses with his nieces and nephews, (from left to right) Bobby Swaim, James "Pete" Swaim, Bill Bell, and Georgia Swaim Cothren of the Roaring River community. (Courtesy of Georgia Cothren.)

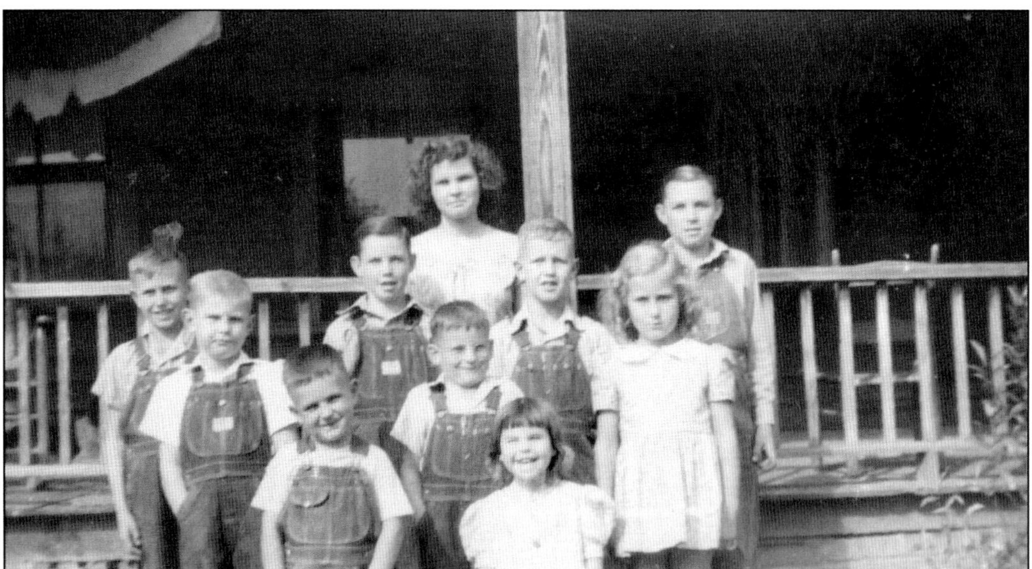

Eller family, 1949. Pictured from left to right are (first row) Bobby Eller and Anne Eller Stallings; (second row) Troy Eller, Vaughn Eller, and Connie Eller Parsons; (third row) Benny Eller, John Clinton Eller, and Harold Eller; (fourth row) Rose Eller Ellis and James Eller. It was taken *c.* 1949 at a family gathering at the home of their grandparents, Troy and Bessie Eller, in Millers Creek. (Courtesy of Sheri Hayes.)

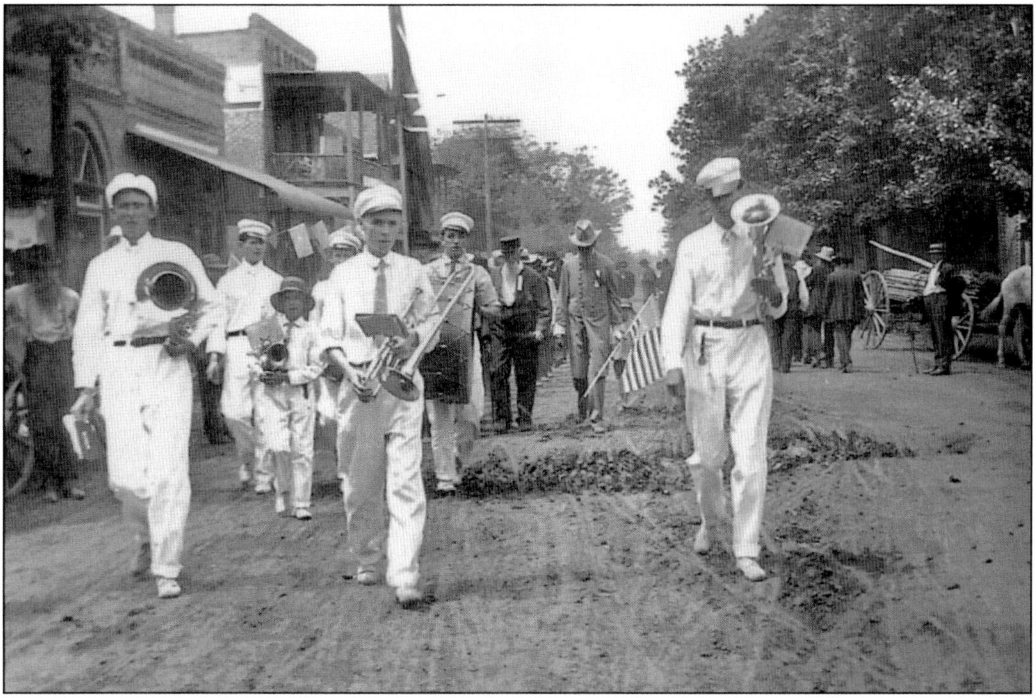

MILITARY PARADES. Military parades were held in Wilkes County to honor veterans of various wars and conflicts. Pictured above is a Confederate Day parade held on the streets of North Wilkesboro. Notice the streets; they have not been paved. Pictured below is the 1919 Fourth of July parade held to honor veterans of World War I, the Spanish-American War, and the Civil War. Business windows were festooned with red, white, and blue, and an arch was raised over Ninth Street in North Wilkesboro. Most businesses closed from 10:00 a.m. until 2:00 p.m. to celebrate the parade. Other festivities included a concert, an exhibition baseball game, and a battalion drill. (Both courtesy of Wilkes Community College Library.)

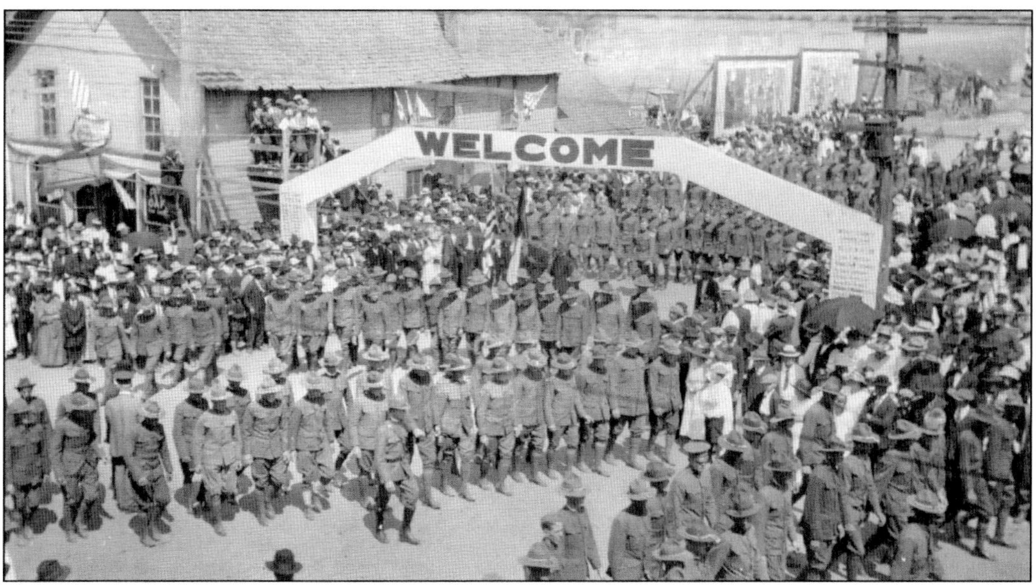

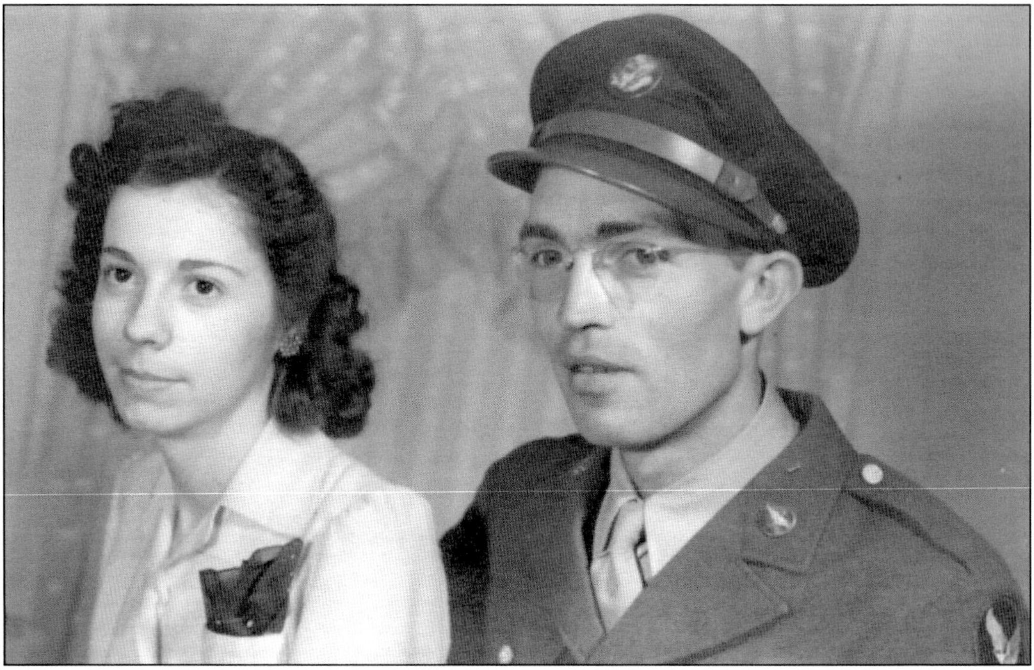

R. J. AND GOLDIE MICHAEL, 1942. R. J. Michael served in the army from 1942 until 1946. As an airplane maintenance technician, he received the American Theatre Service Medal, the Pacific Service Medal, the Good Conduct Medal, and the World War II Victory Medal. He was honorably discharged at the rank of sergeant. R. J. is pictured with his wife, Goldie Jordan Michael. (Courtesy of Goldie Michael.)

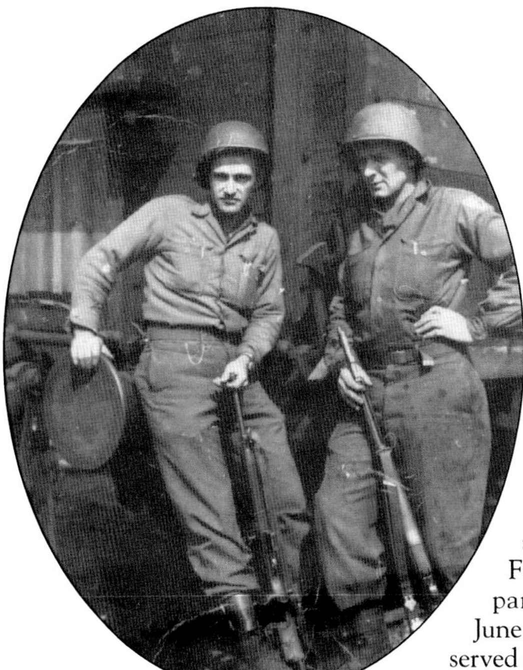

PAUL PARDUE, 1940S. Paul Pardue of Wilkesboro, left, enlisted in the army in 1942 and served in campaigns in Holland, northern France, Rhineland, and Central Europe. He participated in the invasion of Normandy in June 1944. Paul's brothers Eugene and Stewart also served during World War II in the navy and the army, respectively. (Courtesy of Gail Haynes.)

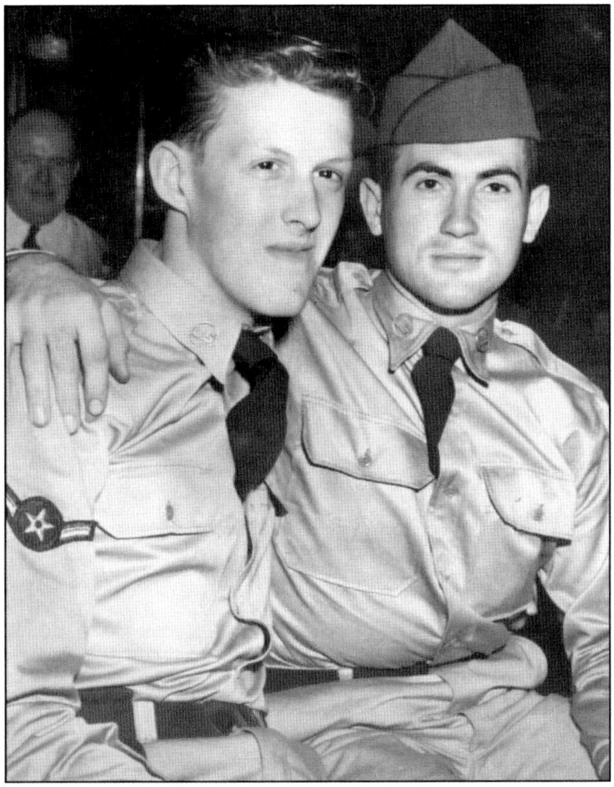

William Hamlin, 1940s. North Wilkesboro resident William Hamlin, right, served in the U.S. Air Force after World War II. His brother, Elmer, received the Purple Heart after his death during the 1944 invasion of the Anzio beachhead. The other soldier in the photograph is an unidentified friend from Chanute Air Force Base in Illinois. (Courtesy of Jamie Hamlin.)

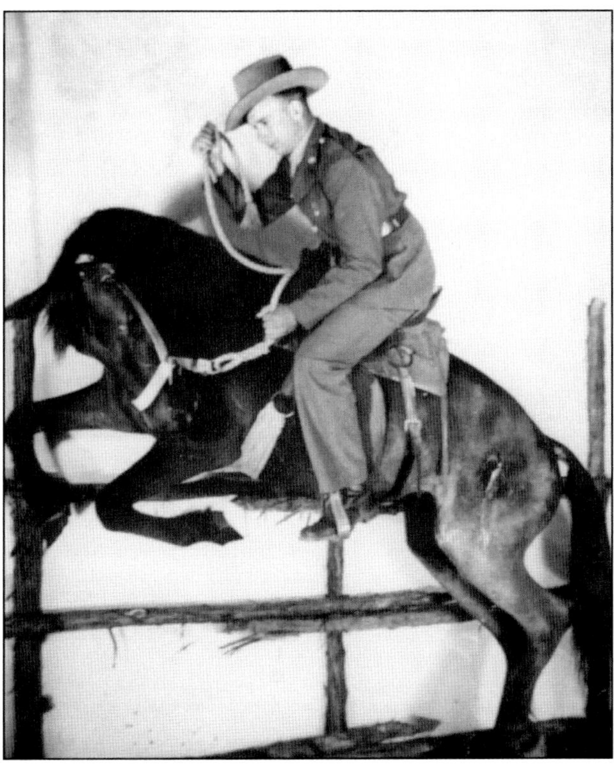

Arnold G. Wagoner. Arnold Wagoner enlisted in the army in 1942 and was honorably discharged in 1946. He served as a searchlight crewman in campaigns at the Bismarck Archipelago, New Guinea, and Luzon, earning several medals, including the American Theater Medal, Asiatic Pacific Theater Medal, and Philippine Liberation Campaign Medal. (Courtesy of Allen Wagoner.)

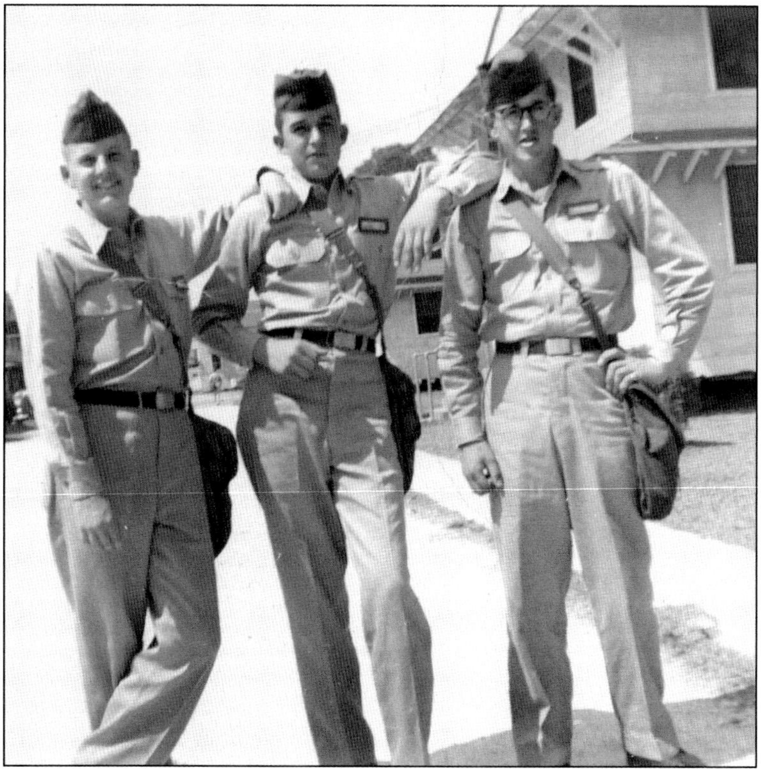

DON DILLARD, 1956. Don Dillard was a radar specialist in the U.S. Air Force. He served in Alaska and Greenland in the 1950s. Pictured from left to right are Marvin B. Crawford, Don Dillard, and unidentified. The photograph was taken in September 1956 at Keesler Air Force Base in Biloxi, Mississippi. (Courtesy of Sheri Hayes.)

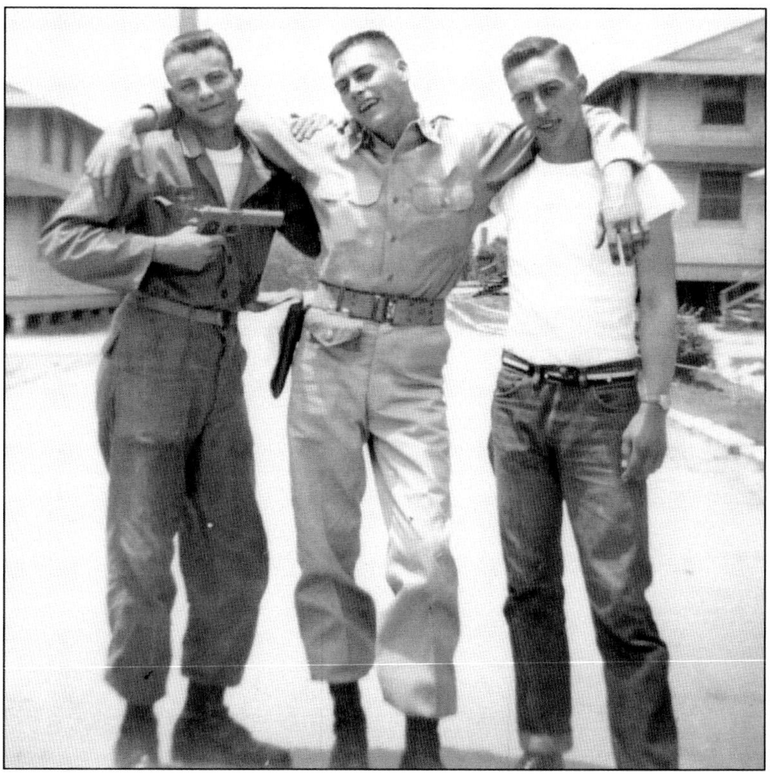

HARRISON BROWN, 1950S. Harrison Brown, center, was drafted into the army in 1954 and served until 1956 during the Korean Conflict. He achieved the rank of specialist 3rd class in the 714th Tank Battalion out of Fort Benning, Georgia. He also served at Fort Polk, Louisiana, in a peacetime maneuver that resulted in the death of 19 servicemen. (Courtesy of Nicole Brown de Bruijn.)

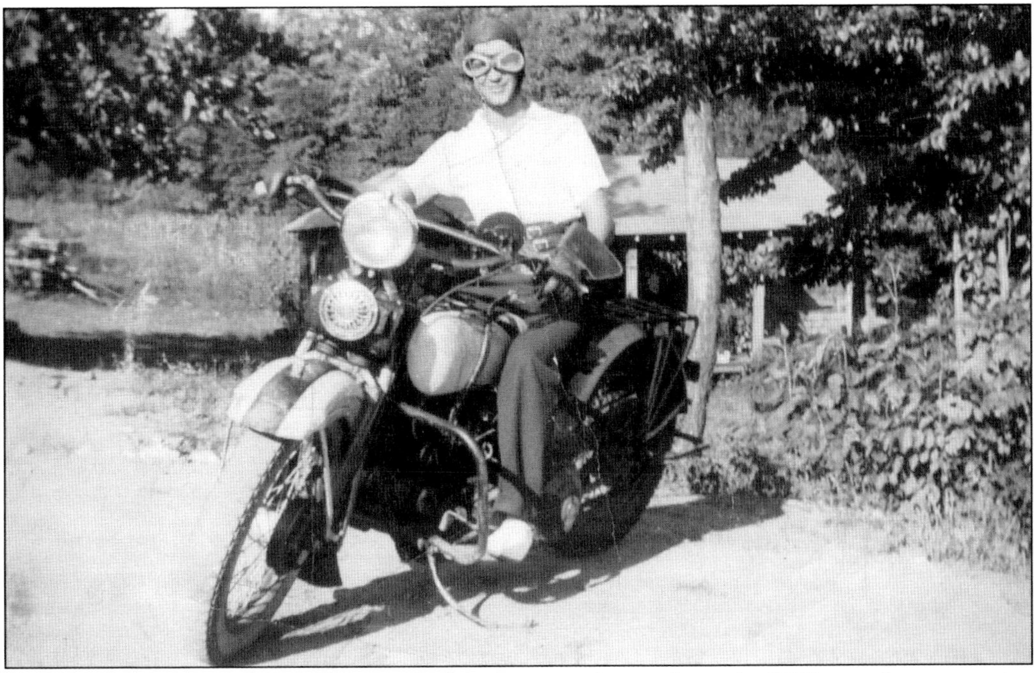

CLIFTON DILLARD, 1930S. Motorcycles became popular in the early 1900s as a less expensive alternative to the automobile, which was often too costly for the general public. Pictured here is Clifton Dillard riding his motorcycle in the 1930s. Clifton, a Wilkes County native, served in the navy during World War II. (Courtesy of Vergie Foster.)

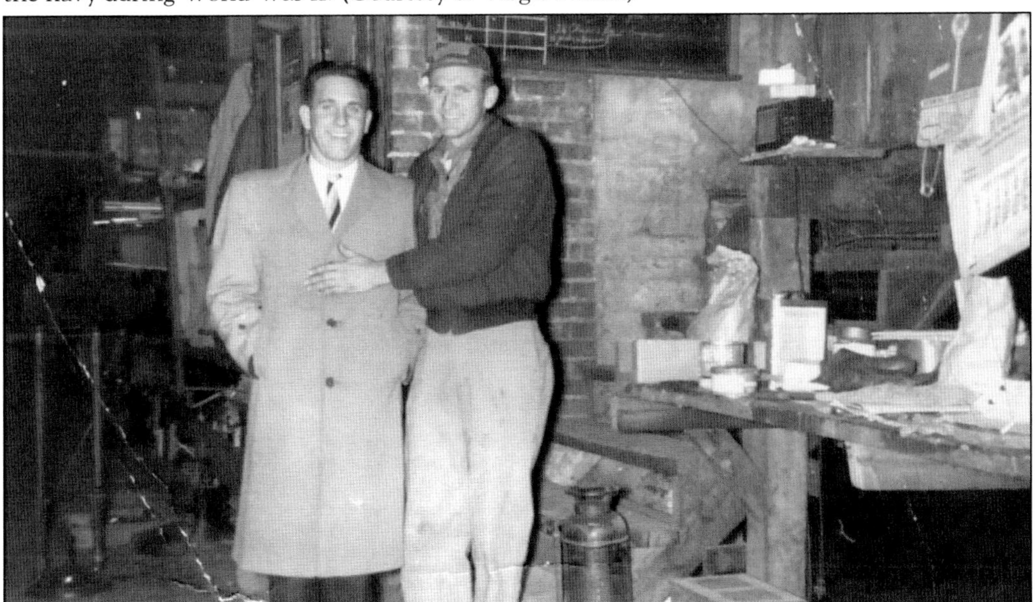

JAMES RICHARDSON AND PAUL JOHNSON. Pictured in the basement of the Sturdivant building where ambulances were parked are Sturdivant Funeral Home employees James Richardson (left) and Paul Johnson. Richardson drove an ambulance, and Johnson handled various aspects of interment. Richardson was later proprietor of the Foster-Richardson Rest Home. (Courtesy of James Richardson.)

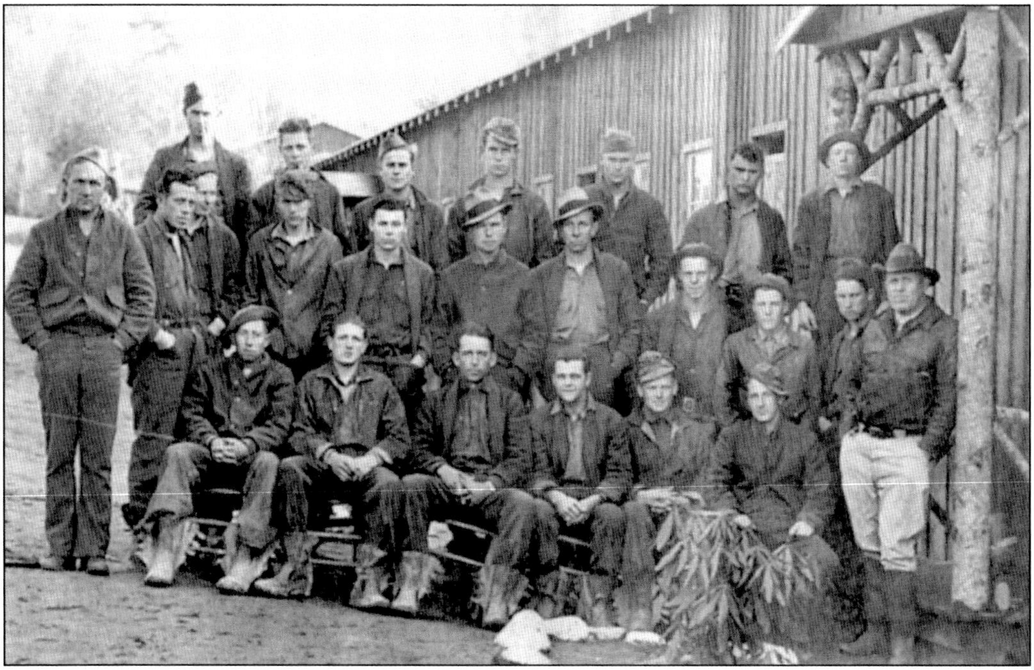

CAMP JAMES, C. 1933. Camp James, a federal Civilian Conservation Corps camp established in Purlear, provided jobs for thousands during the Depression. Projects included the fire tower on Rendezvous Mountain as well as a number of roads in the area. The camp included a mess hall, kitchen, stables, officers' quarters, a boxing ring, tennis courts, and a post exchange. (Courtesy of the *Wilkes Journal-Patriot*.)

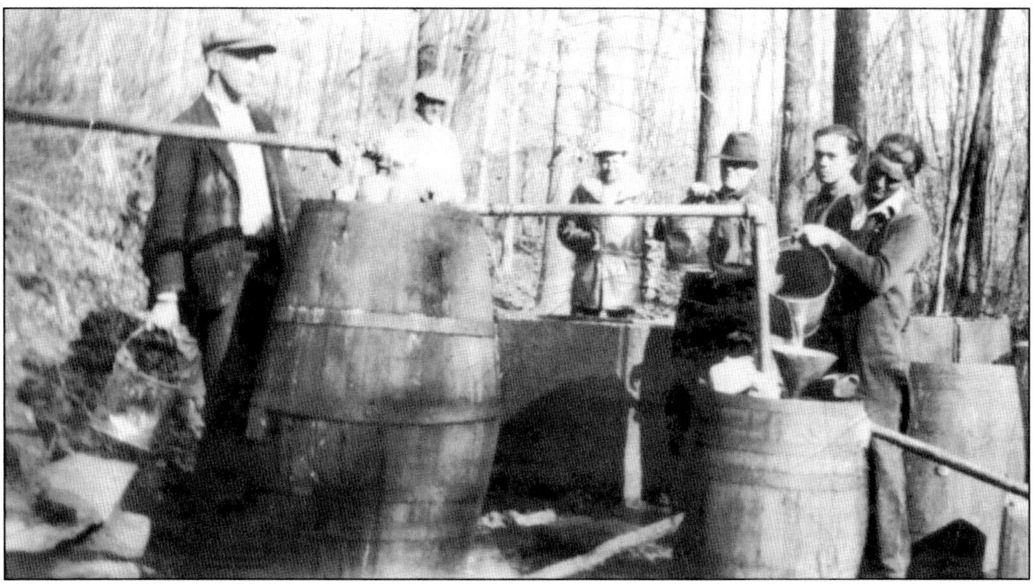

MOONSHINERS, 1930S. Some bootleggers simply enjoyed the thrill of illicit activity, but for many, moonshining became a means of survival after corn markets bottomed out during the Depression. The process involved distilling liquor using heat, sugar, and yeast. Because moonshiners did not pay taxes on their liquor, the process was done in secret, wooded locations by moonlight to avoid detection by law enforcement. (Courtesy of Jason Duncan.)

Nine

Celebrating Life

Wilkes County has always found an occasion to celebrate. From musters, barn raisings, molasses boilings, log rollings, and quilting bees to political rallies, charity auctions, parades, galas, and fund-raising events, residents seldom pass up an opportunity to gather together. In early years, work and play were combined with events like corn shucking and hog killing followed by dancing. Camp meetings were a means of celebrating spirituality with friends and neighbors. Court days brought entire families to the courthouse lawn to sample the wares of drummers and hear the gossip. Political meetings were held under the Tory Oak. More recently, fund-raising and networking have been added to the list of reasons to have a fete.

St. Cecelia's Music Club held recitals, the Great State Stage Company performed comedies and dramas, and the Wilkes County Fair Association hosted annual extravaganzas. At pageants, beautiful young ladies were crowned Miss Scarlett O'Hara, Wilkes County Dairy Princess, and Miss Wilkes County. Commissioners commemorated the county's bicentennial in period costumes and white powdered wigs. Holidays like the Fourth of July have always been festive occasions with parades and fireworks. Birthday parties, watermelon feasts, Easter egg hunts, bonfires, church suppers, cookouts, showers, pool parties, pig pickings, and Saturday trips to town were occasions to celebrate. Food, naturally, has been an important part of the occasions, including barbecued chicken, potato salad, baked beans, fried catfish, lemon pound cake, iced tea, and homemade ice cream.

Events like the Brushy Mountain Apple Festival and the Wilkes Heritage Festival honor artisans, crafts, and traditions. Carolina in the Fall, Chickenfest, and MerleFest celebrate traditional music. The John A. Walker Center, Benton Hall, and the Stone Center provide settings for parties and formal events. From fairs and horse races in the 1910s, to professional baseball games in the 1940s, to NASCAR races in the 1990s, the people of Wilkes County have always loved to get together to share a good time.

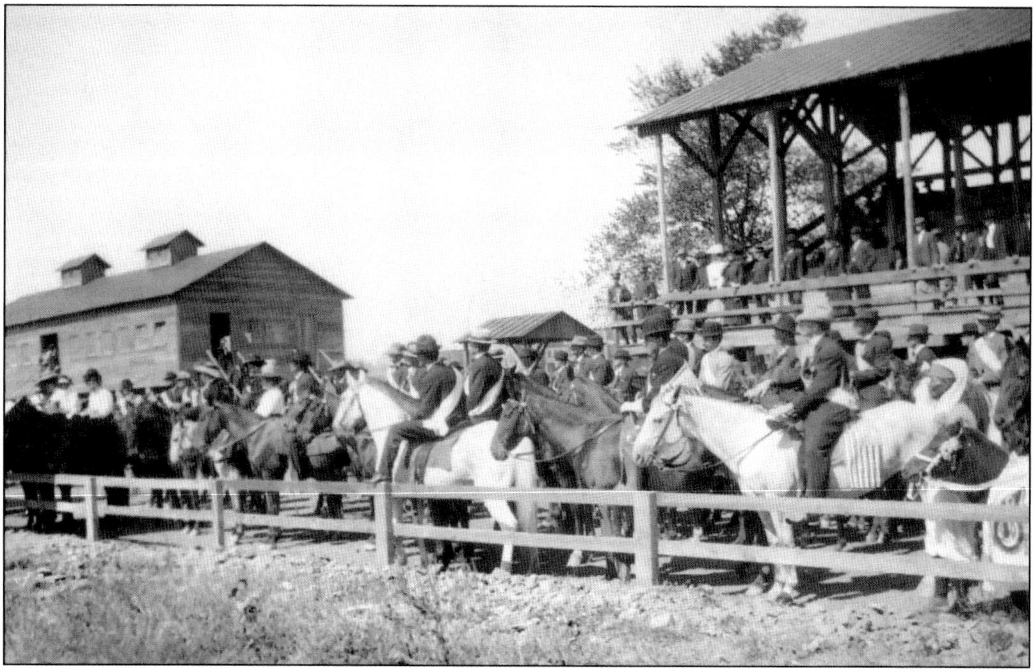

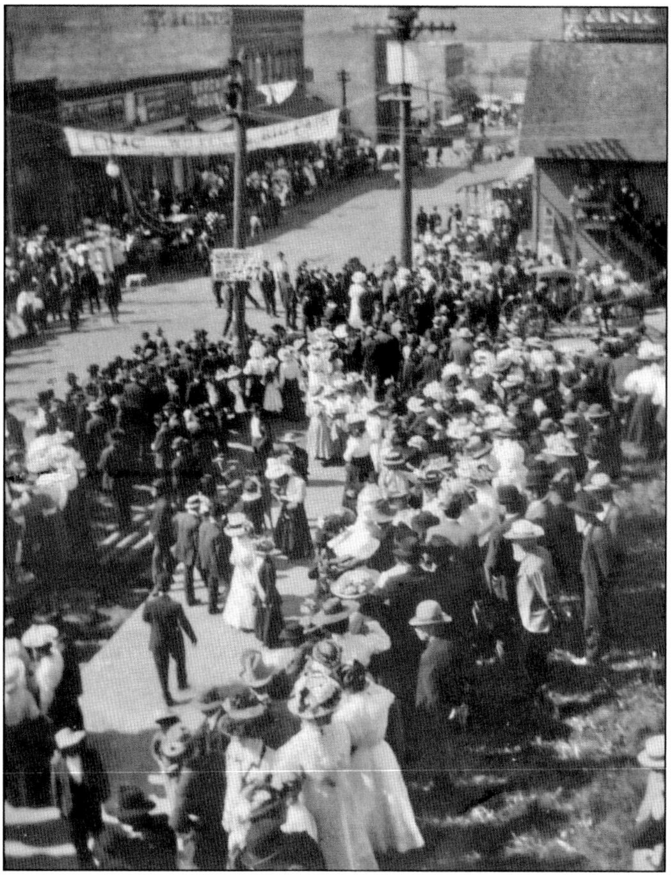

WILKES COUNTY FAIR, 1909. The Wilkes County Fair Association was founded in 1908 to showcase all aspects of agriculture, including gardening, stock raising, and fruit growing. The association wanted to instruct, entertain, and provide a forum in which people could meet old friends and make new ones. The Second Annual Wilkes County Fair was held September 28–30, 1909. Along with agricultural and craft displays, each day featured trotting and pacing races, driving team races, mule races, ox races, and awards for best driving pony and best lady horseback riding. Pictured above are marshals assembled at the grandstand (with the exhibit hall to the left); pictured at left is a crowd scene from the fair. (Both courtesy of Wilkes Community College Library.)

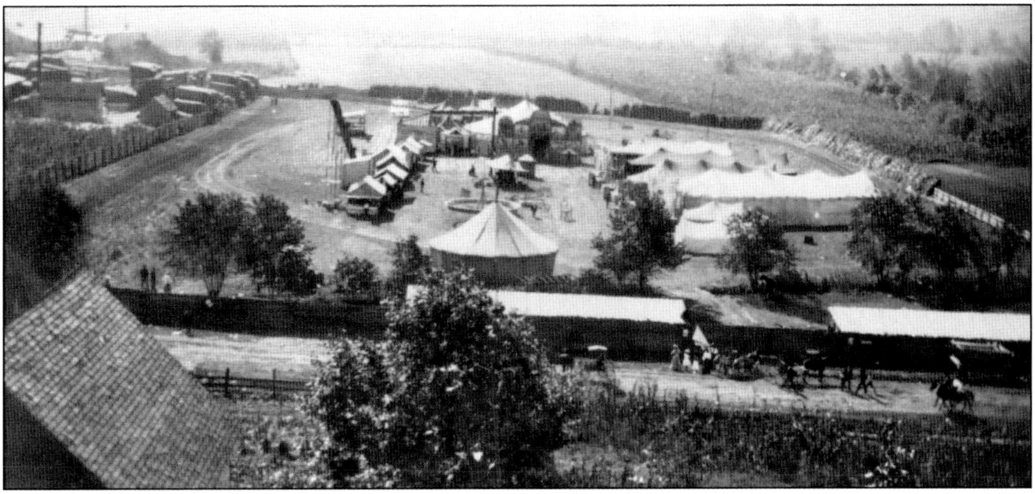

SPARKS SHOWS, 1910S. Wilkes County was a stop on the circuit for the Sparks World Famous Shows traveling circus from 1908 to 1916. The show included sea lions, grease-painted humans and powdered dogs, men that walked on their hands, and clowns. The star of the show was Mary, a 5-ton Asian elephant alleged to be larger than Barnum and Bailey's Jumbo. John and Charlie Sparks, the proprietors of the circus, performed together for years before buying a hotel in Winston-Salem. The fairgrounds of the day were located at the present site of Memorial Park in North Wilkesboro. (Both courtesy of Wilkes Community College Library.)

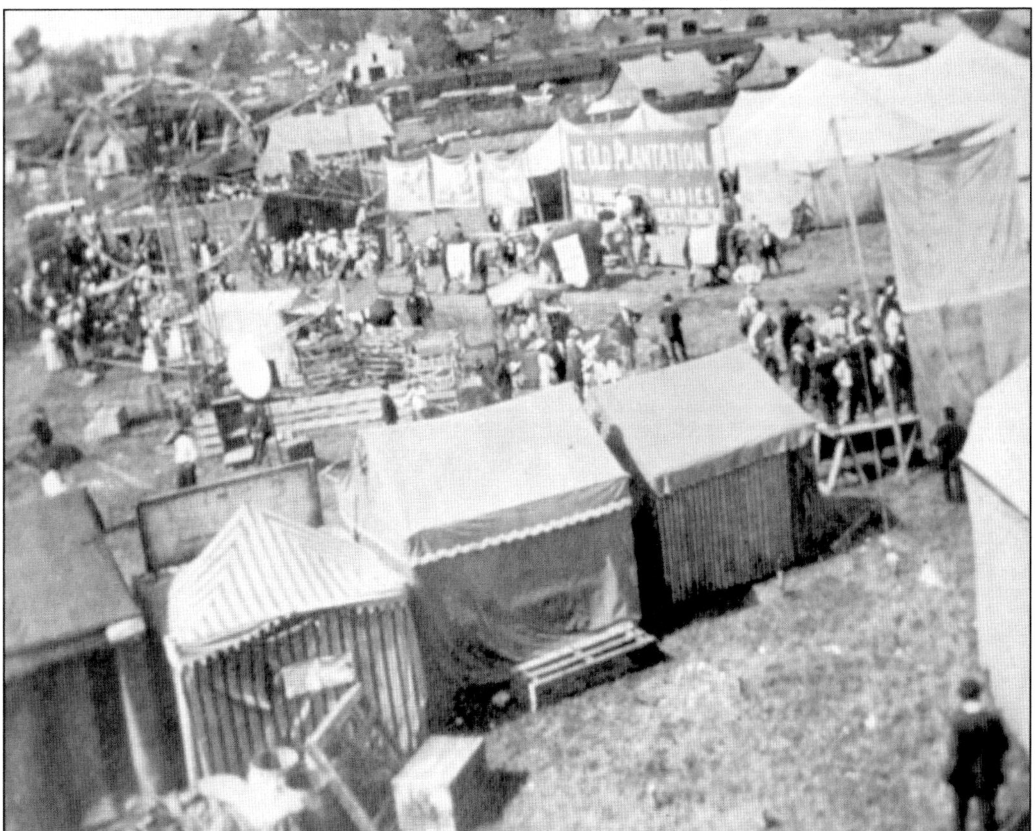

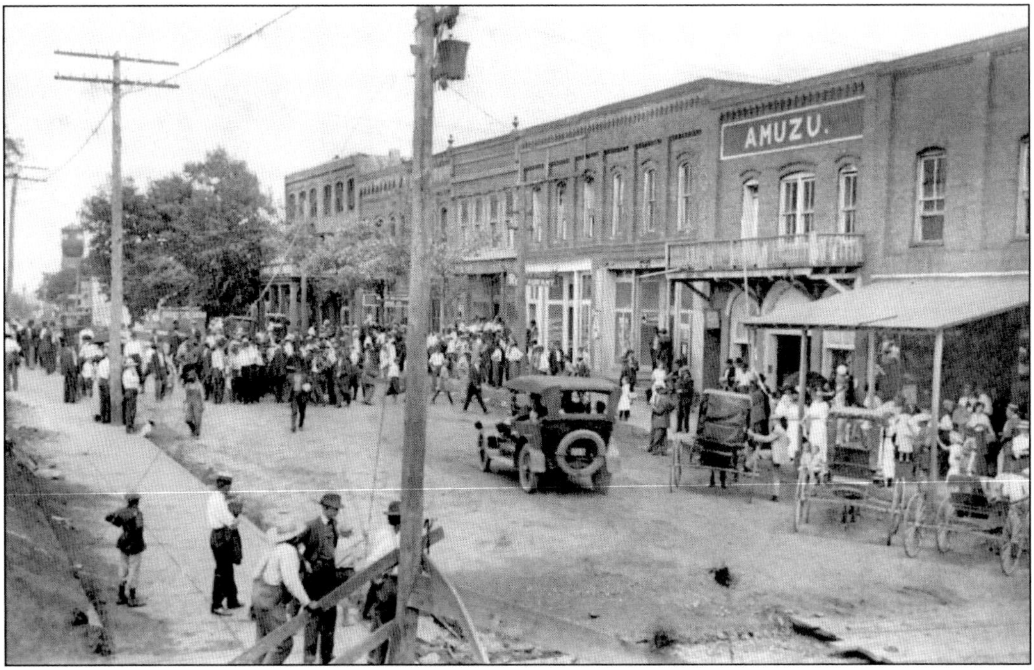

AMUZU THEATER. The first theater in North Wilkesboro, the Amuzu, was located on Main Street. Gus Mitchell established the theater; he later sold it to Jesse Miller who changed the name to the Strand. Miller sold the Strand to W. J. Allen, who would later operate the Allen Theater. (Courtesy of Wilkes Heritage Museum.)

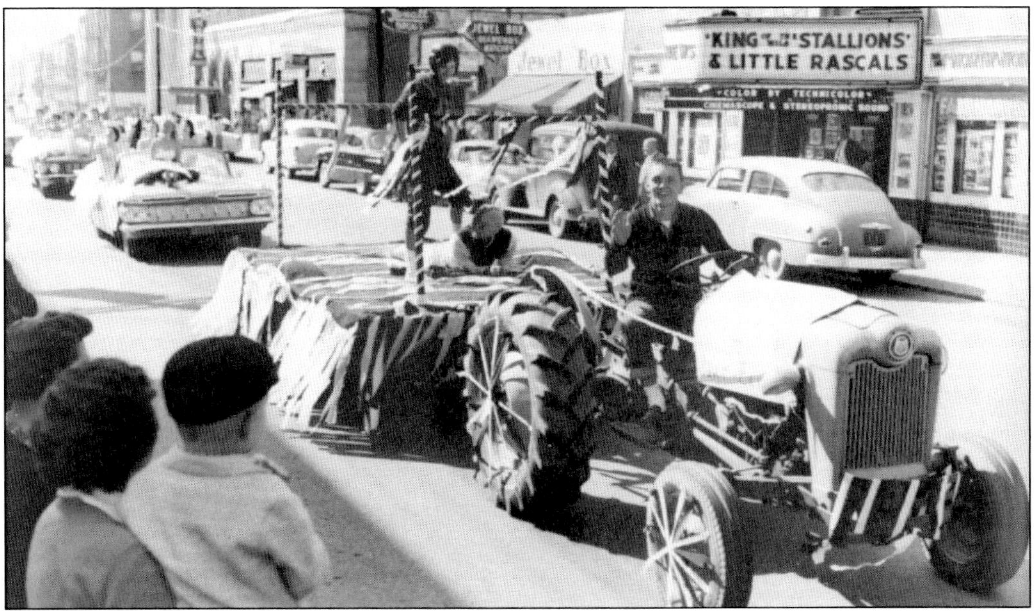

HOMECOMING PARADE, 1960. The Farmers' Day Parade was a September tradition during the 1940s and 1950s. Festivities included musical performances, storefront decorations, and competitions, including pie-eating contests, husband-calling challenges, and even greasy-pole climbing. This entry in the 1960 homecoming parade harks back to the Farmers' Day Parade decades earlier. (Courtesy of the *Hawkeye*.)

North Wilkesboro Flashers. The Flashers were organized in 1948 as part of the Blue Ridge Baseball League. They played six games a week with home games held at Memorial Park. Some Flashers were recruited from out of town, but most players were locals. Enthusiasts enjoyed games until 1950, when a polio epidemic forced local governments to cease public gatherings. (Courtesy of Jamie Hamlin.)

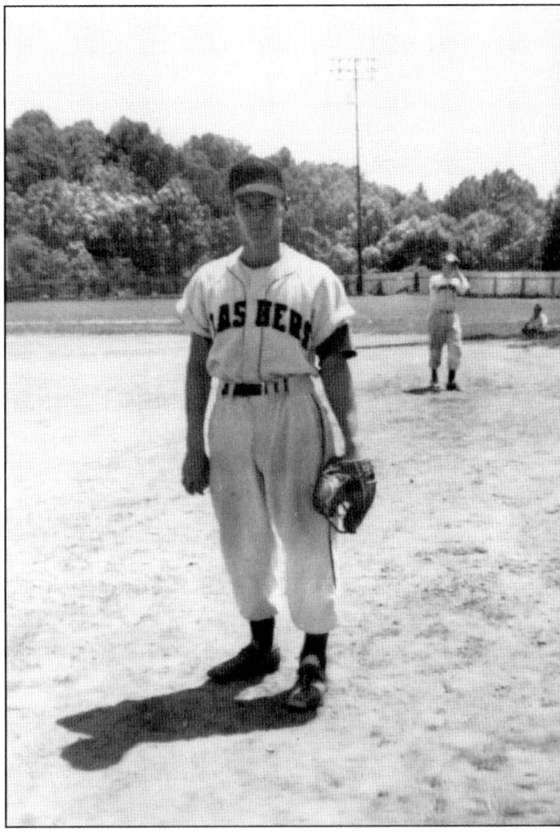

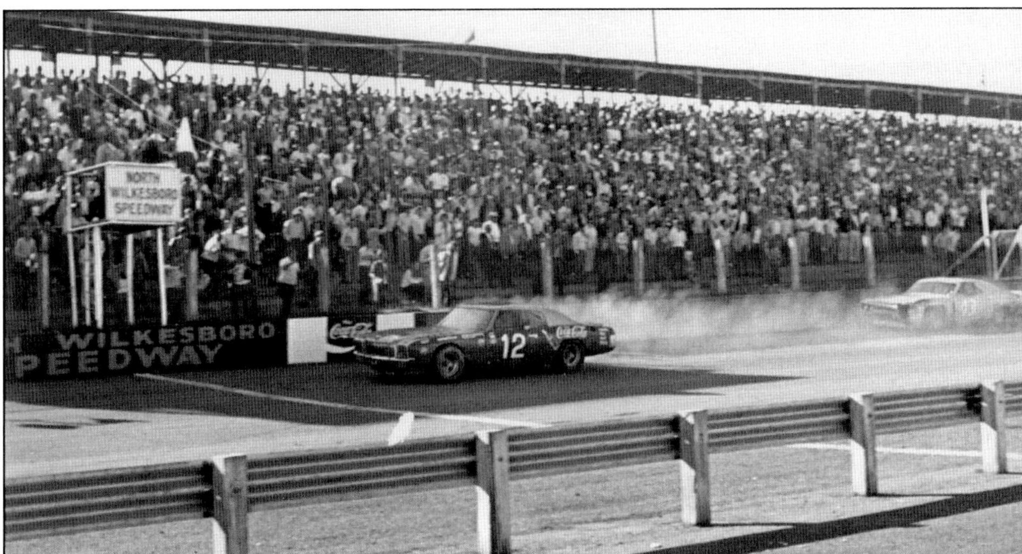

North Wilkesboro Speedway. Racing was born during Prohibition. Local farmers made moonshine and distributed it in cars modified to outrun revenuers. Stock car racing grew from this practice. Enoch Staley, Lawson Curry, Jack Combs, and Charlie Combs purchased farmland in North Wilkesboro for a track that was completed in 1946. The first race was held in 1947, and the track closed in 1996. (Courtesy of Gail Haynes.)

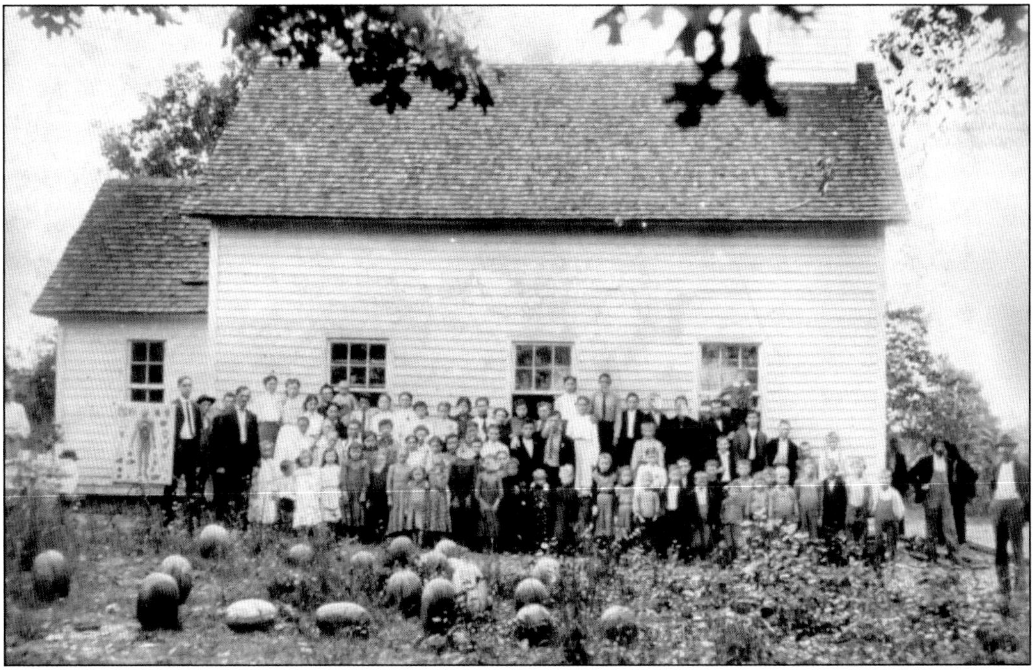

WATERMELON FEASTS. Watermelon feasts were common social celebrations in the South. Often picnic lunches, games like drop the handkerchief, seed-spitting contests, watermelon races, and other festivities accompanied the opportunity to enjoy a slice of chilled watermelon with friends and neighbors. The Fourth of July was a popular time for watermelon feasts, though churches and organizations enjoyed the tradition throughout the summer months. Pictured above is a watermelon feast at Peach Orchard Academy in the Thurmond community on September 26, 1906. Pictured from left to right below are (first row) Christine and Delores Foster; (second row) Vergie Foster and Eula Dillard as they all enjoy slices of watermelon. (Both courtesy of Vergie Foster.)

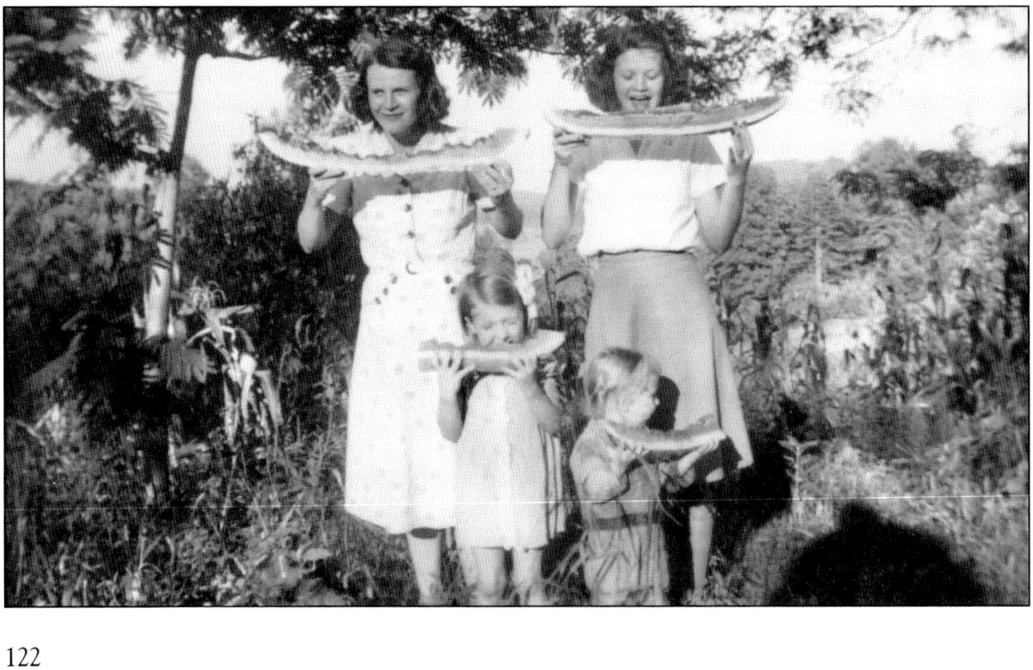

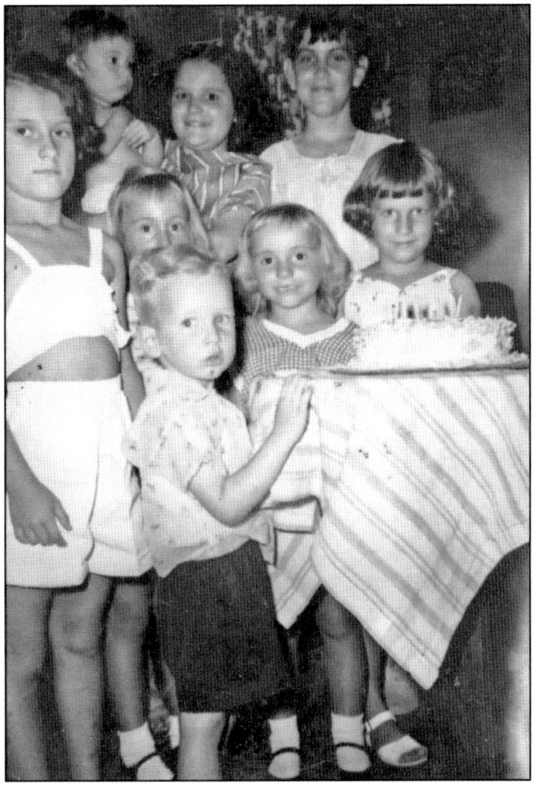

BIRTHDAY PARTY, 1950S. Birthdays became mainstream during the post–World War II years of prosperity. Children played games like pin the tail on the donkey and musical chairs. Pictured at a party from the mid-1950s are, from left to right, (first row) Doris Pardue, Wanda Pardue, Gary Pardue, Gail Pardue, and Peggy Pardue; (second row) Terri Canter, Fay McDaniel, and Helen Moore. (Courtesy of Gail Haynes.)

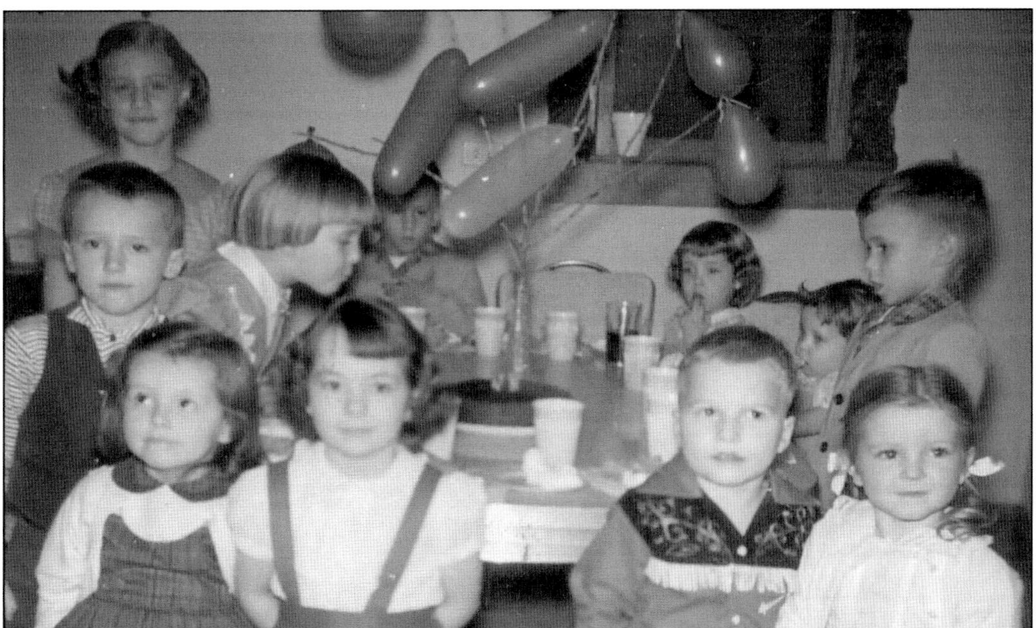

BIRTHDAY PARTY, 1960S. Balloons, papier-mâché streamers, and party favors are other popular traditions. Included in this picture at a celebration in the Millers Creek community are Gayle Foster, Lois Dawes, William and Phyllis Clark, Bruce Hayes, Teresa Foster, Dick and Fred Bumgarner, and three unidentified children. (Courtesy of Vergie Foster.)

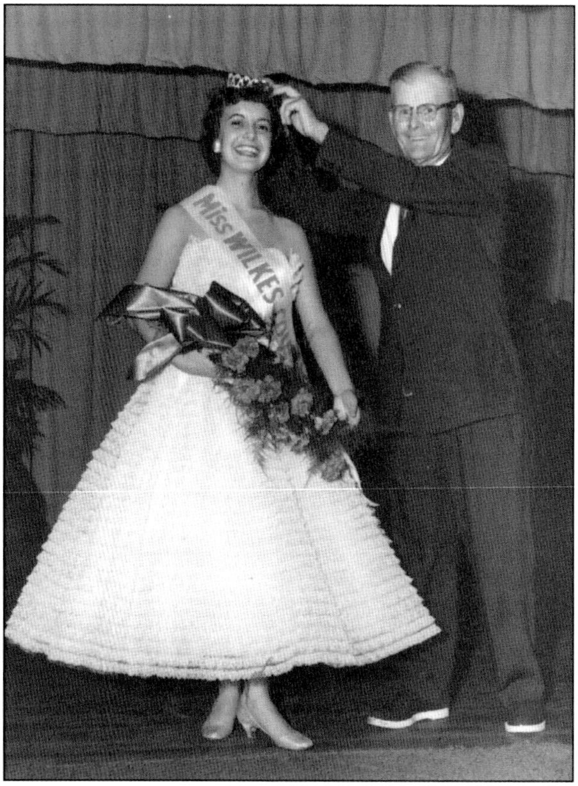

MISS WILKES COUNTY, 1958. Julia Ann Elledge was crowned Miss Wilkes County 1958. Sponsored by the Wilkes Jaycees and the North Wilkesboro Woman's Club, the pageant was followed by a ball. In 1958, the event held at the VFW Hall drew 350 spectators. (Courtesy of Wilkes Community College Library.)

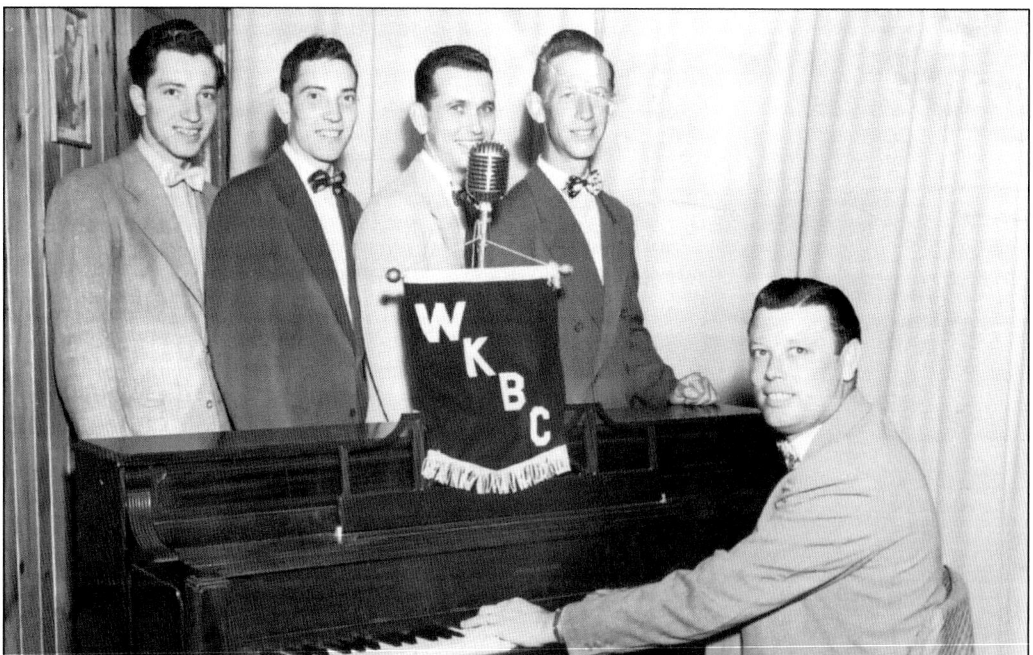

WKBC RADIO. WKBC premiered on June 1947. Broadcast from studios on the corner of Hinshaw and Trogdon Streets, WKBC was owned by Doris Brown and John Cashion. WKBC was also the birthplace of the Friday morning Hometown Opry. (Courtesy of Wilkes Heritage Museum.)

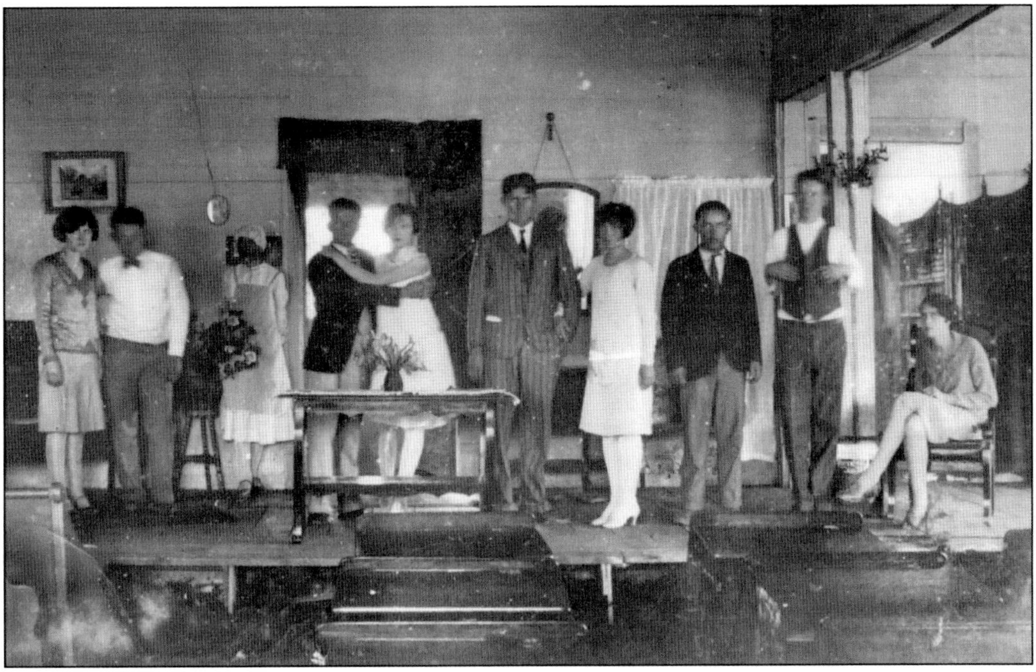

Community Theater. Theater has long been an important part of the cultural scene in Wilkes County. In the late 1940s, Apphia Finley directed the Community Little Theatre in such productions as *Dulcy* and *Night Must Fall.* The drama department of Wilkes Community College has long provided students with opportunities to hone their craft. And the Wilkes Playmakers, founded in 1990, has a growing reputation for excellence in community theater. In 2006, a group from the Wilkes Playmakers premiered *The Scarlett O'Hara Complex* on the New York stage. Pictured above is a production of Wilkesboro High School during the 1920s; pictured at right are (from left to right) Alison Mann Pipes, Harold Bass, and Randy Ashley in a 1981 WCC production of *Annie Get Your Gun*. (Above, courtesy of Vergie Foster; below, courtesy of Harold Bass.)

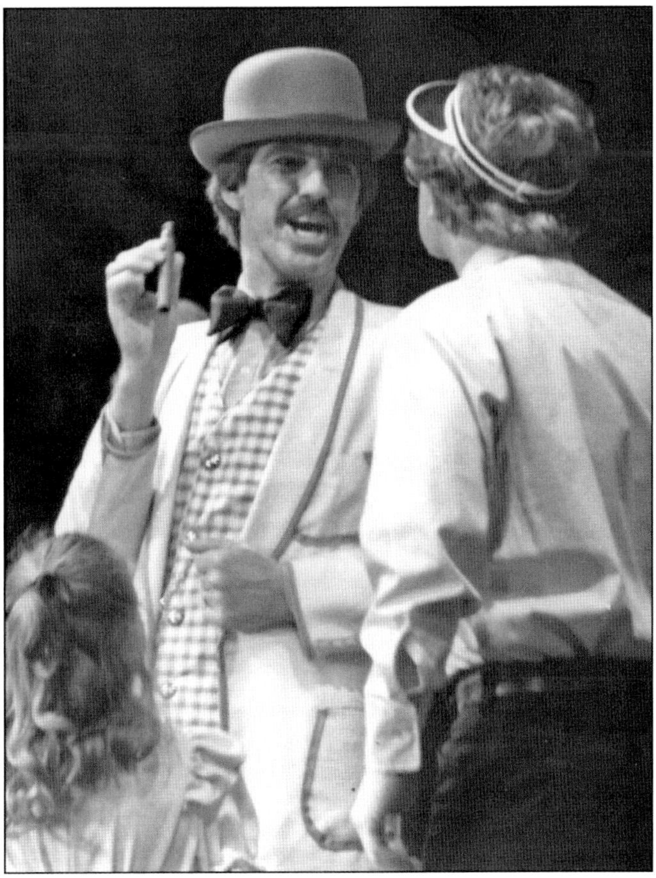

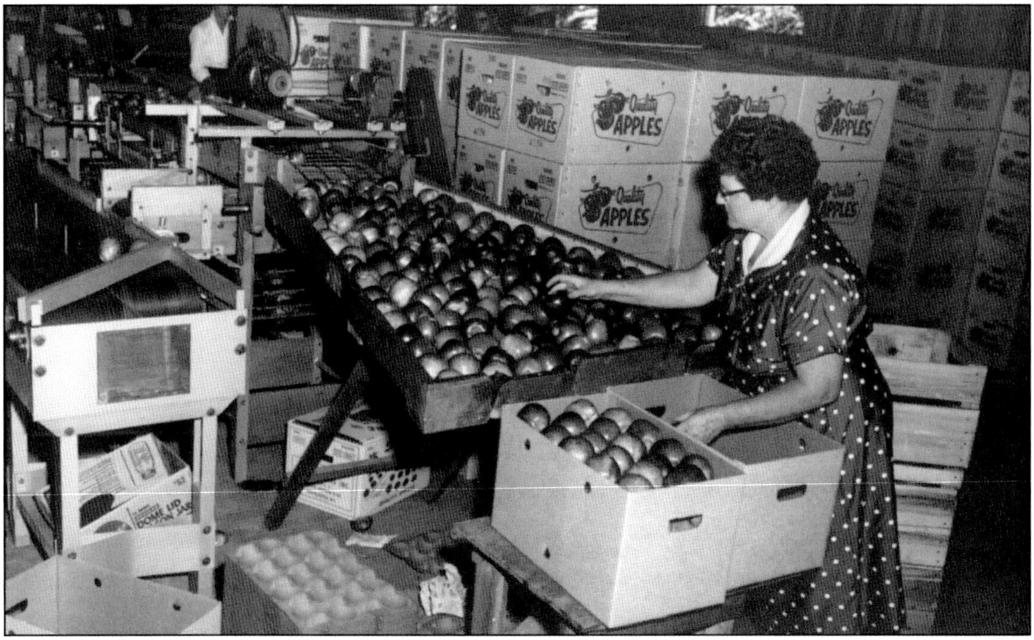

BRUSHY MOUNTAIN APPLES. The climate of the Brushy Mountain community is ideal for apple orchards because an isothermal belt in the area renders them less vulnerable to frosts. The first Brushy Mountain Apple Festival was held in October 1978; the event has become an annual tradition. Pictured above is a worker grading apples. (Courtesy of Wilkes Community College Library.)

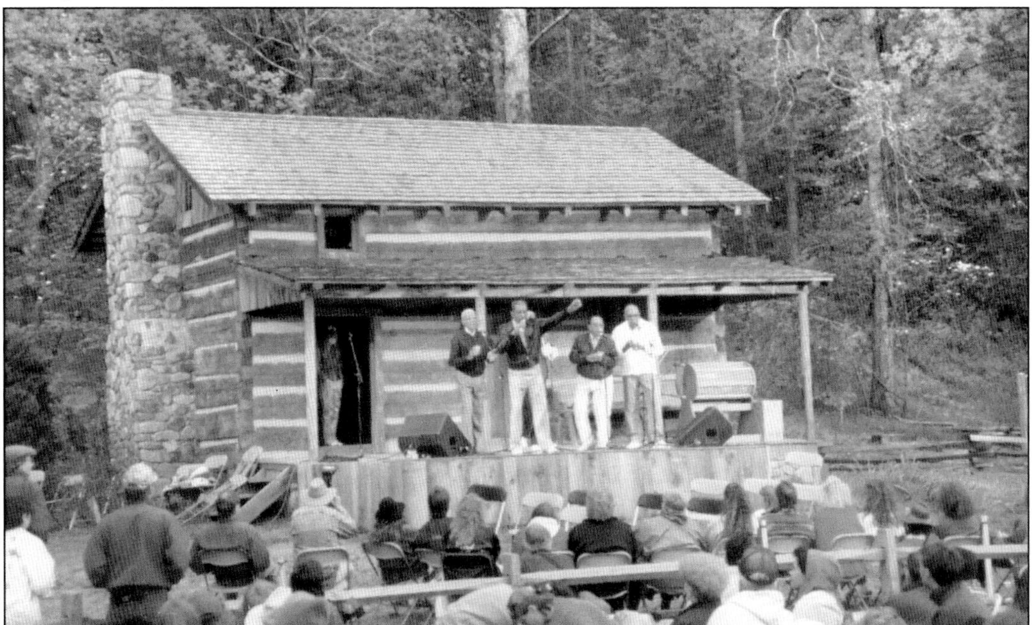

MERLEFEST. The first Watson Festival was held on two flatbed trucks at Wilkes Community College in 1988 and has since grown into a musical extravaganza with 13 stages, drawing more than 80,000 visitors the last weekend of April each year. In 1996, the name was officially changed to MerleFest. (Courtesy of Wilkes Community College Library.)

BIBLIOGRAPHY

Absher, Mrs. W. O. *The Heritage of Wilkes County*. North Wilkesboro, NC: Wilkes Genealogical Society Inc., 1982.

Anderson, J. Jay. *North Wilkesboro: The First Hundred Years, 1890–1990*. North Wilkesboro, NC: North Wilkesboro Centennial Committee, 1990.

Bishir, Catherine W., Michael T. Southern, and Jennifer F. Martin. *A Guide to the Historic Architecture of Western North Carolina*. Chapel Hill, NC: The University of North Carolina Press, 1999.

Brooks, Pat. *Remember Our Heroes: A Tribute to Veterans*. Boone, NC: Minors Printing Company, 2005.

Davis, Pat Hadley. *The Good Old Boys and Memories Unraveled: Stories of the Lives of the Citizens Who Made Wilkes County Great*. North Wilkesboro, NC: Self-published, 1990.

Hayes, Johnson J. *The Land of Wilkes*. Wilkesboro, NC: Wilkes County Historical Society, 1962.

Hickerson, Thomas Felix. *Happy Valley*. Chapel Hill, NC: Self-published, 1940.

Hubbard, Fred C. *Old Town: When Wilkesboro and I Were Younger*. Wilkesboro, NC: Old Wilkes, 1988.

———. *Physicians, Medical Practice, and Development of Hospitals in Wilkes County, 1830–1975*. Wilkesboro, NC: Wilkes Medical Society, 1978.

Moore, Jim. *Wilkes County Remembers World War II*. North Wilkesboro, NC: Carter-Hubbard Publishing Company, 2000.

Phillips, Laura. *North Wilkesboro Historic Inventory*. Unpublished, 1980.

Simpson, Nancy W. *The Heritage of Wilkes County, Volume II*. North Wilkesboro, NC: Wilkes Genealogical Society, Inc., 1990.

Views of North Wilkesboro. Moravian Falls, NC: Yellow Jacket Press, 1906.

Wilkes County Retired School Personnel. *Lest We Forget: Education in Wilkes, 1778–1978*. Winston-Salem, NC: Hunter Publishing Company, 1979.

Wilkes Journal-Patriot. North Wilkesboro, NC: Carter Hubbard Publishing Company, 1933–2006.

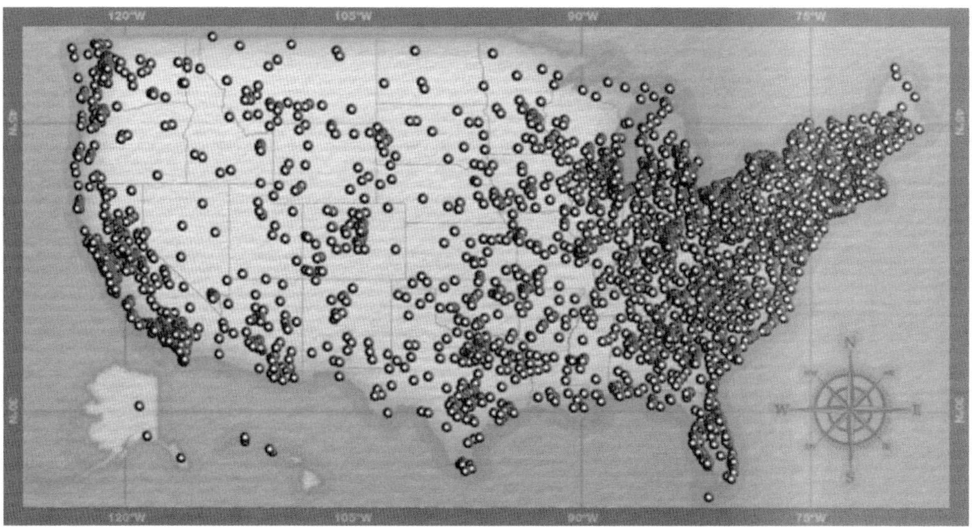